DEFENDING INDIA

Defending India

Jaswant Singh
Deputy Chairman
Planning Commission of India
New Delhi

First published in Great Britain 1999 by
MACMILLAN PRESS LTD
Houndmills, Basingstoke, Hampshire RG21 6XS and London
Companies and representatives throughout the world

A catalogue record for this book is available from the British Library.
ISBN 978-1-349-27193-1   ISBN 978-1-349-27191-7 (eBook)
DOI 10.1007/978-1-349-27191-7

First published in the United States of America 1999 by
ST. MARTIN'S PRESS, INC.,
Scholarly and Reference Division,
175 Fifth Avenue, New York, N.Y. 10010

ISBN 978-0-312-22066-2

Library of Congress Cataloging-in-Publication Data
Singh, Jaswant, 1938–
Defending India / Jaswant Singh.
p.   cm.
Includes bibliographical references (p.   ) and index
ISBN 978-0-312-22066-2 (cloth)
1. National security—India.   I. Title.
UA840.S45   1998
355'.033054—dc21   98–42210
                                                           CIP

First published in India 1999 by
MACMILLAN INDIA LTD
315/316 Raheja Chambers, 12 Museum Road,
Bangalore 560 001

ISBN 978-0-333-93210-0

This edition is available only in India.

10   9   8   7   6   5   4   3   2   1
08   07   06   05   04   03   02   01   00   99

Dedicated to the
soldiers, sailors and airmen of India

CONTENTS

Introduction   viii

Acknowledgements   xxvii

Preface   xxix

1 **Strategic Culture**   1

2 **Armed Forces**   61

3 **Independent India's Military Operations**   142

4 **Defence Spending and Force Structure**   213

5 **The Future**   265

Index   295

Postscript   306

INTRODUCTION

This book is a significant contribution to the growing debate in India on national security and the country's role in the emerging international system. The author, Mr Jaswant Singh, now the Deputy Chairman, Planning Commission is the political leader of highest standing to address the issues of security and foreign policy in the last 50 years of Indian independence in an analytical way in a book and not as a compilation of speeches. Since the party to which he belongs, the Bharatiya Janata Party, has overtaken the Congress Party in the votes polled in the country and in the seats in the parliament Mr Jaswant Singh's views are bound to have ever growing influence on future security policy evolution. The book is very timely with its appearance at a time when there is a discontinuous change of power in Delhi. While there is worldwide recognition that with the end of the Cold War and emergence of a unipolar system which is under pressure to be transformed into a polycentric one there is an imperative need to evolve a new flexible framework for foreign and security policies for major powers like India, large sections of this country's political, bureaucratic, academic and media elite still find it difficult to free themselves from the shibboleths of the last three decades.

Jawaharlal Nehru formulated nonalignment as the optimum security and foreign policy strategy for a country like India in a nuclear bipolar world. Though he himself did not articulate it in that way nonalignment was in fact a modernized version of the classical balance of power in a bipolar world locked in hostility but unable to go to war because of the existence of nuclear weapons. China too played the balance of power game; firstly aligning itself with the Soviet Union against the US and then with the US against the Soviet Union. But its way of playing the game was radically different from India's. Unfortunately in this country whether it is Gandhiji's nonviolent struggle against the British colonialism or Nehru's nonalignment the strategies which are eminently justifiable on the basis of strict rationality have been diluted by mixing them with moral choices and in the process the further evolution of strategic thought has been smothered by platitudinous verbiage. Gandhiji's nonviolent credo did not stand in the way of his strongly supporting the use of the Indian Army in Kashmir nor did Nehru's nonalignment prevent him from accepting military assistance from both US and the Soviet Union in 1963 when the country's security compulsions demanded it. Both Gandhiji's nonviolence and Nehru's nonalignment have been sought to be used by sections of our political class as alibis for not thinking through the problems this country faces as the international environment changes continuously. The views of Gandhiji and Nehru were converted into a kind of dogma ignoring that those living in the present cannot find solutions for their problems on the pronouncements of the leaders gone by, however eminent and farseeing they might have been, and those leaders themselves would not have approved of such escapist behaviour. That is particularly unfortunate in India which does not have a tradition of prophethood or belief in dogmas among the overwhelming majority of its population. Not only did Jawaharlal Nehru put aside the puristic interpretations of nonalignment in 1963, so did Indira Gandhi in 1971 when she concluded the Indo-Soviet treaty to create a sense of deterrence for the Chinese and the Americans. Nonalignment was meant to give such options when crises situations demanded them. It is understandable the Americans could not distinguish the nuances of difference between nonalignment and neutrality but it is unfortunate that many Indians too failed to do so. The essence of nonalignment was the freedom of exercising options on the basis of perceived national interests. Nor was the Indian policy on Afghanistan – private disapproval of Soviet intervention and publicly refraining from condemnation – a violation of nonalignment. Even as the US was arming Pakistan and being permissive of Pakistan acquiring nuclear weapons with China's assistance it would have been utter folly to have alienated the Soviet Union, the only source of reliable arms supply to India.

Nonalignment was meant to be a national strategy to serve India's national interest. It was not intended to be a moral code of conduct in international relations as was sought to be interpreted in the post Nehruvian era. Mr. Jaswant Singh's analytical quest is therefore to be welcomed as an attempt to carry on the Nehruvian approach without making Nehru a prophet. In the Indian tradition the best way a pupil is expected to repay the teacher is to excel him. A true Nehruvian should try to advance India's national security and interest by adapting Nehru's strategy for a bipolar world to one most appropriate for a polycentric world. That must necessarily begin with a critical analysis of pluses and minuses of Nehruvian policy and more so of its deep frozen version in the decades that followed after his death. Mr. Jaswant Singh's is an attempt to do that.

In the recent times Mr George Tanham's provocative monograph published by the Rand Corporation which highlights that India does not have a tradition of strategic thought has initiated a very healthy debate in the country about the Indian strategic culture. Some have tried to be defensive about it. Mr Jaswant Singh has attempted a survey of Indian thought and practice on conduct of war down the millennia. The tradition of strategic thought referred to by Mr Tanhan relates to that of modem nation states, the oldest of which came into being four centuries ago. India joined the ranks of independent nation states only fifty years ago. Therefore it is unrealistic to expect any tradition of strategic thinking in India elite over centuries. The British Indian Raj thought strategically about its security. That was from the point of view of British imperial interests and no Indian took part in that exercise. The absence of Indian strategic tradition is an inevitable consequence of India not being sovereign. Before the arrival of the British in India the rulers of various empires, kingdoms and principalities should have thought about the security of their respective possessions vis a vis threats posed to them by neighbours and powerful challenges from within. But one wonders whether those thought processes of rulers and their courts to counter those threats can be appropriately termed as part of a tradition of strategic thought. Nations needed an aristocracy or a middle class owing allegiance to the nation state to have a continuing tradition of strategic thought. This was not obtained in India in the centuries before the British or French arrival or during the colonial era. Mr Jaswant Singh has rightly emphasized that in India the state was not as important as the society unlike the case of China. We have a millennia old aphorism 'What matters if Rama or Ravana ruled?" For the common citizen it did not matter who ruled so long as he did not upset the societal framework. The British understood this and therefore when the British crown took over from the East India Company there was a proclamation from Queen Victoria promising that there would be no interference in observance of faiths or social practices. For the Indian people it did not matter whether the ruler was a Muslim from Central Asia or a Christian queen from Britain or a native Hindu king. Mr Jaswant Singh has drawn attention to the fact that during most of the Muslim rule the senior ministers and generals were Hindus. The East India Company won India mostly using the Indian soldiers.

On this issue there is need to have an objective view of our history. Till 16th century mercenaries offered their services to the side that paid them better and there was no sense of nationalism in most of the countries of the world. One should be careful in applying the present day value system retrospectively to times several centuries ago and judging those people by these standards. Nationalism developed with a series of wars in Europe, the collapse of feudal order rise of mercantile capitalism and to some extent conflicts over religion and sectarian beliefs. There is no need to feel apologetic that the spirit of nationalism started to develop in India a century or two later than in Europe. After going through centuries of wars and the Holocaust the European nations are coming together today to build a European Union which will be multilingual, multi religious, multiethnic and multicultural.

As Professor Johann Galtung wrote in the early seventies Europe is attempting to progress towards the concept which India has represented over the millennia and is today. When the Europeans were prisoners of a chauvinistic nation state system they decried that Indians did not reach their level of national chauvinistic consciousness. Now that the European nations are moving towards a multinational union they are preaching that nations should rise above nationalism.

There have been continuous movements of populations from one area to another all through history. One view is that Aryans came from Central Asia into Indo-Gangetic plains. Whether that thesis is accepted or not it is an established fact there were successive waves of populations in search of better environment and more congenial climate where availability of good soil and water favoured settled life. While masses of people came into the Indian plains over centuries there were very few instances of people from India moving enmasse into other lands, except in the British period when they were taken to distant lands as indentured labour. Those waves of immigrants into Indo-Gangetic plains were absorbed and became part and parcel of Indian civilizational inheritance. This was largely true of Islam's interaction with India too. Except Babar and Humayun among the Mughals, and the first Islamic rulers in Delhi other Islamic rulers would all be eligible to vote in today's Indian elections and aspire to become India's Prime Minister or President if we are to apply the criteria of today's Indian Citizenship Act. Aurangzeb may be considered a tyrant and fanatic by many but he is part of our history and is a genuine Indian tyrant and Islamic extremist. Such movements of populations happened all over the world. In many cases the immigrants committed a holocaust on the native populations as in the Americas and Australia. In India the indigenous population and civilization prevailed and absorbed the invaders.

Professor Samuel Huntington is not wholly wrong in talking about the clash of civilizations. It has always been there in history. The conflict between Islam and Christianity has been well chronicled. The talk of Yellow peril by the Europeans was a subliminal expression of similar conflict. The colonial conquests of the Europeans and the wiping out of Aztecs, Incas, Mayans and Maoris were all conflicts of civilizations. So also decolonization. Therefore the Huntington thesis is generally valid on the basis of global historical experience. In India we have reacted strongly against it because of our historical experience of Islam coexisting with the indigenous civilization and that resulting in some of the glorious instances of synthesis between two civilizations exemplified by the Taj Mahal, Hindustani dance, music and painting, architecture and even cuisine. Some would even argue that Bhakti movement in Hindu culture was at least partially due to the impact of Islam. Where two civilizations, both based on religions derived from revelations and prophethood came into contact with each other it inevitably led to a violent clash. On the other hand in India Islam came into contact with Hindu civilization which was not based on revelations, dogmas and prophethood. The latter did not proselytize. It was based on the view "Truth is one and the learned expound it in many ways". *(Ekam sat; Viproh Bahudha Vadanthi).* Therefore it could accommodate Islam, Christianity, Zorastrianism and Judaisam and felt no compulsion to convert the "unbelievers" to its belief. Therefore Islam could coexist peacefully with Hinduism in India for over a millennia and that would explain the opposition of the Indians in general to the Huntington thesis on "clash of civilizations".

However it cannot be denied that Jinnah's two nation thesis was the original delineation of the "clash of civilizations" doctrine and preceded the Huntington thesis by half a century. One could even argue that the British were the originators of this thesis when they introduced the separate electorates and sowed the seeds of partition. In India there was and continues to be an asymmetric situation. While Hindu civilization and culture, irrespective of its many flaws and shortcomings in societal terms is basically secular and nonexpansionist as it is a non-proselytizing one, Islam was used by the British and cultural and religious chauvinists in a confrontational mode leading to the partition. The rest of India continues to be secular.

The Indian subcontinent is recognized as one of the self contained civilizational areas of the world. For the Hindu kings of ancient times India consisted of 56 kingdoms and one of them became a *Sarva Bhauma* (Emperor) if he was acknowledged by others to be such and he performed an *Aswamedha* sacrifice. One could think of it as a kind of Westphalian system of those days, all bound by a common *Dharma*. No one thought of areas beyond India except in terms of trade. Even when there were Muslim rulers in India, in spite of their contacts with Iran, Arab areas and South East Asia they never thought of expansion of their territorial jurisdiction beyond traditional Indian civilizational area.

The British strategic tradition could not be passed on to the new Indian republic because, from the time of Waterloo up until the 1930s, Britain was the sole superpower in the world. It could hold sway over the entire Indian Ocean arc and convert Tibet, Afghanistan, Iran and Thailand as buffers to protect its empire in India. While Pakistanis and some others have charged Jawaharlal Nehru as having inherited the mantle of the British Indian empire he knew very well that India could never exercise in the rapidly decolonizing world the power the British Indian empire could as part of the then sole superpower of the world. It does not make sense to expect the Indian elite at the dawn of independence to have any tradition of strategic thinking derived from the British imperial perspective. Jawaharlal Nehru's nonalignment was his contribution to Indian strategic thought and today it is widely recognized that irrespective of all developments in security sphere in the last half a century nonalignment was the appropriate strategic doctrine for India. However a perusal of the debates in Parliament in the fifties would show how difficult it was to reach a consensus on it. The Left denounced it as toadying to the imperialists and the Right as being unrealistic and anti-West. Even in 1963 there were many in India including sections of military and civil bureaucracy and political class who urged that India should ally itself with the West. It is only after the death of Nehru, the US letting down India on its military preparedness against China, its not condemning Pakistan when it used US weapons in the battle in the Rann of Kutch, the Indo-Pakistan war of 1965 and the steady flow of Soviet armaments in mid-sixties nonalignment achieved national consensus.

While Mr Jaswant Singh has been justifiably critical of Jawaharlal Nehru's failure to pay adequate attention to security issues and to build institutional structures for decision making and opinion making in the sphere of national security one has to guard against the monarchical approach so widely prevalent in the country and hold one leader responsible for all failures and all successes. It is true that the Congress Party left foreign policy entirely in the hands of Nehru. While there were a number of very articulate exponents of foreign policy perspectives in the Parliament - H. V. Kamath, N. G. Ranga, M. R. Masani, Nath Pai, Frank Antony, Ram Manohar Lohia, J. B. Kripalani, Pandit H. N Kunzru, Ashok Mehta, H. N. Mukerji, Bhupesh Gupta and many others - in retrospect are we in a position to say that there was a critical mass of people with knowledge and background on strategic issues? Mr Jaswant Singh has quoted Mr B. K. Nehru on the paucity of knowledgeable and competent diplomats in our foreign service of that time with the exception of Sir Girija Shankar Bajpai. In the armed forces there were very rapid promotions in the forties and fifties, in order to Indianize the top ranks and their limitations in terms of knowledge, experience and competence in the fifties are highlighted in the book. General Thimmaya talking about the impossibility of defending against China on the Himalayas, the total lack of consideration of use of Air Force in 1962, lack of Army-Air Force coordination in 1965 and the Chiefs preferring to have the trapping of a theatre Commander-in-Chief instead of playing the role of planners of national security all establish the inadequacies in the armed forces. In 1962-63 there was no appreciation about the nature and extent of the Sino-Soviet dispute and most of the military and civilian bureaucracy used to talk about 'commies' and 'commies' would always be together and therefore India should firmly join the western camp. History is witness to how much support we got from the West in facing Mao's China.

The civilian bureaucracy of that time were competent in administering India as they demonstrated in managing the aftermath of the partition and consequent refugee rehabilitation. They had no clue to international relations and national security management. They had no idea that long range security management had to be based on a comprehensive assessment of threats. There was no intelligence failure in 1962 as is commonly believed. A stream of reports on Chinese build up in Tibet in the months ahead of 1962 attack came in. But the reports were not put together and assessed. Even today it is ironic that while there are justifiable demands for publication of the Henderson-Brookes report on the debacle in Sela-Bomdila there are very few observers who realize that one of the two authors of the report was General Prem Bhagat who was the Director of Military Intelligence till early 1962, and whose duty it was to demand regular assessments. He was a Victoria Cross winner in the Second World War and was undoubtedly one of our ablest of commanders. But he was a cog in a system which just did not function.

Jawaharlal Nehru, as Mr Jaswant Singh brings out did fail and died a broken man. But the odds were against him. He was facing a leadership in China which had fought more than two decades of war. Even in the thirties John Gunther in his *Inside Asia* described Mao Dze Dung and Zhou en Lai as 'Red Napoleons in Blue'. Today Mao Dze Dung's military thought has been overtaken by political and technological developments. In late fifties and early sixties his prestige in military affairs was high. The Chinese had thrown back General Douglas

MacArthur and the American Eighth Army from Yalu to 38th parallel. What military and diplomatic assets did Nehru have against them? At that time the Indian Army headquarters did not even have materials on the Korean war to be issued to our training institutions.

While Nehru's failure should be critically analysed we have to look at the larger national failure as well. More than that we have to look at the continuing failure on effectively managing our national security in the last thirty-four years after Nehru passed away. There has no doubt been some improvement. Our armed forces are today far more professional, and a little more aware of international security environment. Our media takes a lot more interest in national security issues and the number of people, including retired service officers, diplomats, intelligence service officials, academics and media persons debating national security issues has expanded significantly though not sufficiently to make a critical mass. However the interest of politicians in national security issues has not gone up. With the rise of regional parties the interest in proportionate terms has in fact declined. Most of them are not interested in foreign and defence policies except where their parochial interests are involved. Tamil Nadu politicians are concerned with Sri Lanka, Bihar politicians with Nepal, West Bengal leaders with Bangladesh and Punjab, Rajasthan, Gujarat and Kashmir ones with Pakistan. The civilian bureaucracy continues to be generalist in its orientation and has significantly lost its stature and credibility and are largely looked upon and treated not as professional advisers but as staff officers.

Therefore there is an imperative need to analyse why this country which faced overt wars with Pakistan in the Rann of Kutch, and Western border in 1965, both on Eastern and Western borders in 1971 and now having to deal with a continuous covert war in Punjab and Kashmir since 1983 and sharing one of the longest land borders with a fast emerging superpower, China is so lackadaisical in its approach to security. This cannot be blamed on Nehru. All over the world it is understood that security, stability and development are symbiotically related and have to be addressed as an integral whole. In India alone we continue to hear the shibboleth 'guns versus butter' as though it was ever an issue in this country the defence expenditure of which had for a long period hovered around 3 per cent and has been declining in the last decade. Mr Jaswant Singh has a very valuable critical analysis of our defence budget and has argued the case for much needed reforms in the budgetary process which is today archaic beyond belief.

Some years back an Hungarian academic told me that large countries like India, China, Russia, US, Canada, and Australia could never understand international relations in the manner in which it is understood in smaller countries like Hungary. A truck driver in Budapest comes across an international border if he drives a few hours East, West, North or South. He had to deal with passports, Visas, foreign exchange, trade and all other aspects of international relations. In the case of countries like India one can fly in a jet airliner for a couple of hours without crossing an international border. So an overwhelming majority of the population, and the politicians representing them have very little interest in international politics. Mr Jaswant Singh refers to inward looking perspectives of Kings and Sultans down the ages and that continues to apply to the ruling classes of today.

Secondly foreign policy and national security interest those nations which have either an aggressive and expansionist foreign policy (such as US, China, Russia) or which are highly insecure (such as Pakistan) or which are interested in large scale trade and commerce and an international role for themselves. (Germany, Japan, UK and France). India does not have an aggressive and expansionist foreign policy and does not have a paranoid sense of insecurity. Until recently India did not evince much interest in international trade and commerce. For these reasons India does not have a foreign and security policy establishment of adequate size.

Thirdly there is a sense of complacency about having muddled though all the security problems in the last 50 years except the 1962 one. In 1965 India could have had a stunning victory if our military establishment had correctly assessed that Pakistan was running out of US supplied ammunition while India had hardly used 7 - 10 percent of its stocks. In 1971 the military victory was not fully exploited and its fruits were thrown away at the Shimla summit. India allowed Pakistan to overtake it initially in nuclear weapon capability and is now in danger of repeating that mistake in the missile field. Indian leadership's handling of politics in Punjab and Jammu & Kashmir and permissiveness of the porosity of our borders which resulted in continuous flow of narcotics, weapons and terrorists exacted a heavy toll in lives and development in covert wars in Punjab and Kashmir. Yet at political and bureaucratic level it is argued that we have come through it all.

Fourthly there is the widespread and largely justifiable view, also shared by the Indian establishment that high intensity inter-state wars deploying regular armed forces have a very low probability of happening and the chances of a nuclear threat or use of nuclear weapons are just above negligible levels. Therefore the Indian political establishment feels there is no need to be very concerned about national security.

The above perspective does not take into account the nature of new threats to security in an increasingly globalizing world subjected to continuing communication and transportation revolutions. A nation attempting to hurt an adversary today, does not launch an overt military attack using organized forces. It initiates a covert war using terrorists, infiltrating arms and explosives into the target country and exploiting all possible fissures in its social fabric. This country has been subjected to such covert war since 1983. Thousands of trained infiltrators have been sent into our country and they have carried out thousands of acts of terrorism inflicting many times the number of casualties India has suffered in all inter-state wars it has fought in the last 50 years. Our cities have been subjected to simultaneous multiple blasts to undermine the confidence of investors or to intimidate voters. Our coastline has been violated and tons of explosives have been landed. It is not beyond the scope of such adversary organizations to land a nuclear device and set it off. Our airspace has been penetrated with impunity and arms dropped on our soil, thousand miles deep into our territory. Fake currency has been sought to be introduced. Narcotics are flowing in and external agencies have established contacts with organized crime in India. Insurgencies within the country are supported with arms and money by such agencies. This is a low cost option for our adversaries which exacts a higher price from us in terms of casualties, development process and expenditure. In 1965 when Pakistan sent in its infiltrators into Kashmir in Operation Gibraltar, India reacted by sending its Army across the Line of Control. Now with the nuclear factor operating that option is not considered an optimal one. Consequently India has suffered enormous casualties and disruption in Kashmir while being deterred from acting in the way it did in 1965.

Mr Jaswant Singh has conceptualized national security in broader terms encompassing economic development, food security, energy security, environment, etc. In the light of happenings in East Asia, safeguarding a country's economy from the kind of currency turbulence that has afflicted that region and some Latin American countries earlier, should also be appropriately considered as part of the national security management. So long as nuclear weapons and missiles exist in the arsenals of some countries – especially war-prone countries – they constitute a threat to Indian security. India faces a unique situation being situated between two nuclear weapons powers China and Pakistan – which have an ongoing collaboration in nuclear weapons technology. India cannot afford to overlook the fact that nuclear weapons have been legitimized by the international community. Such legitimization of the most horrendous weapon of mass destruction has tended to nullify the existing ban on less horrendous weapons of mass destruction – biological and chemical. This is especially true of use of weapons of mass destruction by non-state actors in a terroristic mode.

Information warfare and revolution in military affairs are today much talked about. In a sense with the global electronic and print media dominated by the rich industrialized nations most of the developing world – particularly India – is already being subjected to well-crafted information campaigns. That has very significant impact on Indian image in the world as well as among our own populations. It is therefore, obvious, given these factors, national security management today is far more complex than it was earlier. We did not manage our security competently earlier and the task has not become easier with the new developments.

It is not as if those who talked about giving a higher priority to development over national security managed our development satisfactorily. After eight five-year plans the country is way behind other developing countries in literacy, availability of basic needs to the population and developmental infrastructure. The country was on the verge of default in payment in 1991. It would perhaps be correct to say that the country's elite has displayed the same degree of incompetence in managing both national security and development.

Countries make mistakes. If India has its 1962, the US has its Pearl Harbor. The difference is the way in which the US establishment quickly learnt from its mistakes and radically altered its approach to security issues. Henry Stimson as Defence Secretary in Hoover Administration shut down censoring of mail by the military intelligence with his remark that 'gentlemen did not read other people's mail'. Yet he proved to be an outstanding Defence Secretary of the Second World War. Americans had to learn a lot about international intelligence collection from the British. In about less than a decade they left the British far behind. They were new to realpolitick in the thirties. By fifties they were leading the world in the practice of realpolitick. In India our problem appears to be the absence of learning process among our elite – whether it be in economic development or national security. In today's context the two will have to be viewed together and dealt with in a comprehensive way.

The lead for this has to come from the government. It is in this context setting up of a National Security Council (NSC) in the government becomes an imperative need. Unfortunately there is not much understanding of the role of such a council among our politicians, civilian bureaucrats, academia, media and even among a large proportion of the service establishment. The Indian NSC cannot be on the US model which is situated in a presidential system. Nor is the Indian NSC can ever function in that role befitting a superpower with an aggressive global foreign and security policy. Nor is India likely to become a paranoid state with military industrial establishment playing a significant role. The Indian NSC is meant to enable the cabinet committee dealing with national security to take a holistic view of Indian development process inclusive of national security which today it is incapable of doing because of the lack of an appropriate mechanism. Secretaries' Committees cannot fulfil the role of a dedicated coordinating and monitoring body which will be able to address a large number of vital issues which are transdepartmental and transministerial.

The Planning Commission has failed when in contrast to other countries it got ensnared into sub-optimal planning having decided to divide the development process of the country into plan and non-plan. There would have been better planning if the entire process including social, political, economic development which would encompass national security had been addressed in an integrated manner. The sub-optimal planning process, resulting from the turf division into plan and non plan spheres purely for bureaucratic reasons, ruined the planning process. Assets created in one plan were neglected in subsequent plans since their maintenance expenditure became non-plan. Social, political and security developments having an impact on economic development were neglected to be taken into account. In fact the Planning Commission became a body to plan new developmental projects and never played the role indicated by its name.

Therefore both our economic development and national security management vital to economic development have been fragmented to all round detriment of the nation. There is no security without development and can be no successful development without security. Among the civilian bureaucrats there are fears that the NSC Secretariat will become a supra government and will infringe into the legitimate spheres of policy making of the ministries. That fear is unwarranted. The NSC is meant to be a staff organization to coordinate and monitor broad issues and should not and in fact cannot supplant the role of the ministries. The opposition to the creation of the NSC as well as some fanciful roles envisaged for it by some academics – such as its being a think tank are all due to inadequate familiarity with national security management in the Indian context among our bureaucracy and academia. Mr Jaswant Singh is a strong protagonist of a National Security Council.

It is only when such a body is set up and our politicians are trained to look at national security and development in their total symbiotic relationship and understand the scope of national security comprehensively they will be able to transmit their perceptions to the parliament, bureaucracy, business community, academia and media. This country does not have bodies analogous to the Council on Foreign Relations or the Royal Institute for International Affairs which knit together a country wide foreign policy and national security establishment. Since our industry was mostly meant to cater to domestic market during the permit-quota-license-Raj our business community has not taken as much interest in international affairs as captains of industry elsewhere in the world do. Nor do they finance academic research in international studies. Our bureaucracy is brought up in the tradition of Vikramaditya's throne. According to this view, wisdom is embedded in the chair a person occupies and once he vacates that chair he has nothing worthwhile to contribute. Most of our bureaucracy believes they have no use for any information or any perception outside the walls of South and North Blocks and they have all the information they need. With that attitude pervading the bureaucracy and with politicians totally dependent on such bureaucracy it is not surprising that the country has not developed a national security establishment even thirty-six years after Sela-Bomdila debacle and thirty-four years after Nehru's death.

Those who read this book will be puzzled that Mr Jaswant Singh has not followed his trenchant criticism of the system with detailed prescriptions of what should be done. His last chapter lists out the areas that needed to be attended to but has not recommended detailed courses of action to be pursued. I suspect the recent elections had something to do with his extreme caution in coming out with his advocacy of his preferred solutions. Since he was one of the major architects of the manifesto of his party and the subsequent National Agenda For Governance of the Bharatiya Janata Party and its allies he appears to be less than forthcoming in his prescriptions than he would otherwise have been. That is no doubt a major loss from the academic point of view since his own specific recommendations, as a senior political leader venturing into the field of national security would be of great interest to all those interested in the subject.

The Bharatiya Janata Party devoted more attention to national security and foreign policies in its election manifesto than all other parties. It has, subsequent to the elections formulated an agreed National Agenda For Governance in collaboration with all its coalition partners. Most of that agenda, but not everything in it, has now been incorporated in the President's Speech to the Parliament and therefore will be the policy of the BJP alliance government. While the BJP manifesto and the National Agenda For Governance talked of National Security Council, formulating a strategic defence review and re-evaluating nuclear policy, since their assumption of office there has been greater emphasis on continuity of policy by the Prime Minister and Defence Minister. It is to be hoped that a National Security Council will be formed to evolve a more comprehensive and coherent perspective on national security than was done in the last fifty years.

If that were to happen Mr Jaswant Singh's contribution would come in handy to focus attention on some of the perennial weaknesses in the Indian approach to national security.

K. Subrahmanyam

30th   March   1998
New   Delhi

ACKNOWLEDGEMENTS

Grateful thanks are due to Sir Dorab Tata Trust for their generous grant in meeting the research costs of this book; to Bharat Karnad for preliminary work, and later for sharing his detailed research analysing India's defence budgets; to the Institute for Defence Studies and Analysis and its Director Air Commodore Jasjit Singh, VrC (Retd) for his advice, for patiently going through the manuscript, sharing his papers, particularly on Air Power and for loaning me two able research assistants Rahul Roy Choudhury (himself an author) and Swaran Singh. Rahul helped greatly with his work on Indian Navy and Swaran with Chapter III.

I am particularly beholder to B. K. Nehru who corresponded on the subject; to Jagat Mehta who shared his insight, experience and papers; to Roderick MacFarqualer for sharing his research and unpublished (yet) material on China; to K. Subrahmanyam for encouraging, advising and for writing an introduction to the book.

I am grateful to the HMSO, Copyright Office, for the permission to quote from the Mountbatten papers.

To Bharat Verma for his invaluable assistance in converting impossible manuscripts into presentable material, and for producing it all in time.

To Magu who ensured that *Defending India* was managed even as I was unavoidably kept away from it; touchingly from a combination of filial duty, interest in the subject and perhaps, part concern about a hopelessly overworked man.

Thank you Vijay and Padmavathi for typing and retyping, always uncomplainingly. And, of course, A. K. Chanana, for the great help in putting it all together finally.

The authorship of a book is a consuming affair, it takes over one's life. K put up with this affair, complaining only occasionally. But then without her, this book as so much else would not have been possible.

PREFACE

The completed manuscript of *Defending India* had already been with the Publishers for some weeks when some momentous events took place in South Asia. On May 11 and 13, India conducted two nuclear tests which were followed by those of Pakistan on May 28 and 30. For a book entitled *Defending India*, to be published without any reference to the post-tests situation, globally and in South Asia, would have been a crippling deficiency. Simultaneously, what was needed was an articulation of the rationale, at some length, behind these tests. Obviously, that could be the Indian viewpoint alone.

This has occasioned the uniting of a Postscript, and of this Preface. But the Postscript, is not really an afterthought, nor simply a hurriedly added explanation. It stands on its own, and attempts to address the issues that today confront the entire international community; the totality of the non-proliferation regime and this whole complex question of disarmament.

One more explanation is needed. Whereas the rest of the book does have a fairly exhaustive index, the Postscript does not. It does not really need one. For that decision (and deficiency) for the purists, the author alone is responsible.

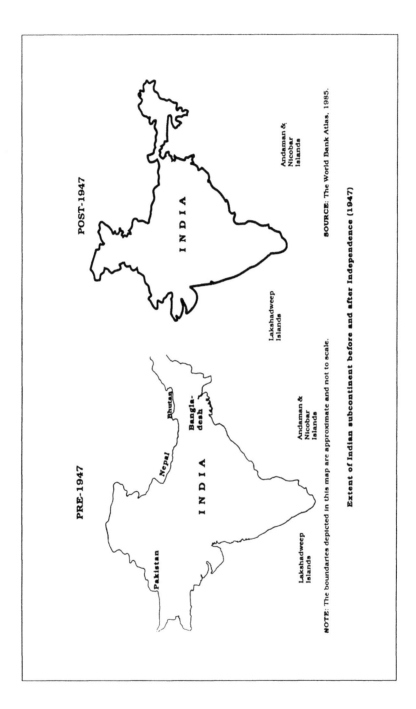

POST-1947

I N D I A

Andaman &
Nicobar
Islands

Lakshadweep
Islands

PRE-1947

Pakistan

Nepal

Bhutan

Bangla-
desh

I N D I A

Andaman &
Nicobar
Islands

Lakshadweep
Islands

SOURCE: The World Bank Atlas, 1985.

NOTE: The boundaries depicted in this map are approximate and not to scale.

Extent of Indian subcontinent before and after Independence (1947)

Strategic Culture

Two axioms, seemingly contradictory, open our enquiry on India's strategic culture. The first, that warfare is not the concern of the military alone. This is a self-evident and an oft-repeated truism. But not so the second: the proposition that strategic decision-making is the function and responsibility of a small political-military class alone. Thus for this class of leaders a culture of strategic thinking emerges as an irreplaceable attribute, no matter what the form of governance. But of them alone? Principally, yes; for though civilizational, cultural, and societal influences shape the thought processes of the leaders, entire societies or a people can hardly be expected to be endowed with a culture of strategic thinking. Of course, today's warfare involves an entire society, all the sinews of a state are stretched, it tests a nation's will, and policy governing such supreme endeavour is unquestionably the concern of a much wider audience: but as audience alone or as commentators and as critics, not architects. Because for formulating and executing that national will, or for meeting the challenge the primary responsibility rests upon a small decision-making apparatus alone. It is in this core of the executive that the attribute of an appropriate strategic sense, culture, tradition, or attendant thought, and the needed ability to first plan, whereafter to efficiently execute is so vital an ingredient. For without this no challenge, military or otherwise, can be met with any recognizable degree of success.

Did India, during the first half century of its independence from colonial rule, rather did the Indian political and administrative class demonstrate this needed attribute? Our enquiry widens even as we proceed. It has to examine the very nature of India's nationhood; the characteristics of its society; and the evolution of its strategic thought over the ages, but, of course, all this has also to be accompanied by an attempt at defining the concept of strategic culture itself. For if there is neither such an attendant culture nor a tradition of strategic thought, then obviously enough no adequate planning of this nature can take place at all.

As assumption that the principal application of strategic thought is in the realm of the military alone is a common error, a simplism, for the culture of strategy is not born in that crucible. It is an intermix of many influences: civilization, culture, evolution and the functioning of a civil society all contribute. It is a by-product of the political culture of a nation, and its people; an extension of the functioning of a viable state, more particularly its understanding of and subscription to the concept of power: the nature of that power, its application and more importantly its limitations. For power is not merely military, it is diplomatic and economic, coercive, or persuasive; power of ideas and thought and example. And in all these ways the power of a state can be used. But, of course, there has first to be an understanding of this 'state power' in the political-military leadership. And that is where history and racial memories influence strategic thought, its culture, as does a sense of geography, and this last much more significantly, for of this is born a sense of territoriality. In which context a question arises: Is geography and a sense of it merely about physical territory or is it more?

Our study is about India, the evolution of strategic culture in Indian society, and in its political decision-making classes, particularly in the last half century, for this is the period (1947-97) of India's fresh endeavours as an independent country, free from alien invasions, occupation or colonialism of about two and a half centuries, of imperial British dominance. Which, in turn, had followed a near ten-centuries-long period of Islamic invasions, conquests of parts of India, and the establishment of successive, foreign ruling dynasties. How could this happen if India was then a developed society, a flourishing economy and had an ordered polity, as indisputably it did have? That is why, to our enquiry an understanding of India becomes central. What or who or which is this India? What sets it apart as a civilization; what are the distinguishing marks of its culture? What are the characteristics of its civil society, the role of the military in it, and the other integrals of strategic culture?

Many have attempted to capture, in words (also physically) this undefinable India. It is ironic that this land got called India simply because it lay East of the river Sindhu (Indus), for in the origins of the name lie the answers to many of our queries. This great river originating in the Himalayas and pouring into the Arabian Sea is the very first major physical obstacle after the bastion of the formidable mountainous north-west is breached and one debouches on the great plains of North India, which, watered by many other great rivers stretch thousands of kilometres to the East and South until the north-eastern hook of the Himalayas interrupts their stretch, and the mighty Vindhyas do the same in the South.

To the river Sindhu there are references in the ancient epics of India but not to any country by such a name. 'In short, in the Indian context, Sindhu started out as a geographical word with strong cultural resonances.'[1] It gave a name to Sind, now a province of Pakistan. India has in turn, lent its name to so many others, in such diverse parts of the globe, as for example to Brazil, where 'Indians' live along the Amazon and there are Canadian and Mexican Indians, too, and, of course, we all know about the Red Indians.

India is also Bharat, which is not simply a constitutional nomenclature,[2] it is the recognition of an ancient verity:

'*Jambu dveepe Bharat-Khande*' (upon the island of Jambu-dveep – Bharat). This, an ancient Sanskrit recitation, is invoked before a ritual even today. It is thus '*Bharatvarsha*', this land inhabited by the descendants of Bharat, which lies at the foot of the Himalayas and is bound by the ocean. But India is also Hindustan: the land in which reside the Hindus, which was not originally at least a denominational description in any sense. It was entirely geographical, for the word Hindu is but a degraded version of the same Sindhu. Over time, this Hindustan gave a descriptive identity not simply to the land or its inhabitants (Hindus), but also to the 'major prevalent beliefs, practices and faith' in it. Thus came into being the description of a religion – Hinduism – which is as undefinable as India. In our search for its strategic culture, the origins of the cultural impulses of India are the first building block. More perhaps than in any other land and amongst people, faith plays a central role in India; shaping its cultural patterns, the norms and structures of its society; indeed even in the attributes of nationhood, for Indian culture and Indian society are at the core of the Indian nation. Thus Hinduism.

'Hinduism – or the plural reality labelled as such – has been a major cultural phenomenon.'[3] It is ancient, it has survived conquest, pillage, war, famine, flood and such other occurrences. It has absorbed influences, transmuted them, 'Hinduized' them; it has travelled across oceans: to the Indonesian Archipelago and Bali for instance, or other lands of Indo-China, not as a proselytizing force, but as an exporter of thought and culture, and its peculiarities. It sustains, supports, directs, and governs the daily life and behavioural patterns of around a billion human beings, of whom 850 million live in India. From its womb have been born Jainism, Buddhism and Sikhism – three great religions. 'Hinduism has influenced the semitic religions of Judaism, Christianity and Islam',[4] too, during the many centuries that these great faiths have found a place in India. Besides here still continue to find shelter the sun-worshipping Zoroastrians. For our purpose, however, an exhaustive treatise on Hinduism is not central. Its influence on the evolution of India's strategic thought is, and that leads us to conclude that 'Hinduism is both a way of life and a highly organised social and religious system . . . quite free from any dogmatic affirmations concerning the nature of God'.[5] It is the 'Sanatana Dharma', that principle which is eternal and is for all; also, despite being so all inclusively formless, the belief has conceptual and structural unity. For a Hindu (though disputation is 'Shastric' tradition) thesis and antithesis lead not to struggle and conquest but more to synthesis. 'That is perhaps why for a Hindu there is no country but theirs, no nation like theirs, no kings like theirs, no religion like theirs, no science like theirs.'

Why so much about Hinduism? For it is this 'ism' that has given birth to a culture, from which we hope to extract the essence of its strategic thought. Is India's strategic thought then essentially Hindu in character? Stephen Rosen offers a thought:

. . . above all else, India is Hindu, and Hindus think differently from non-Hindus. This statement, of course, acknowledges the presence of non-Hindus in India and has been modified to take into account the existence in India today of an elite that is relatively less traditional in its religious outlook. . . .

But accepting that qualification, is it important that India is Hindu? If it is important, that could form one basis for arguing that there is a Hindu strategic culture.[6]

We need to go back a bit, attempt a definition, or as near a definition of strategic culture as possible. Does, for example, the strategic culture of Britain differ from that of, say, Germany or Russia? Does America then have a distinctly separate strategic culture? And Canada and New Zealand, too? What about the 'suicidal defenses of the Japanese in World War II'? Were these the outcome of Japanese concepts of honour and shame

as Ruth Benedict in *Chrysanthemum and the Sword*
suggests? Is that then a part or constituent of Japanese
strategic culture? And thus our search widens to enquire
about China and other nations. In each we find that
national cultural attributes do contribute to the ability
of a people to conceptualize, then plan for the actual
demands of war; whereafter to execute, successfully or
otherwise, the war itself.

If one looked more closely, this time at areas of
clear differences, obviously enough if the major characteristics
of a society differ from another then the attributes
fielded for meeting the demands of warfare shall also
be markedly different. There is a more modern version
of the same thought whereby,

> Intellectually, strategic culture is related to the
> specific idea of a Bolshevik "operational code",
> as advanced by Nathan Leites and the concept
> of "political culture" advanced by Lucian Pye,
> Sidney Verba, and others. Leites' concept of the
> operational code was subsequently elaborated during
> the cold war to explain different approaches by
> the Soviet leadership toward nuclear weapons.[7]
>
> The other source of the concept of strategic
> culture is the more general concept of "political
> culture"; which, in turn is the product of "non-
> political beliefs – such as feelings of basic trust
> in human relations, orientation towards time and
> the possibility of progress, and the like – [which]
> can be of overriding importance" in shaping political
> institutions. These sets of beliefs constitute, in
> each country, that nation's political culture. Political
> culture is not uniform across cultural boundaries,
> [and] even if countries adopt common forms of
> economic organisation, because [they] would be
> overlaid on older systems of beliefs and would
> not simply replace them. Particularly as Western
> colonial patterns of government receded in time
> and prestige, local "subjective attitudes, beliefs,
> and values prevalent among the dominant groups

in the society" would increasingly shape the political development. . . .[8]

This Stephen Rosen calls 'a short-hand expression for a "mind set" . . .'[9] And this 'mind-set' as '. . . societies organized themselves differently . . . might lead to differences in the amount of military power they could generate.'[10] That is why 'whether or not culture, defined as the dominant set of beliefs, matters for strategy, domestic social structures could still affect the generation of military power.'[11] But whereas an entire society will obviously have its distinctive attributes, not all constituents (of it) are expected to contribute to a formulation of its strategic thought, not even the 'entire political class, only that 'subset' who are 'political-military decision makers. [It is] their beliefs and assumptions,' which determine 'military behaviour, in particular, the choices concerning decisions to go to war; preferences for offensive, expansionist, or defensive modes of warfare.'[12]
Alastair Iain Johnston, refers to the

assumptions, symbols, myths, and beliefs held by national leaders that affect their perception of available acceptable strategic options, "a nebulous ideational milieu which limits behavioral choices" and "which acts to establish long-lasting strategic preferences by formulating concepts of the role and efficacy of military force in interstate political affairs . . . the role of domestic politics in shaping the attitudes of a society toward its military and the political views of the military with regard to its host society, all while acknowledging the importance of the internal culture of the professional officer corps, a culture that was not determined by the distribution of domestic political power. The problem [however] with strategic culture tends to lie in its application. In a proper understanding of power, in the ability of a people and society to generate power; thereafter, to have the necessary social will and ability for a full and effective employment of that power.[13]

How does India rate when we apply these broad criteria? To start with, the essence of Indian civilizational thought engages itself more with the other-worldly than this. As a great Indian philosopher and sage expressed early in this century:

> India's central conception is that of the Eternal, the Spirit. . . . involved and imminent in it and evolving on the material plane by rebirth of the individual . . . till in mental man it enters the world of ideas and realm of conscious morality, Dharma. India's social system is built upon this conception; her philosophy formulates it; her religion is an aspiration to the spiritual consciousness and its fruits; her art and literature have the same upward look; her whole Dharma or law of being is founded upon it. It is her founding of life upon this exalted conception and her urge towards the spiritual and the eternal that constitute the distinct value of her civilization.[14]

Yet another philosopher, Dr Sarvepalli Radhakrishnan, who was independent India's second President and whose views one could assume to be more current, has, as have many others before and after him, expressed that India through centuries venerated the sage against the statesman, a learned man instead of a warrior. That is why 'India has failed to give political expression to its ideals. The importance of wealth and power though theoretically recognized, was not practically realized. India has suffered for this negligence.'[15] And he proceeds to analyse, 'but spiritual unity is a large and flexible thing and does not insist like the political and external on centralisation and uniformity; rather it lives diffused in the system and permits readily a great diversity and freedom of life.'[16] Here we touch on the secret of the difficulty. And Myron Weiner takes hold of it, he is direct and much more to the point:

The absence of analytical continuity among ancient [Indian] political theorists, the relatively small role of political theory in the dense fabric of Hindu philosophical and religious writings, the historical break in this literature caused by the Muslim invasions, the introduction of European political ideas and institutions in the nineteenth century . . . all suggest the irrelevance of classical Hindu thought.[17]

We thus have a set of criteria against which to examine an entire range of questions. Does India at all possess the needed attributes? How did they evolve historically through the ages? How has the Indian civilizational and cultural ethos influenced them? Other questions pertain to the existence and effectiveness of the Indian state, and India's own and acquired military concepts or, in brief, India's military culture. Whereafter, the entire question is about history, its recording; about geography and territoriality: the British period and the Indian military revolution; the period of independence, transforming social, political and civil-military relations and what these did to the development of a suitable strategic culture. Internally and internationally, what were the strategic challenges to an independent India and did the political-administrative-military leadership of this period – 1947-97 – anticipate, understand and address itself effectively to them? This is our canvas for an enquiry into India's strategic culture.

INDIAN STATE

It is significant that whereas early Indian writings abound in a variety of treatises on statecraft, or on the duties and obligations of a citizen, about kings and kingship yet there is scarcely any material on the political institution of a state, also not so much about the craft of war either. This is largely so because the concept of State itself was alien to Indian political thought. It could not be otherwise. Civilizationally, the Indian nation is a unity, a whole: diverse, multilingual, with numerous shades and varieties of faith and kaleidoscopic cultural distinctions, also varieties of beliefs, languages, dialects, dress, food – but always with that indefinable, civilizational oneness: an Indianness. Thus civilizationally, there is but one India; politically, however, there has been greater diversity. From 'satrapies and kingdoms to village republics' this diversity of India has found expression in myriad and oft-transforming political forms. This geographical entirety of India has never been one unified and monolithic state; not under the great and all-conquering emperors like Ashok and Chandragupta Maurya, or later during the period of conquest when there were Sultanates in Delhi, or during the reign of the Mughals. But all this is perhaps superfluous; for in the centuries and periods of which we talk, the concept of a nation-state itself was non-existent. It is after all a post-industrial-revolution, occidental derivative. That is why in the British period we witnessed a distinct advancement in the direction; the establishment of many of the attributes of a modern state: one currency; uniform tax regime; common foreign and defence policy, one law and an overarching philosophy of jurisprudence with attendant legal systems. Yet, even then, large parts of the country like the North-West of India – today's NWFP (North-West Frontier Province) of Pakistan, along with at least a third of India remained outside of this unifying, imperial effort (as Indian states, nearly 600 of them – some larger than many members of the UN today). An Indian state came into existence, for the whole of India, though admittedly for a divided India, for the first time ever only after 1947. To mind comes an ancient truism about two of the great civilizations of Asia, Indian and Chinese, that 'India has always existed without a state, but that China cannot exist without one'. But whereas this modern Indian state, in the post-British colonial period was the inheritor of many of the transferred attributes of statehood there remained a deeper cultural layer in its consciousness.

These subsumed layers, as integrals of thought and concepts, in formulation of policy and in governance acquired importance. The ethos of governance altered in the process.

India is routinely described as a peace-loving nation. Yet, it is a troubled state. And herein lies a cruel paradox. The Indian state, since independence, has been prone to internal violence. This could possibly be a consequence of the very acquisition of statehood; equally, of course, a result of inadequate experience of statecraft, combined with enhanced means of violence at the disposal of the state. In the process an old judgement is reaffirmed: that the principal security challenge to India has historically been and remains the imposition and maintenance of internal order. That had been the preoccupation of the rulers like even Chandragupta Maurya, as we shall presently see; or the Mughals; later even the British. This preoccupation has fixed attention, prevented the growth of a proper security thought, truncated the concept of power and left little military surplus either. This inability to develop a 'surplus of military power', beyond that which was necessary for internal control of existing possessions is noteworthy.

As Marshall Hodgson has noted, both the Ottomans and Safaid Iranian Muslim empires could and did make use of their imperial revenues to purchase an overwhelming amount of artillery, which they used first to overwhelm internal opposition and then to expand, despite the divisions among religious and ethnic groups within their empires. But contrary to Hodgson, students of the Mughal Empire have argued that the empire in India was not able to consolidate its internal control and expand outward in the way that the Ottoman Empire did.[18]

That is why in the famous *Arthasastra* of Kautilya there is an obsession with 'spies, secrets, and treachery'. When listing the virtues of a king, Kautilya includes, along with energy, controlling his sensual nature, cultivating his intellect, and associating with his elders, the need to keep 'a watchful eye by means of spies'. Who should be the counsellors of kings? Those whose 'integrity or the absence of integrity' has been ascertained 'by means of secret tests'.[19] We need to digress only slightly and attempt here a comparative evaluation of three military-strategic classics: of Sun Tzu's *The Art of War*, Carl von Clausewitz's *On War*, and Kautilya's *Arthasastra*. What do we find? And this even at the cost of some simplification:

> Clausewitz focused on fighting battles and military campaigns, whereas Sun Tzu was more concerned with the strategic problems of national leadership. *Arthasastra* is on the training to be given to kings.[20]

But just as subterfuge features in all the three as an essential aspect of war; Sun Tzu is more akin to the *Jataka Kathas* or *Panchatantra* of India, emphasizing attributes of leadership of which, yet again, deception and secrecy are a part; Kautilya, on the other hand, is all about gathering intelligence (in today's parlance, that is) through a network of spies. And being Indian he goes into benumbing detail. This establishment of spies to be created to serve the king should include 'the apostate monk, the seeming householder, the seeming trader, the seeming ascetic, as well as the secret agent [the brave, the poison-giver, and the benign nun]'. They should spy on

> the councilors, the chaplain, the commander-in-chief, the crown-prince, the chief palace usher, the chief of the palace guards, the director, the administrator, the director of stores, the commandant, the city judge, the director of factories, the council of ministers, the superintendents, the chief of the army staff, the commandant of the fort, the commandant of the frontier-fort, the forest

chieftain, too, and that also in his own territory.

What characterized Kautilya's Bharat was true of British India as we shall see subsequently. But as a comment on the Indian state, society and kingship we can venture a generalized conclusion. India's strategic culture got internalized, remained fixated upon curbing within rather than combating the external, and created a yawning chasm of mutual suspicion between the state and the citizen. This signal failure, the establishment of a confident, viable and efficient Indian state, nourished by effective institutional instruments, and sustained by a willing and cooperative citizenry has become a political and cultural trait; it both prescribes the form and constricts the functioning of the Indian state, even today. In the process it has prevented India from developing its true power.

The ethos of the Indian state was crippled by another great failing. Not just occasional, often an excessive, and at times ersatz pacifism, both internal and external, has twisted India's strategic culture into all kinds of absurdities. Many influences have contributed to this: an accommodative and forgiving Hindu milieu; successive Jain, Buddhist, and later Vaishnav-Bhakti influences resulting in excessive piety and, much later, in the twentieth century – *ahimsa* or non-violence. An unintended consequence of all these influences, spread over many centuries, has been a near total emasculation of the concept of state power, also its proper employment as an instrument of state policy, in service of national interests. War was shunned, a linear consequence of both Jain and Buddhist logic and a belief in non-injury; but it was deprecated by

Somadeva, a Jain Scripturist even as a 'tool of state craft' because it was so uncertain [in] its outcome, to be resorted to only when intrigue had been tried and had failed. He advised rulers instead to engage in kutayuddah, translated in this contextas'treacherous fighting', and tushnidanda, translated as 'silent fighting', involving the uses of poison and intrigue. Another Jain author, Hemachandra, similarly advised against the risks and costs of open war, favouring the use of bribery, conciliation, and efforts to promote dissension in the enemy camp.[21]

The remarkable aspect is not that this pacifist thought developed but that despite it so much else about warfare as an instrument of policy, about the craft of war, about valour and heroism remained. That despite the combined cultural influences of such pacifist faiths, Islamic conquest of just parts of India needed many centuries of strife; that even at the height of its glory and spread the Mughal Empire did not encompass the whole of India, and that it was in reality not so much a 'Mughal' empire as a political-military alliance, a coalition of the principal Rajput feudatories of the period and the Mughals. Despite the earlier Delhi Sultanates, the Vijaynagar Empire flowered in the South. Later still, the Maratha Confederacy checked Aurangzeb and upon his demise carried its sway deep into the Indo-Gangetic plains and other parts. Much further to the North the tenets of Sikh faith, infused by the martial spirit of Guru Gobind Singh, gave birth ultimately to an empire that planted its standards in Kabul; the Dogras, later, went deep into Tibet; the Jats of Bharatpur, Dholpur and regions around Mathura-Agra in the heart of the Indo-Gangetic plains provided early checks to the British. These were, by any standards, achievements which were not possible without a highly developed sense of the military craft; but of a larger strategic culture, alas, they remained largely innocent.

As Jadunath Sarkar, the foremost Indian historian of ancient and Mughal military affairs, has observed, 'these armies were largely levy, improvised for national defence under threat of invasion', and while 'the Indian defenders were brave. . . each man fought to the death in isolation . . .' At the strategic level, the leadership was composed of disunited tribal leaders, and thus, in consequence, 'divided we fell'. This aspect of lack of unity is a point that has been made often. In turn this was in itself both a cause and a consequence. Disunity was amongst the principal causes that resulted in conquest and military defeat, yet, it was an inevitable consequence of the absence of an Indian state; of a sense, therefore, of the territorial geography of such a state; an absence, too, of a sense of history which otherwise would have carried the lessons of the past.

That is why even as India and its many constituents were each of them separately self-governed, also well governed and prosperous, the country at large assured in the steady functioning of a highly developed civilization and culture, where art and science and music and literature flourished, yet they failed to 'serve for the national and political unification of India and failed in the end to secure it against foreign invasion, the disruption of its institutions and an age of long servitude'.[22] The political system (as derived from a larger political culture) of a society has to be judged, no doubt first and foremost by the stability, prosperity, internal freedom and order it ensures to the people, but it must also be judged by the security it erects against other states, its unity and power of defence and aggression against external rivals and enemies.

It is not perhaps altogether to the credit of humanity that it should be so and a nation or people that is inferior in this kind of political strength, as were the ancient Greeks and mediaeval Italians, may be spiritually and culturally far superior to its conquerors and may well have contributed more to a true human progress than successful military states, aggressive communities, predatory empires. But the life of man is still predominatingly vital and moved therefore by the tendencies of expansion, possession, aggression, mutual struggle for absorption and dominant survival which are the first law of life, and a collective mind and consciousness that gives a constant proof of incapacity for aggression and defence and does not organize the centralized and efficient unity necessary to its own safety, is clearly one that in the political field falls far short of the first order. India has never been nationally and politically one. India was for close on a thousand years swept by barbaric invasions and for almost another thousand years in servitude to successive foreign masters. It is clear therefore that judgment of political incapacity must be passed against the Indian people.[23]

As a constituent of strategic culture, a sense of history, of a recording of it, evaluating and assessing it, and then utilizing it as an input in decision-making has not been there. This absence of a written historical account of India can be variously explained: on account of a lack of unity, there being no one India; that the Indian tradition is more oral; that religious texts, in any event, have always had greater merit. No matter what the causes, the consequence of this absence (of a sense of history) has significantly affected the development of India's strategic thought. For this sense of history is an integral part of military science. That is why, as already observed, whereas ancient Indian texts on every conceivable subject abound – on art and dance and drama, most abundantly on philosophy – there are none, other than Kautilya, that have detailed the military science of India. There is another factor: of geography, of a sense of territory. Indian nationhood, being largely cultural and civilizational, and Indians being supremely contented with what was theirs feared no loss of it, for it – the civilizational – was as unconquerable as is the spirit. Thus, both were absent: a territorial consciousness, and a strategic sense about the protection of the territory of residence. Romila Thapar, a historian of renown, observes upon the phenomena:

Perhaps the most popular of the major sacrifices was the *Ashvamedha,* or horse-sacrifice, where a special horse was permitted to wander at will, the king claiming the territory over which it [so] wandered. . . . an illustration of non-territoriality, arbitrariness, shifting frontiers determined by the grazing impulses of horse freed from its stable and keepers.[24]

But we judge harshly for the times and its demands were altogether different.

There were some other, militarily more damaging, consequences of these misattributes. Adversaries were confronted but only after invasion, then too, on a ground of the former's choosing; they were never, of course, pursued, and threats were not recognized until they actually occurred; they were neither anticipated nor neutralized beyond the territory, before they could actually materialize. This too was perhaps an aspect of near total preoccupation with management of internal order. This absence of a sense of geographical territory persisted from ancient India down the ages, to the medieval period and even later. Of none of these periods does there exist even a suggestion of a reliable map, even though there are descriptions, but with only the unmistakable landmarks being fixed – say, of rivers, the mountains, or the ocean. It is only during the British reign that territory, its survey, settlement, and mapping came recognizably to India. And yet after Independence it faded again, the 'older cultural verities' surfacing. For independent India this can only, in part, be explained away on grounds of a division of the country. The ill is deeper, as we shall see in subsequent chapters. But one thought merits attention. It is this twining of the historical and geographical (senses) that has contributed to a such a sharp and clear response to the invasion and annexation of parts of Kashmir. However, this is not so in the case of the dispute in the North-East and Ladakh with the People's Republic of China. That is why the proposition that historically India is not a fact, more an idea is so routinely made:

Even today, despite the fact that it has acquired the lineaments of a State, even a Nation-State (the qualifying attribute being a matter of disputation). This State was the creation of the British during the two hundred years of their rule: they first gave it a territorial, pan-Indian jurisprudential, political, economic and administrative identity superimposed on the several plural identities of the subjects of an imperial conquest of an area of subcontinental proportions. The sovereign republic of India that inherited this entity by an Act of the British Parliament fifty years ago is still grappling with the ambiguities of this legacy. There is no difficulty in agreeing that, despite the Mauryan, Gupta and Moghul empires that rose in different centuries of pre-British Indian history, there was no pan-Indian state, certainly not on the scale of the British empire in India or with the same reach of authority of the Central power. And since enforceable power is the basic attribute of a State, there indeed was no political fact called India before the British established their rule in India.[25]

What did this British period impart to India? 'A defined territory . . .; a national armed forces; uniform philosophy of jurisprudence, a common civil service, a judiciary.'[26] But that was not all: of course, the railways were introduced, but that could have been as a facilitator to trade and telegraph – an additional aid to internal order? For our enquiry, more relevantly, they introduced the basics of a modern nation state in whose wake came the various institutions and apparatus of it. This notwithstanding, the British left India with around 600 states. Empire builders as they were, the British conducted extensive and perhaps the first detailed surveys of India. They mapped it indefatigably, often at great risk and over the entire terrain of India: its land, rivers, mountains, and passes. They conducted censuses and published highly informative gazetteers of the districts that they administered.

Inveterate diary-keepers, and note-takers, they kept accounts of what they saw and did. But in the military field they brought uniformity of recruitment, of fixed, assured (much more important) pay and pay scales. They introduced drill and training, military law and acts governing the conduct and discipline of troops and officers. Independent India is yet to replace this antiquated imperial anachronism. But the most significant contribution was this practice of surveys and map-making; of recording all that happens; a law for the military and a detailed system of military administration; and most important was the progress from dependence on conquered territory to a system of integral logistical arrangements about all the supplies needed. They recognized that for the defence of India, strategically, the adjacent lands were vital. Thus, preventing ingress into India became a strategic objective; hence Tibet, the Great Game, Afghanistan, Burma, the Indian Ocean and always a consciousness about Russian designs. As the Empire was a child of British trade, Indian Ocean and ocean routes came into Indian strategic thinking for the first time. They built a 'surplus of military power' in India which, if ever the occasion arose, could be employed outside of India, as we shall see in the next chapter. With this accumulated and often confusing inheritance, how then did Independent India fare?

The British period had given to India an opening to more current military science. During this period, the Indian Army got an exposure to warfare outside the country. Its natural fighting abilities were tested, honed and a large number of officers and men acquired experience in modern (then) warfare; tactical skills of battle management up to the level of companies and battalions (seldom, and only in exceptional cases, up to a brigade) improved greatly through combat experience. Though the Indian Army participated with great distinction in both the great wars (First World War and Second World War) of the twentieth century, its conduct during these conflicts is not central to our enquiry but for one singular fact. Field Marshal Slim's XIVth Army, which stopped the Japanese invasion of India at Kohima and Imphal, was very largely an Indian Army. The Japanese till then had been an invincible force, sweeping away all that confronted them: Russia, China, Great Britain and the USA. This seemingly unstoppable Japanese force was halted, turned back and eventually defeated by the Indian Army; officered preponderantly by British officers, but comprising almost entirely of Indian soldiers.

Within just about two years of the first ever (and hitherto only) use of an atomic bomb during war resulting in victory in both Europe and over Japan, India gained independence. India was divided and Pakistan was born. The era of the end of colonial rule opened; in 1949 communist revolution swept across China; a great cold descended between the West and the East; Churchill at Fulton and Truman about the Atlantic Charter and Truman Doctrine on 12 March 1947 drew the first sketch map of a 'policy of containment'. The Second World War ended but only to become the Cold War.

Each of these events (and it is not an exhaustive catalogue this) exemplified a strategic challenge to the statecraft and strategic thinking of a nascent India. How did India measure up to these challenges? And were these the only challenges? An explanation is necessary. For the entire period of British rule, policy about the defence of India and its external relations had been the preserve, total and exclusive, of the British alone, and that too from Whitehall. No Indian was involved in conceptualizing foreign and defence policies; or even in subsequent strategic planning. In 1947, the resource pool, therefore, of thought, talent and personnel specializing in these fields was almost entirely non-existent.

But independence brought in its wake a number of other, more domestic, problems too. They were social – coping with the vast millions (estimates vary between 20 and 25 million) that had been uprooted by partition; economic – tackling simultaneously the challenge of partition and post-war restoration of growth; integration – of the states (numbering around 600), their various administrative systems and norms; of their Armies(the State forces), and above all stabilizing the Indian armed forces themselves from the multifaceted consequences of the end of war; INA trials; demobilization; division and reorganization consequent upon partition; separation and splitting up of units, and of course assets. The British withdrawal from India was not, as is often asserted, an act of high statesmanship. A war-ravaged Britain was no longer in a position to hold India in bondage; its intelligence network in India had in any case been warning of great disorder and public upheaval to follow if India did not gain independence; besides, British economic conditions in 1944-46 simply could not have permitted any continued occupation of India. The process of granting independence itself was, therefore, a greatly hastened and a hasty process. On 15 August 1947 when Independence arrived, the country was partitioned but exactly where the new boundary line ran was not announced until three days later – an act of near unbelievable insensitivity and administrative arbitrariness.

In these circumstances the formidable and daunting tasks confronting independent India's political-administrative-military leadership were multidimensional. At the level of strategic planning and execution they included, amongst others, at least the following:

• Formulation and enunciation of India's foreign policy.
• Organizing the higher defence and military organizations.
• Approach to the dawning of the age of atomic weaponry.
• Assessment of the dawning of the Cold War and India's response.
• Evaluation of the geopolitical realities of a post-colonial Asia.
• Evolution of India's post-Independence armed forces.
• India and its newly independent neighbours in South Asia, particularly Pakistan.
• India and China.

This can by no means claim to be an exhaustive catalogue. It suffers from another major deficiency: that of vision improved by the focus of hindsight. Yet, how else, if not through such distancing, can any historical evaluation of independent India's strategic culture be conducted?

The first priority was, of course, the economic growth of India. This, by any reckoning, is a vital integer of any nation's power and India's first prime minister, Pandit Jawaharlal Nehru, accepted this as his first challenge, his first responsibility. There is, however, only one and retrospectively a cruel criterion that can be applied. Did he succeed in achieving what he had so eloquently described 'the establishment of a just society through just means'? Not significantly. The other criterion, even more significant and challenging, was the establishment of an effective, efficient, caring and an accountable state of India with the institutions of such a state functioning truly as the 'steel framework' of it, no matter what. This too, regrettably, did not happen. Governance regressed, the concept of power became personalized, sinking subconsciously into an older reality. Consequences, all too visible now, were thereafter inevitable. But Pandit Nehru had as his own preserve what he most coveted: the sphere of independent India's foreign, and, by deduction, also its defence policies. How did he fare? This focussing on only one of the more than ten premiers of independent India in the last fifty years is not a bias. It is a recognition of the stamp that that first premier, Pandit Jawaharlal Nehru, has left on the entire political consciousness of India. That is why a focus on his policies – foreign and defence – is the appropriate measure of evaluating India's strategic culture in the first half century of its independence.

Jagat Mehta, a former Foreign Secretary of India, a career diplomat of distinguished service who had worked in Pandit Nehru's office, and with him, has commented on some of the various aspects of our enquiry. In the early phase of independence, the principal foreign policy challenge was that of giving conceptual definition to India's foreign policy. I rely for that on his personal observations. For Nehru's defence policy I depend on the Congress party's official history of the period, and *Nehru's Defence Policy* by K. Subrahmanyam. But there is one other, equally valuable, source. Late Pandit Nehru's nephew, B. K. Nehru, himself of distinguished diplomatic and foreign service, has shared his assessment. But first he qualifies.

As a precautionary statement . . . I might explain that I was not by any means a regular adviser . . . to Panditji. My own interest lay only in economic affairs for the reason I have explained in my memoirs which was that the only aim before us at the stage our society has reached, and even more at [that] earlier stage at which Panditji guided our destiny, was to make ourselves economically strong. Foreign affairs in which I got involved as a result of my interest in economic affairs was for me a secondary interest and so was our defence policy. The result was that our discussions on these subjects whenever they took place were neither deep nor detailed.

I might also explain that my own view of Jawaharlal was, as I have expressed elsewhere, that he was an English nobility. He was himself so pure of all guile and the pursuit of self-interest that he found it difficult to appreciate that there were people in the world not quite as pure as himself. His father knew this weakness of his and used quite often to tell me that he had no judgment of men because he assumed that they were all as good, as honest, as unselfish as he was. It is remarkable that in spite of his seventeen years of ruling our country, which is a long enough period to disillusion even the noblest of souls and in which he had found dishonesty in plenty, he still could not tarnish his idealism with realism. More than once I said to him that the weakness in his policies was that he thought that the whole country consisted of Jawaharlal Nehrus. His answer, of course, was that he was not fool enough to believe in such a thing. But the fact nevertheless remains that he continued to trust the words

of his countrymen as well as those of the world.
The reference of Kashmir to the U.N. was a
typical case of his trust in the goodness and
honesty of humanity. His economic policy, his
foreign policy and consequently his defence policy
was based less on a cool, calm assessment of
facts giving due weight age to human greed
and human deceit than on idealism.[27]

The independence of India on 15 August 1947 was
an event of major global significance. It marked the
beginning of the end of the 'Age of Imperial Civilization',
that evocative and felicitous phrase of André Malraux's.
But as Aung San, the President of Burma, now Myanmar,
was to remark on 4 June 1947, the day after Mountbatten
announced the partition plan: 'A divided India augurs
ill not only for the Indian people but for all Asia and
the whole world.'[28]
Jagat Mehta adds:

Indian independence set in motion the era of
decolonisation. Indeed, India actively supported
the process and became its spokesman in the
UN, even before its own freedom. There were
hopes amongst governments and liberal thinkers
that India's advent to the international democracy
where, new nations and old, as equal partners,
would create a new force against international
conflict and provide an impetus for enlightened
cooperation amongst independent nations. As a
country with old traditions of ethnic and religious
assimilation, and regional and linguistic diversity,
the Indian civilisation had been a kind of a
cultural melting pot. It had no tradition of isolation
and superiority as in China, no nostalgia for
an empire as in Vietnam towards Cambodia and
Laos and as Europeans had towards their old
colonies. Its self-confidence had been reinforced
by Mahatma Gandhi's political leadership, which
aroused a mass political awakening but combined

it with a movement for social reform. India was seen as likely to prove a bulwark of peace and stability in the world.[29]

Such at least were the high aspirations. This gave to Indian foreign policy a harmony with its prevalent social philosophy (and beliefs), a continuity with the impulses of non-violence of the freedom movement and provided Pandit Nehru, as the first premier of an emergent India, a natural platform from which to be the voice of the Third World. To a query whether Nehru had actually sought any such leadership, B. K. Nehru has given his personal, subjective reaction.

I would totally disagree with the thesis that Nehru had 'assumed a Third World leadership role' because of the respect in which India was held by the decolonised countries. He assumed no role whatever, the leadership of the Third World was thrust upon him out of respect for his life long struggle for independence and for his real concern for freedom from colonial rule not only for India but for all the countries who were subject to imperialism. I can personally vouch, from my experience from 1949 onwards for the fact that the respect which the entire world, including the imperialistic world, showed for Jawaharlal was not due to any respect for India at all. Indeed the exact contrary of it was true; the respect shown for India was merely the reflection of the respect shown to Jawaharlal. It was in fact one of the greatest mistakes of those involved in our foreign policy, including the whole lot of our foreign service officers, that they thought that the respect in which they were held abroad was because they were Indians. This was not true at all; the realists of the world respected [and respect] only power and India had none. Nevertheless, the position of spokesman for the conscience of the world which Jawaharlal

occupied till 1961 was due to his idealism and
vision and not to his being an Indian. The voice
of Sir B. N. Rau which reflected the voice and
ideals of Jawaharlal was held in high respect,
the voice of Krishna Menon which was recognisably
not that of Jawaharlal was not respected at all
– no matter what our newspapers said.[30]

Echoing Aung San's fears, Jagat Mehta expresses
a view that much of this downgrading of India
in its international position can be traced back
to the fragmentation of its geographical unity which
damaged the historical synthesis of its old civilization.

Had the partition of the subcontinent taken place
even a decade earlier, India and Pakistan, with
or without a reunion, might in 30 years have
rediscovered the logic of their interdependence and
developed by now a relationship of trust and
cooperation between them. If [now] the beginnings
of such a denouement is no more than a distant
goal of public policies, it is very largely because
the artificial division of India got fused into
the other great divide – the postwar bipolarity
of power politics.[31]

The partition took place in bitterness, left a legacy
of suspicion and started a kind of cold war between
India and Pakistan, which continues with

periodic conflicts [and] persisting militarisation,
[which] has resulted in the economic emasculation
of both the countries. The contenders in this
little cold war exploit competitively, but in different
ways . . . their respective relationships with
major powers. The end result today is that there
is neither a natural relationship of harmony within
the subcontinent nor are the powers comfortable
or confident with their relations with the countries
of the subcontinent.[32]

The subcontinent remains one of the most tense if not explosive regions in Asia and the world.

The reason is not entirely due to the inability of India and Pakistan to resolve their problems (as argued by the major powers) nor the quarrel of the great powers (as exploited in the subcontinent) but the interaction of the two cold wars.[33]

The partition of India has many similarities in the division of the Western world (to which Russia also belonged). Both divisions were artificial. They separated natural geographical and economic entities which over the millennia had evolved a distinct common civilization and culture different from other major regions of the world. In both cases a universalistic faith – Marxist dogma in one case and Islamic political theology [in the other] was introduced against the emerging secularisation of the politics of nation states. What has not been noticed is that the critical decision which led to these divisions, and started these two cold wars were taken in almost the same hundred days in the Spring of 1947. This accidental synchronisation may well have been responsible for the myopia and failure to foresee the consequences for the subcontinent and the prospect of balance and stability in Asia.[34]

Did Pandit Nehru see all this or anticipate the likely course of events? Certainly not in the early years before and after Independence. Though one of the principal architects of the partition, he remained largely unconvinced by the viability and sustainability of Pakistan as a nation state. As B. K. Nehru has shared:

Who then was he to turn to for advice or for a debate on foreign policy? The only one to whom he could was his evil genius Krishna Menon, whose claim to knowledge of foreign policy vested very largely on his membership of the extreme left-wing of the Labour Party. The effect of this was to strengthen his innate dislike of the brashness, the crudity and the "vulgarity" of the United States and increased his trust in the words of the communists who continuously stressed the threat from Pakistan and invariably underplayed China.[35]

The partition of the country lent support to this kind of expression; it came more easily than an immediate or early acceptance and a proper assessment of the short- and long-term strategic consequences of an Islamic Pakistan, carved out of India and living in a state of tense hostility with it. Pandit Nehru laid the foundation of India's early attitude, which over time events fixed, and which subsequent political leaders could not or did not significantly alter. Pandit Nehru was his own foreign policymaker, and

I am not at all sure that Panditji had any fixation on Pakistan in regard to any threat into our national security. If there was any fixation it was that of Krishna Menon, not his. Judging from conversations on various occasions I had with the Prime Minister, his attitude on Pakistan always seemed to be that Pakistan's internal problems would prevent it from lasting for any length of time. He was in fact somewhat contemptuous of the ability of Pakistan to continue to exist. "Let us see how long it lasts."[36]

This early mental attitude and approach to Pakistan and the first conflict of 1948 perhaps lie at the root of current Indo-Pak difficulties. Which is not to suggest that the attitude of Pakistan was more conciliatory or tolerant; it could not be, for Pakistan had sought a separate existence and after partition endeavoured consciously to give to itself altogether a different – a more unIndian and a purely Islamic and West Asian – identity. That it has not succeeded in these goals, except in maintaining tense hostility is altogether a different point not central to our current enquiry. What is an indisputable fact is that this Indo-Pak standoff has caused untold and avoidable suffering to over 1.2 billion humans: it has quartered the creative energies of both the countries, and has held to ransom the economic growth of the entire South Asian region. But is Pandit Nehru alone to answer? Perhaps not, but he was certainly responsible for not having adequately assessed the long-term strategic consequences of such a standoff and confrontation. Nehru spoke of Asian solidarity and stood for Third World unity, but when it came to Pakistan and other neighbouring countries he was singularly indifferent. It is as if he had a blind spot, or found the neighbourhood too messy; thus he sought the larger platform and revelled in the spotlights of that platform. In his first major international effort, the Asian Relations Conference that he had organised in March 1947,

> Nehru presided over it, delivered an inspired address to the delegates, spoke of his vision of a confederation of emergent Asia, and unity around the Indian ocean; but sadly he gave voice to Asian unity even as India was [being] torn [apart] by disunity and [was] headed for partition.[37]

Did his approach prevent an unemotional and a better critique of the emerging strategic situation in India? The answer has to be yes.

There was one other failure, rather curious, of great long-term significance; that which could have altered the course of the history of the entire subcontinent. It is, of course, speculative and benefits from time – distance also lending post-facto clarity to analysis – yet it is worthy of thought. I refer to the Atlantic Charter which had been proclaimed by Truman on 12 March 1947.

The Indian leadership must have read the reports

of it; certainly Pandit Nehru who had maintained a deep interest in international developments during the inter-war years. But he did not foresee the likely consequences of the looming global cold war, and its relevance as a factor on whether or not to acquiesce in the division of India. The non-official Asian Relations Conference started on 23rd March 1947 – the day after Mountbatten's arrival in India. Despite his responsibilities as head of the interim government and as principal leader of the Congress party, Nehru presided over the Asian Conference. He delivered one of his most inspiring speeches to the delegates, who had gathered from all over independent and colonial Asia. His theme was the emergence of Asia; he foresaw an Asian Federation and unity around the Indian Ocean. But he did not foresee that the chances of such hopes were, at that very moment, being jeopardised by the Cold war heralded by the Truman doctrine. He did not see that his dreams for India would be enfeebled by accepting partition – which had not yet been decided. He did not raise with Mountbatten (a former Supreme Commander with a feel for Asian resurgence) or with the US, the possible international consequences of the division of India in the light of Truman's speech. Had he done so, there might have been a pause before the fateful decision which was to be taken in the next two months. . . . Only Maulana Azad, the then President of the Indian National Congress, had some premonition of the disastrous international consequences of the vivisection of India.

On 5th June 1947 (two days after the British decision on the partition of India was announced) as a result of work . . . under George Kennan, General Marshall in his Harvard commencement speech made an American offer for a European recovery programme. The Marshall Plan (as Truman wanted it to be called) symbolised the end of the quest for coordination in post-war economic and political policies between the wartime allies. The Truman doctrine and the Marshall plan were the critical milestones leading to the global Cold War. The integration of the three western zones, the bifurcation of Europe, the creation of the NATO and the *Warsaw Pact, indeed the whole political Armageddon of post-war bipolarity* which followed were implicit in these decisions.[38]

The implications, however, of a divided South Asian subcontinent, on Asia, on a post Second World War polity, on the strategic calculus of an emerging bipolar globe did not feature in the reflections of any of the parties involved.

The partition of India and the dawn of the Cold War coincided in time. The effect of the second was experienced almost immediately – in Jammu & Kashmir. This had foreign policy implications, and should immediately have been assessed as such. A military conflict had followed the Pakistan-inspired tribal invasion of the state. Nehru authorized an appeal to the United Nations Security Council to secure their withdrawal – a critical strategic error which we shall assess in some detail subsequently. What needs to be emphasized here are two aspects: that a reference was made to UN in a 'spirit of internationalism', and that Western powers, under advice of British 'expertise', sought to treat the Kashmir question as if it was still some kind of an internal pre-independence problem – to determine whether Kashmir, with a Muslim majority, should be a part of India.

Germane to our analysis is a recall of other important international developments, particularly in China. In September 1947 an answer to the Truman doctrine and the Marshall Plan was found in the launching of the Cominform. The world, it was announced, was facing a struggle between the 'imperialist and capitalist forces' and the 'socialistic democratic anti-imperialist camp' and that there could be no coexistence.

By the end of 1947 and early 1948 it had also become clearer (as it was not in early 1947) that Kuo-min-Tang (KMT) could not defeat the People's Liberation Army (PLA) in China; in fact, observers began to foresee the eventuality of a Communist victory over the whole of China. The prospectus of a US-Communist China rapprochement and a KMT/CPC coalition had been abandoned when General Marshal returned from China in December 1946. However by the end of 1947, Mao-tse-Tung was to claim that the civil war had reached a turning point. It was only a little later that Mao was to make plain that he saw no middle or third way between the two camps and China must tilt towards the USSR. But by the end of 1947 it was on the cards that China would become an ally of the USSR and the world scene would become the playground of two mammoth ideological and military blocs.[39]

This background and analysis is of significance for it was against this evolving international backdrop that independent India's foreign and defence policies took shape. Besides, these events dictated, even if indirectly and at first unknowingly, Indian responses, for involved were the four corners of the country's foreign policy: what shape was to be given to the bilateral relations between an emergent India and Pakistan; how was India to approach a new Asian giant, China, then and in the long term; how was it to approach that northern superpower, the USSR; and finally, what shape was to be given to Indo-US relations?

India's answer to global bipolarity was the principle of non-alignment: an appropriate response which gave India the needed flexibility. It provided the correct policy platform for an assertion of the sovereignty of a newly independent India in international relations; it echoed accurately the sentiments of the emergent, post-colonialism Third World; and it adequately subserved India's national interests. In practice, however, and with the passage of time – even though non-alignment was not equidistance – the responses of the Nehru government to global issues like Hungary (1956) or Czechoslovakia robbed the non-aligned platform of the lustre of principle and (some) moral authority.

The socialist bloc became the natural allies of the non-aligned; at least in pronouncements, but notwithstanding that, for Indo-Soviet relations and despite Stalin during the early years of Independence, yet again non-alignment was the correct policy.

In the locked-in position of global bipolarity and given the Dullesian categorization of non-alignment as 'immoral', unavoidably thereafter, Indo-US relations suffered.

And it is here that the fourth corner, that of Indo-Pak relations, not only suffered the most through neglect and prejudice, these bilateral relations, in turn, got intermeshed with a mushrooming global bipolarity and thus the Indo-Pak factor became an aspect of superpower rivalry.

Their (the superpowers') attitude on Indo-Pak problems became almost the touchstone of India's international friendships, but, even so, the world has tended to remain neutral on intra-subcontinental problems.

Africa and the Arab world [themselves] look to India's support in their regional or continental problems. India still has a preeminent position in the nonalignment movement and the group of 1977. But the Third World [continues to] shirk from [a] categorical or full throated support for India on subcontinental problems.[40]

Meanwhile, the [self-] evident has to be restated:

Democratic India, not enfeebled by [this] subcontinental cold war, would have been a far more powerful bulwark of stability in the wider context of Asia. It would have been a more credible spokesman for international detente.[41]

The second major challenge was undoubtedly the emergence of the People's Republic of China, the possibilities and the potential of it. Though we will examine this question in greater detail subsequently, and in other chapters too, nevertheless a brief reference here to the reality of the Sino-Indian dispute, standoff, conflict and the present tepidity of relations, combined with unresolved problems, is essential. The second President of India, Dr Radhakrishnan in an uncharacteristic rebuke from that high perch of philosopher-president, had found it necessary to admonish Nehru's government of 'credulity' in the conduct of its China policy. Nehru himself explained his position to the Indian Parliament, as quoted extensively in Chapter Three of this book. But the core of his position on China, 'Hindi-Chini Bhai-Bhai' and 'Panchsheel', perished on the bleak heights of the Aksai Chin, and the high passes of North-East India in the late autumn of 1962. This was a major strategic error for which successive generations of Indians have paid, indeed are still paying.

These two significant foreign policy errors were the direct outcome of Nehru's idealistic romanticism and also, because he did not encourage the institutionalizing of strategic thinking, policy formulation and implementation. This point has been made repeatedly: what is shared here is B. K. Nehru's assessment and interpretation of Pandit Nehru's foreign policymaking:

It is true that "he made foreign policy almost extemporaneously". I remember him once telling me that *"Taar aate hain to main wahin par jawab likh deta hoon"* (Telegrams arrive and I write a reply on the spot) and "then you fellows come along and tell me that I was wrong". But please remember the fact that there was nobody, literally nobody, in India who, till Independence, knew anything at all about foreign affairs. Nor did our Foreign Office realise that foreign policy meant the relentless pursuit of one's own national interest and not only the establishment of a

just world order which, till long after Nehru's death, seemed to continue to be our primary aim. There was no politician in Panditji's cabinet (except Krishna Menon) who knew anything or cared anything about the world outside India – except for what had only then technically become foreign territory i.e. Pakistan. The people who manned the Foreign Office, all of whom I knew well, were [like myself] ignorant of foreign affairs. [The sole exception among them was Girija Shankar Bajpai.] Such knowledge as they had of diplomacy came from the reading of history books and memoirs of diplomats and was in fact theoretical and antiquated. The result was that they accepted fully the international consequences of the Prime Minister's idealism and regarded justice and fairness for the downtrodden and exploited of the world as the objective of Indian foreign policy.
. . .

As for China, as I have said above, he refused to accept till the last moment that there was any military threat from it at all. If he bent backwards in accommodating China it was not out of fear of what it would do but out of the belief common among gentlemen . . . that human nature being essentially good, one-sided favours done to our neighbours would fill them with gratitude and would cause them to reciprocate. The ease with which, in the Treaty with China, we gave up every single right of ours in Tibet was due not to any fear that China might get its will through force of arms but from the feeling that our rights in Tibet were imperialistic and imperialism being by definition bad we had no right to continue to claim any of the various concessions which had been extracted by the imperialists from a weak and defenseless country.[42]

Strategically, the concept of non-alignment in all

respects eminently suited independent India's conceptualization of a policy plank; also for the conduct of its international relations. The determination, however, of the success or failure of this vital plank of our national strategy can only be our relations with the neighbours, the superpowers, and the Third World.

During these decades whenever there were moments of actual conflict within the subcontinent or periods of hopeful improvements in Indo-Pak relations, both superpowers showed a parallel interest not to exacerbate the problem but to encourage the easing of tensions in the region. As we have seen, neither power foresaw in the partition (1945-47) any future advantage for their national interests even though they were ranging themselves in global confrontation.

During Stalin's lifetime the ideological prescription of proletarian internationalism only banked on the economic determinism of Marxist philosophy to bring a socialist transformation in Asia. Coexistence between different social systems, endorsement of non-alignment and inter-governmental economic relations only developed after the visit of Khrushchev and Bulganin to India in 1955. What is relevant to recall is that following the India-China conflict and the dramatic improvement of India's relations with the West – when the USA and the UK sought to mediate and resolve the Kashmir problems through the shuttle diplomacy of Averill Hariman and Duncan Sandys – the USSR did not try to frustrate the efforts. Indeed according to Prof. J. K. Galbraith, the then American Ambassador to India, his Soviet colleague showed no jealous concern at the emergence of the US as the dependable friend of India. The tables were turned at the time of the next Indo-Pak war in 1965. The USA seemed to have actually prompted the USSR to play the honest broker between India and Pakistan. In any case the USA and the UK welcomed Kosygin's skillful efforts which resulted in the Tashkent agreement. Similarly both the USA and the USSR made the same kind of approaches urging India and Pakistan to subscribe to the Non-Proliferation Treaty and sought to discourage nuclear explosions by both countries. Instability and tensions was not the goal of their policy but it was the unintended consequence of their policies.[43]

Neglect of relations with the neighbourhood resulted in an 'internationalisation of the problems of the subcontinent', which could under no circumstances be treated as being beneficial to Indian national interests. After all, superpower policies were then determined by their own strategic and political perceptions, that is their own national interests, which is not, and cannot be a synonym for Indian interests. This tendency was exacerbated

> because the countries of the subcontinent while denouncing the cold war yielded to the temptations of trying to take advantage of this competition even when Pakistan's real fears and ambitions were *vis-à-vis* India. But Pakistan was accepted as a military ally and armed in the pursuit of the American policy of military containment of USSR and China.[44]

Inevitably thereafter the Soviet response was to 'choose India'.

> In fact, both India and the Soviet Union found a convergence of interest because of the ill-conceived US policies. Pakistan befriended China disregarding its obligations as a member of SEATO, before and during the Vietnam war, when China was even more hostile to the US than the USSR. The USSR provided arms to Pakistan including tanks in 1968 even when Pakistan was a US ally. This was not to encourage belligerence against India but as a part of its own strategy to

neutralize Chinese standing in Pakistan. In other words, every country tried to use the other but did not foresee the danger and limitations of trying to do so.[45]

'The arms race' thesis is popular but not tenable. Both countries have been reducing defence expenditure – India since 1987 and Pakistan since 1992. And serious deterioration of bilateral relations came in the wake of the Soviet invasion of Afghanistan. The Soviet move – probably one of the most fateful mistakes in its foreign policy – was to contain a local situation which had uncontrollably gone awry. The Soviet intervention outraged Afghan nationalism and invited strong reactions from the entire Third World. The Soviet Union clearly ignored or underestimated the adverse reactions in South Asia, including those in India. But this error was compounded in the instant reactions of the US in linking the Soviet move to the hostage crisis and the oil crunch, and concluding that the Soviet action was a move to control the Gulf and was, as such, directed against the West.

The Soviet invasion led to the US constituting the RDF and urging a strategic consensus. Once again Pakistan got US arms. As for Pakistan, its arms acquisition was not to combat the USSR but essentially for 'defence' against India. The Soviet Union in turn sought to use Western reactions as a post facto justification to save the 'Democratic Republic of Afghanistan' from Western machinations. In consequence, even though Afghanistan has now all but dropped out of the agenda of both the US and Russia, Pakistan and India continue to pay a price for their respective interventions. The real damage from these misconceived interpretations and policies continues to be a danger to the prospects of stability in South and South-West Asia.

Thus as at the time of Dullesian policy, the superpowers acting or reacting in their own interests, have unwittingly revived sub-continental tensions and, in the process, only complicated their own diplomacy and long term interests.[46]

And that other major security consideration for India, after decades of being a factor in international power play, has all but vanished; the USA courts the People's Republic of China just as assiduously as does the Republic of Russia. All these complications and a compounding of India's strategic complexities, including the nuclear conundrum, can be traced back to those early errors; to the partition, to those misperceptions which yielded to the 'temptation of inviting or imposing the cold war into the region, and an absence of institutional framework for policy determination'.[47] Strategically, Nehruvian foreign policy did not leave a legacy of a stable security environment, or even secure frontiers; what it did confer as a legacy was ambivalence, ambiguities and an uncertain and apprehension-filled future.

The other major component of independent India's strategic thought – defence policy – did not receive even that treatment. Foreign policy as the forte of Pandit Nehru had a certain cachet, a glamour. Not so defence, astounding as that assertion may sound. There are many factors that contributed to this neglect, but the result was inevitable. Till 1995, a good thirty years after Nehru's passing away, India was unable to articulate an intelligible defence policy. That is why, in 1995, the Prime Minister could do no better than enunciate the country's defence policy with characteristic ambivalence to contend that the country did in fact have a defence policy (contrary to a belief on the contrary). He asserted that the policy included guidelines for the preservation of India's sovereignty and territorial integrity and to that extent exercise such influence over our neighbours as would promote our national interests. Further, he asserted that this policy would effectively contribute towards regional and international stability and prevent destabilization of small nations in the neighbourhood which in turn would prevent adverse security implications to ourselves.

The foundations of this neglect had, of course, been laid well before Independence: they lay in the cultural and civilizational roots outlined earlier; the British monopolization of this responsibility; the neglect by successive generations of Indian thinkers of this vital area of national endeavour; and a deliberate relegation of the importance of defence by post-Independence political leadership. Once again responsibility devolves upon Nehru. He had a sense of history but few of his colleagues or his successors shared that sense. The consequences of such a lack have been damaging. For obviously, a people devoid of a sense of history, and an awareness of the lessons of it, will be at a disadvantage when dealing with nations that do.

This absence (of a sense of history) is, of course, best exemplified by the fact that as yet there are no published official accounts of the various conflicts independent India has had to face, except of the first, the 1948 war. This is largely because

> those empowered to take a decision on declassifying the report are mostly generalists who hold their respective official positions for very short period[s]. They have neither an adequate background on the historical evaluation of the country's policies nor a perspective on the interrelationship between our history and that of other countries. . . . History of the 1948 Kashmir war was published [only] in 1988. Though an attempt is being made to compile a history of Bangladesh war, so much of the documentation and data is still being withheld from those entrusted with the task that the outcome could hardly be termed [as] official history. This attitude towards history stems from the generalist and adhocist approach that pervades our polity.[48]

K. Subrahmanyam, writing about Nehru's defence policy in the official history of the Congress Party, has expressed a viewpoint shared by many.

In order to develop an understanding of our defence policy in post-independence India, it is essential to look at the roots of that policy during the freedom struggle . . . since Gandhi was a fervent advocate of non-violence, Indian defence preparedness was not given the attention it deserved. . . . There is also the view that Jawaharlal Nehru was anti-militarist in his orientation and, as an advocate of peace and non-alignment, neglected the role of military power in international relations. During the early years of the first cold war, what India was advocating at that stage could easily have been justified in real-politic terms and strategic rationality. However, given the Indian environment and the traditions of the Indian freedom struggle, the argument advanced by Indians was couched in moralistic and ethical terms. The dividing line between strategic rationality and international morality is very fine indeed.[49]

Subrahmanyam then cites a conversation between the first Indian C-in-C of the independent Indian Army and Mahatma Gandhi:

General Cariappa sought a clarification from Gandhi just a month before his death. "I cannot do my duty well by the country if I concentrate only on telling troops of non-violence, all the time subordinating their main task of preparing themselves efficiently to be good soldiers. So I ask you, please, to give me a 'Child's guide to knowledge' – tell me, please, how I can put this over, i.e. the spirit of non-violence to the troops, without endangering their sense of duty to train themselves well professionally as soldiers," he asked. Gandhi replied, "You have asked me to tell you in a tangible and concrete form how you can put over to the troops the need for non-violence. I am still groping in the dark for the answer. I will find it and give it to you some day."[50]

Jawaharlal Nehru, in his speech to the Constituent Assembly (Legislative) on 7 September 1948, had said:

When this question [of the invasion of Jammu & Kashmir] first came up I sought guidance, as I often did in other matters, from Mahatmaji and I went to him repeatedly and put to him my difficulties. The House knows that the apostle of nonviolence was not a suitable guide in military matters and he said so – but he undoubtedly always was a guide on the moral issues. And so I put my difficulties and my Government's difficulties before him; and though it is not proper for me to drag in his name at this juncture in order to lessen my own responsibility or my Government's responsibility on this issue, which is complete, I nevertheless mention this matter merely to show how the moral aspect of this question has always troubled me.[51]

What is this 'moral aspect' that troubled Nehru then, also subsequently, in the face of the other challenges that his premiership faced? The question is of importance in assessing the evolution of a proper strategic culture in independent India, for it was Nehru's stewardship that set the tone, established almost all the hitherto undefined reference points, not just internally but internationally too.

This 'moral aspect' was in essence a confusion; it periodically afflicts other nations too, for example, the United States of America. It is a search for the 'moral' in the realm of international affairs, a reconciliation then of that 'moral' with the demonstrated reality of the conduct of nations in pursuit of their respective national goals and interests. It is a confusion that arises from not differentiating between individual human morality and ethics, and the reality of national interests.[52] It is also a consequence of not recognizing that between high idealism and the hard stone of a pursuit of national goals what will splinter is always this 'moral aspect'. Time and again Nehru demonstrated the same tendency: a vacillation born of his search for the idealistically moral. He appropriated the responsibility of Jammu & Kashmir, as distinct and apart from the portfolio of princely states held by his deputy prime minister, Sardar Vallabhbhai Patel. Nehru was hesitant and tentative not simply about Kashmir but on the issue of relations with China and the vital question of Tibet as well. Witness, for example, the late Sardar's clarity on the Sino-Indian question, or his firm directness about Hyderabad.

Always being 'troubled' by the individual 'moral aspect' resulted in serious long-term consequences, for India and its successive generations, in four more specific areas of critical importance: Tibet; Sino-Indian relations; Indo-Pak standoff relations as exemplified by Jammu & Kashmir; and the nuclear armament question. Ambiguity and a lack of clarity about national purpose on all the four became the national stand – as a direct legacy of the Nehru stewardship, and as a result of his leaving a stamp of his personality and thought on successive generations of the Indian political class. There was yet another major deficiency. Because Nehru so towered others around him, he, not through any act of will, more as a cultural consequence, prevented an alternative thought from emerging. He did not stifle dissent and disagreement – he was too much of a democrat for that – he just overpowered by his position, personality and standing. This, in turn, prevented healthy institutions from emerging; such established centres of policy (within and outside the government) as would provide independent, iconoclastic thought, and which could act as instruments for the implementation of policy as well.

To Nehru's influence was added the legacy of Gandhi. Subrahmanyam has trenchant views on this.

Gandhi's idea of a non-violent Indian state was based on his conviction that such a state could

be built as was done by Ashoka (*Harijan,* 12 May
1946). It was not an immediate prescription. It
was an idealistic, long term goal. But [a] major
problem in India has been that Gandhi's precepts
and practice of non-violence have not been studied
in the overall international context of the use
of the violence in offensive and defensive modes.
It has generally been assumed that the Gandhian
prescriptions of non-violent mass action would be
applicable, irrespective of the context. Recently,
after Attenborough's film, Gandhi, was released,
questions have been raised whether Gandhian
methods would have succeeded against Hitler, Stalin
and the like. . . . In strategic parlance, offence
and defence are different. While the former aims
at changing the status quo, the latter attempts
to preserve it. In India, the British Raj was on
the defensive, while the freedom movement was
on the offensive. While in the offensive mode,
the leader of the movement had the choice of
strategy, including use of massive non-violent
mobilization of the people. If the State were to
be on the offensive, the populace could not have
[been] allowed non-violent mass mobilization. .
. . That is why non-violence could not have succeeded
against Hitler, Stalin and Mao Zedong. Secondly,
there was no doubt that the Britain-India relationship
was unique and not a stereotype colonial situation.
A comparable instance of non-violent mass action
was that of Martin Luther King and the civil rights
movement in the US. There, again, Dr. King was
on the offensive to change the status quo and
he succeeded.[53]

Standing against the evolution of any comprehensive
strategic doctrine for independent India was 'Nehru's
dislike of militarism'. Accounts by contemporaries report
that when General Sir Robert Lockhart, the first
Commander-in-Chief of the Indian Army, presented a
paper to Nehru as the first Prime Minister, outlining

a plan for the growth of the Indian Army, in light of an assessment of threats, Nehru retorted: 'We don't need a defence plan. Our policy is non-violence. We foresee no military threats. Scrap the Army. The police are good enough to meet our security needs.'[54] Nehru,

> unlike his father, did not take much interest in the Indianisation of the military and problems of defence. Combined with this attitude was the high priority he gave to development and in-dustrialisation and his assessment that, in the prevailing international situation, India constituted a high enough stake to ensure that no single power would attack India as, in such an event, the other powers would combine to frustrate the attack.[55]

But there is a telling admission in Nehru's own words; writing of the Japanese advance upon India he said:

> Much as I hated war, the prospect of a Japanese invasion of India had in no way frightened me. At the back of my mind I was in a sense attracted to this coming of war, horrible as it was to before India. For I wanted a tremendous shakeup, a personal experience for millions of people, which would drag them out of that peace of the grave that Britain had imposed upon us, something that would force them to face the reality of today and to outgrow the past which clung to them so tenaciously, to get beyond the petty political squabbles and exaggeration of temporary problems which filled their minds; not to break . . . the past, and yet not to live it; realise the present and look to the future – to change the rhythm of life and make it in tune with the present and the future. The cost of war was heavy and the consequences full of uncertainty. That war was not of our

seeking but since it had come, it could be made
to harden the fibre of the nation and provide
those vital experiences out of which a new life
might blossom forth. Vast numbers would die,
that was inevitable, but it is better to die in
war than through famine; it is better to die
than to live a miserable, hopeless life. Out of
death, life is born afresh and individuals and
nations who do not know how to die, do not
know also how to live. Only where there are
graves are there resurrections.[56]

Moving, stirring words, but alas not followed when
the challenge confronted himself in 1962, and when
he as premier had to take decisions and provide the
lead.

For Nehru, India's international role was the real
test of its independence. As he put it to the Constituent
Assembly on 8 March 1949,

What does independence consist of? It consists
fundamentally and basically of foreign relations.
That is the test of independence. All else is
local autonomy. Once foreign relations go out
of your hands into the charge of somebody else
to that extent and in that measure you are
not independent.

And he had a vision of India's rightful place in
the world. In *The Discovery of India* he wrote:

Forgetting present problems then for a while
and looking ahead, India emerges as a strong
united state, a federation of free units, intimately
connected with her neighbours and playing an
important part in world affairs. She is one of
the very few countries which have the resources
and capacity to stand on their own feet. Today
probably the only such countries are the United
States and the Soviet Union – China and India

are potentially capable of joining that group –
no other country, taken singly, apart from these
four actually are potentially in such a position.
It is possible of course that larger federations
or groups of nations may emerge in Europe or
elsewhere and form huge multinational states
. . . whatever happens, it will be well for the
world if India can make her influence felt. For
that influence will always be in favour of peace
and cooperation and against aggression.[57]

In thought and in expression, inspiring and unexceptionable sentiments; when judged, however, against
the hard test of policy formulation and implementation,
sadly, our judgement has to be markedly different.
In December 1947, speaking in the Constituent
Assembly, he stated:

If there is a big war, there is no particular
reason why we should jump into it. Nevertheless,
it is little difficult nowadays in world wars to
be neutral. Any person with any knowledge of
international affairs knows that. We are not
going to join a war if we can help it; and we
are going to join the side which is to our interest
when the time comes to make the choice.[58]

Yet again a realistic and sound appraisal and a
fine pronouncement, but what of action when required?
Though he abhorred war, Nehru was not totally
averse to the use of force in defence of India's national
interest. On 11 August 1951, replying to the debate
on the President's address in Parliament, Nehru declared
that, whatever happens, India is not going to be invaded.
'Even if there is war, do you imagine that we will
wait idly to be invaded? Certainly not.' In the same
speech he said,

I have ruled out war as a measure for the
easing of Indo-Pakistan relations, but I cannot

rule it out independently or unilaterally. Since the other party brings it in and talks and shouts so much about it, I have to be perfectly ready for it.

In fact, at that stage, following the fighting speech of Pakistani Prime Minister Liaquat Ali Khan and his shaking of his fist in public demonstration, the Indian Army was moved to the border in an exercise of coercive diplomacy.[59] But this was a demonstration against Pakistan; no such firmness was, however, shown in the Sino-Indian standoff.

Between 1949-50 and 1962, the strength of the Indian armed forces almost doubled from 280,000 to 550,000. The Indian Air Force, with seven combat squadrons at the beginning of independence, expanded to 18 squadrons by 1962. During this period India became a major importer of military hardware. These were all the decisions of the Nehru government.[60]

And of this humiliating diplomatic and military failure an analysis is needed. This we shall do in the next chapter. Here what is required is Nehru's own explanation of it; for it is his defence policy that we examine. Speaking in the Parliament (Rajya Sabha) on 3 September 1963 Nehru explained: 'There was enough equipment but spread out all over India. It may not have been available at a particular place, because we had to face the situation rather suddenly and we did not have time.' He was also candid: 'There had been a slant in our minds that China would not attack us. It is perfectly true. There had been a slant in our minds in the past, not completely but partly.' There was an assessment of the Intelligence Bureau that, based on the past experience that the Chinese had not used force, when they came up against an Indian post, they were not likely to use force against a line of Indian posts set up to prevent their further encroachment.

No one raised the question, "What if there was a discontinuity in the Chinese pattern of behaviour?" But this query does not absolve, it merely explains, and is an extenuating circumstance only. For this 'slant originated in the minds of senior military men and probably influenced the thinking of Jawaharlal Nehru' too. This thinking was reflected by General Thimayya who wrote in an article in July 1962:

> Whereas in the case of Pakistan I have considered the possibility of a total war, I am afraid I cannot do so in regard to China. I cannot even as a soldier envisage India taking on China in an open conflict on its own. China's present strength in manpower, equipment and aircraft exceeds our resources a hundred-fold with the full support of the USSR, and we could never hope to match China in the foreseeable future. It must be left to the politicians and diplomats to ensure our security. . . .

And what did they do?

> The possibility of the Chinese launching a very carefully controlled limited operation, with very limited political objectives, appears to have been overlooked altogether, both in the services and political circles, and by the prime minister.[61]

Also there was an insufficient appreciation of the problems of operating aircraft from high altitude airfields. If those problems had been thought through then there would not have been as much reluctance to use Indian air power in support of our operations 1962 as there was. Perhaps it can, and with some justification, be asserted that these after all were almost entirely military issues, to be handled by the military alone. What, however, about the larger strategic issues, where diplomacy and foreign policy act as instruments of national security interests? And here the responsibility rests squarely with

Nehru. The aspect of the Sino-Soviet rift of the sixties, the withdrawal of Soviet technicians from China, the great famines, the disaster of the cultural revolution, and the combat effectiveness of the Chinese air force, none of these aspects were fully appreciated.

> What is quite evident today is that despite Nehru's reference to the possibility of a war with China for over three years – from the autumn of 1959 to the autumn of 1962 – hardly any professional thought had not been devoted to the problem of war in the Himalayas.[62]

But there were other assessments too of this second great strategic failure of Nehru; the first being obviously, Kashmir, and thus implicitly the Indo-Pak question. Michel Brecher, who spent several years in India, is recounted by Subrahmanyam as having written:

> With the Chinese occupation of Tibet, their [India's and China's] interests met in the heart of Central Asia. A conflict of interests in these circumstances might well lead to direct clash as it almost did over Tibet in 1950. But in its present position of weakness India is determined not to become embroiled in a dangerous conflict with its neighbour, unless its vital interests are openly threatened such as control over the Himalayan border states of Nepal, Bhutan and Sikkim.

It should not be inferred, however, that Nehru was dominated by these assumptions or that unqualified trust was the basis of his China policy. Indeed, he was disturbed by the evidence of Chinese penetration into the Himalayan border states and had made it abundantly clear that he considered them to be in India's 'sphere of influence'. Nor was he oblivious to the inevitable long-run rivalry between Democratic India and Communist China for the leadership of Asia. He knew fully well, but never admitted it in public, that the ideologically uncommitted countries of the area were watching the contest between Delhi and Peking, particularly in the economic realm, to see which system could 'deliver the goods'. He knew that the fate of Asia hung in the balance and hoped that sympathetic Western statesmen would realize the implications of the contest before it was too late. Thus far he had been disappointed with the evidence of [any] such imaginative understanding. It is in this context that one must evaluate Nehru's policy.[63]

Goa is yet another question that troubles us about Nehru's strategic thought. Why the attack? Besides, in December 1961, Goan operations had revealed that the Indian Army's logistics were unsatisfactory. Our soldiers did not have the necessary clothing, items or equipment when they marched into Goa.

> The railway schedules in the western and mid-western part of India were greatly dislocated on account of troop movement – and all this to carry out an operation which involved [just] one division and that too in the plains. A dispassionate assessment of the Goa operation and an attempt to draw lessons from them might have helped in avoiding the terrible mistakes that were committed in the 1962 operations.[64]

It is not as if Nehru had no understanding of essentials – he did; what was absent was that other important internal of strategic culture: effective planning and implementation. In a speech in Parliament on March 1956 he said:

> What is the equation of defence? In what lies the strength of a people for defence? Well, one thinks immediately about defence forces – army, navy, air force. . . . They are the spear points of defence. . . . How do they exist? What are they based on? The more technical armies and navies and air forces get, the more important

becomes the industrial and technological base of the country. You may import a machine or an aircraft or some other highly technical weapon and you may even teach somebody to use it, but that it is a very superficial type of defence because you have not got the technological background for it. Thus in spite of your independence you become dependent on others, and very greatly so. . . . From that point of view probably there are very few countries in the world that are really independent, able to stand on their own feet against the military strength of others. Therefore, apart from the army, navy and so on, you have to have an industrial and technological background in the country. . . . Supporting all this is the economy of the country. If the country's economy is not sound, it is a weak country. I can give many examples. The equation of defence is your defence forces plus your industrial and technological background, plus, thirdly, the economy of the country, and fourthly, the spirit of the people.[65]

He reiterated the same approach in the Lok Sabha in November 1962 while moving the resolution on the Chinese aggression. He said:

What is the war effort? People think of the soldiers on the front, which is perfectly right. They are bearing the brunt of the danger. But in the kind of struggle in which we are involved, every peasant in the field is a soldier. Our war effort essentially, apart from the actual fighting done, is in ever greater production in the field and the factory. It is an effort which depends greatly on our development. Today, we are much more in a position to make that kind of effort in the field and the factory than ten or twelve years ago. We are not still adequately developed. I hope this very crisis will make us develop

more rapidly . . . [And later he said,] . . . defence
and development were two sides of the coin.[66]

This formulation then became the basic foundation
of India's defence policy, and remained not simply
unaltered but also unquestioned. That the proposition
itself was an error, as we demonstrate in Chapter
Four, never featured. This is a tragedy because Nehru's
thinking was modern, his grasp acute, his vision
comprehensive. He was also the first head of government
outside the socialist bloc to initiate centralized planning
in economic development, that too at a time when
such centralized planning was looked upon as halfway
house to communism, but he did not initiate defence
planning, he encouraged no institutional mechanism
either.

An effective countering of the Chinese threat did
not call for the acquisition of very many sophisticated
weapons and equipments. Communications had to be
opened and measures initiated for the early development
of an adequate and effective road network all along
our borders, stationing of our men on high altitudes
and getting them acclimatized, provision of adequate
clothing and shelter at those altitudes, communication
equipment and rifles, carbines, machine guns, mortars
and light mountain artillery. This the Nehru government
did attempt. From 1950, when the Indian administration
in Arunachal Pradesh was introduced and began its
consolidation, efforts were made to develop communications.
Earlier, the Military Engineering Service was entrusted
with the responsibility of constructing roads in these
areas. Because of inadequate progress, the project was
later withdrawn from them and entrusted to the Public
Works Department but it was found by 1958-59 that
they also could not cope with this challenging task.
And thus was formed the Border Roads Organisation,
covered more extensively in Chapter Two. It was as
a consequence of 1962 that the first attempt at defence
planning commenced in 1964, just before Nehru's death.
It was under his premiership that India sought US

military assistance.[67]

A short comment alone remains to be made upon the early establishment of India's strategic thinking about neighbouring countries other than Pakistan. The attitude and approach voiced by Nehru in respect of Nepal on 17 March 1950, is telling. He informed the Constituent Assembly that

> it is not necessary for us to have a military alliance with Nepal. . . . But the fact remains that we cannot tolerate any foreign invasion from any foreign country in any part of the subcontinent. Any possible invasion of Nepal would inevitably involve the safety of India.

And this became a kind of yardstick. In consequence the treaty signed with Nepal on 31 July 1950 remains. Historians comment that this was all occasioned by a 'perceptible shift in Nepal's policy towards China, though India herself [had] initially encouraged diplomatic relations between the two countries'. The telling points, however, about these developments are: one, that the strategic definition of the 'subcontinent' got established by the Himalayas; and, two, that whereas India (then Nehru) acted when it came to Nepal, the very same Nehru did nothing when it came to neighbouring Tibet. For which last, an explanation that India did not then (in the fifties) have the resources is adequate until one examines the neglect of subsequent years. Such a distinction in approach, however, and for whatever reason, bred uncertainty and apprehensions, in the smaller neighbours, not any sense of faith and reassurance. The treaty with Bhutan in later years; the annexation of Sikkim even later; the aid to the Maldives in the late eighties; or the two military assistance programmes with Sri Lanka, in 1971 and 1987, are all part of that same strategic culture of which the root lies in 1950.

A consciousness about the power of the Indian state, its role, relevance and limitations, is the final aspect that we repeat through an examination in our scrutiny of India's strategic culture. During subsequent premierships, challenges were faced by the country and conflicts were encountered. Mrs Indira Gandhi demonstrated an extension of state power during the war for the independence of Bangladesh; she displayed a sense of it by commissioning the first underground nuclear test. Yet, in the destructive decade of the eighties, during her second premiership, the policies that were pursued by her successively in Assam, Punjab, Jammu & Kashmir and in respect of the ethnic and linguistic strife in North Sri Lanka, particularly in relations with the LTTE, were destructive in the extreme. It is as if all understanding about the nature of state power – and its limits – was by then lost by her; how else, otherwise, do we rationalize the commissioning of the first nuclear explosion and thereafter nothing at all; decade after decade it was a vacuum, a hibernation of policy and options. The approach to the entire nuclear, or strategic armaments questions has, for India, thus got trapped between Nehru's call for ban on nuclear tests made in 1954 and the first peaceful nuclear explosion conducted underground in Pokharan in 1974. And between these two identifying landmarks it still oscillates. Thus India's stated position: universal disarmament; the global reality of a fixed and near unbreachable nuclear asymmetry; and the country's strategic options remain in a situation of near permanent discord. Yet again, a consequence of this yawning absence of a sufficiently well developed culture of strategic thinking, planning and execution or even any institutional mechanism for that. K. Subrahmanyam is scathing in his commentary upon this lacuna.

> [Nehru] lent powerful support to the international peace movement [perhaps befitting] his role as an international statesman, a leader of the non-aligned and an ardent champion of peace and international development. Such pronouncements at leadership level [however,] should not have inhibited intensive [internal] debates on [the] country's security

problems and a detailed, professional consideration of measures to safeguard the country's security. But the innate sycophancy, mediocrity and indolence of political leadership at various levels, the civil and military bureaucracy, academia and media, converted Nehru's pronouncements into a convenient alibi for inaction and a lack of cerebration. These weaknesses still persist in the Indian polity and the risks are far higher now than in the Nehru period.[68]

How did the relevant right process emerge? Perhaps a fair inkling is available. Talking of the formulation of the Congress viewpoint, Nehru says,

Gandhiji found himself unable to give up his fundamental principle of non-violence ever in regard to external war. . . . He could not give up the faith of a lifetime . . . He wanted Congress to declare its adherence to the principle of non-violence even for a free India. . . . He realized that a government of free India was not likely to discard violence when questions of defence were concerned and to build up military, naval and air power. But he wanted, if possible, for Congress at least to hold the banner of non-violence aloft and thus to train the minds of the people and make them think increasingly in terms of peaceful action. He had a horror of seeing India militarized. He dreamt of India becoming a symbol and example of non-violence and by her example weaning the rest of the world from war and the ways of violence.[69]

How then were we to live in a violent world upholding the banner of non-violence, without the spine of Gandhi? This was the difference, the cause of much hesitation, vacillation and ambivalent purpose.

Nehru describes his meeting with Iqbal, whose thought has laid the foundation of the state of Pakistan.

A few months before his death, as he lay on
his side-bed, he sent for me and I gladly obeyed
the summons. As I talked to him about many
things I felt that, in spite of differences, how
much we had in common and how easy it could
be to get on with him. I admired him and his
poetry and it pleased me greatly to feel that he
liked me and had a good opinion of me. A little
before I left he said to me: "What is there in
common between Jinnah and you? He is a politician,
and you are a patriot."[70]

Apparently, Nehru was rather fond of himself for
being considered a patriot in preference to a politician.
Sir Nirad Chaudhary has this to say about Nehru:

Yet, the man who on the day of independence
became the dictator of India, was not himself
a scoundrel or even a counterfeit. He was wholly
genuine, as an Englishman of radical views. But
he was not endowed with practical political capacity.
As soon as with independence he abandoned his
former role of demagogue, he became an ineffable
ideologue, flapping his wings against the bar of
the cage in which he was put by the bureaucracy.
The political programme which he himself wished
to put into effect was to make India a Soviet
Union in technology, and a parliamentary democracy
in governance. He alone did not realize that he
was really a dictator without the will to exercise
his dictatorial power. I said so publicly in an
article published when he was living.
    But just as he would not act like a dictator,
he could not also become a practical democratic
statesman. He took refuge in escapism. He shunned
all policies and actions in which he knew he
would have to face the massive stability of the
Indian messes and the cunning self-seeking of
politicians of his party. He began to build national
structures like dams with the help of American

engineers and public buildings with the help of Le Corbusier. His object was to bypass all realities in India. I called these material structures the pyramids of Nehru; alas! not as long lasting as those at Gizah.

So, the task of actually governing and legislating India passed to the officials and Congress politicians, both of whom were hard-boiled opportunists and adventurers, the most hard-boiled to be seen anywhere in the world.[71]

If seemingly disproportionate space has been devoted to the legacy of Nehruvian strategic culture it is not on account of any bias; it is in the very progression of independent India as a viable state and an examination of the foundations. There alone, in the Nehru period that is, during this entire stretch of half a century was demonstrated any original thought. Nehru's legacy, whether still relevant or not, remains dominant, in the process providing a kind of continuity to independent India's strategic culture, even if that continuity be of negative attributes like veneration of the received wisdom; an absence of iconoclastic questioning; a still continuing lack of institutional framework for policy formulation; lack of a sense of history and geography; an absence of sufficient commitment to territorial impregnability; and a tendency to remain static in yesterday's doctrines, even form.

NOTES

1. Julius Lipner, *Hindus: Their Religious Beliefs and Practices* (London: Routledge, 1994) p. 8.
2. Ibid., p. 8.
3. Ibid., p. 8.
4. Ibid., p. 8.
5. Ibid., p. 8.
6. Stephen Peter Rosen, *India and its Armies, Societies and Military Power* (Delhi: Oxford University Press, 1996) p. 33.
7. Ibid., p. 15.
8. Ibid., p. 17.
9. Ibid., p. 18.
10. Ibid., p. 19.

11. Ibid., p. 22.
12. Ibid., p. 17.
13. Ibid., pp. 18, 19.
14. Sri Aurobindo, *The Foundations of Indian Culture* (Pondicherry: Sri Aurobindo Ashram Trust, 1959) pp. 2, 3.
15. Dr Sarvepalli Radhakrishnan, *The Supreme Spiritual Ideal* (Delhi: Oxford University Press, 1974) p. 368.
16. Ibid., p. 368.
17. Myron Weiner, *Ancient Indian Political Theory and Contemporary Indian Politics* (details not available) pp. 37, 38.
18. Stephen Peter Rosen, op. cit., p. 67.
19. Ibid., p. 67.
20. Ibid., p. 67.
21. Ibid., p. 67.
22. Sri Aurobindo, op. cit., p. 362.
23. Ibid., p. 363.
24. Romila Thapar, *A History of India,* Vol. I (New Delhi: Penguin Books, 1966) p. 54.
25. N. S. Jagannathan, *The Book Review Journal* (Delhi, September 1997).
26. Ibid.
27. B. K. Nehru in correspondence with the author.
28. Jagat S. Mehta in correspondence with the author.
29. Ibid.
30. B. K. Nehru, op. cit.
31. Jagat S. Mehta, op. cit.
32. Ibid.
33. Ibid.
34. Ibid.
35. Ibid.
36. B. K. Nehru, op. cit.
37. Ibid.
38. Jagat S. Mehta, op. cit.
39. Ibid.
40. Ibid.
41. Ibid.
42. B. K. Nehru in correspondence with the author.
43. Jagat S. Mehta, op. cit.
44. Ibid.
45. Ibid.
46. Ibid.
47. Ibid.
48. K. Subrahmanyam, 'Evolution of Indian Defence Policy 1947-64' in *A History of the Congress Party* (Delhi: AICC and Vikas Publishing House, 1990).
49. Ibid.
50. Ibid.
51. Constituent Assembly Debates.

52. K. Subrahmanyam, op. cit.
53. Ibid.
54. Major General. D. K. Palit, VrC, *Major General A. A. Rudra, His Service in Three Armies and Two World Wars* (New Delhi: Reliance, 1997).
55. K. Subrahmanyam, op. cit.
56. Ibid.
57. Ibid.
58. Ibid.
59. Ibid.
60. Ibid.
61. Ibid.
62. Ibid.
63. Ibid.
64. Ibid.
65. Ibid.
66. Ibid.
67. Parliamentary debates, Rajya Sabha, 3 September 1963. This is the most extensive explanation that Nehru ever offered to country for what was a humiliating military policy. He was forgiven by a tolerant India. This explanation, therefore, from the platform of a parliamentary debate is a must for any analyst (Rajya Sabha Secretariat, New Delhi, 1963).
68. K. Subrahmanyam, op. cit.
69. Jawaharlal Nehru, *The Discovery of India.*
70. Ibid.
71. Sir Nirad C. Chaudhary, *Three Horsemen of the New Apocalypse* (New Delhi: Oxford University Press, 1997).

2

Armed Forces

EVOLUTION

Though our focus is on the armed forces of independent India, their evolution obviously predates 1947 by many millennia. Organization, structures, arms and capabilities all evolved with time. More relevant to our purpose is the military tradition, its ethos, the evolutionary process itself, almost as a continuum from ancient to medieval India, then to the British period, whereafter to partition, its consequences and thence to the armed forces of an independent India.

Evidently we cannot dwell for long in those times, ancient or medieval; though British India – whose direct descendants are the Army, Navy and Air Force of independent India – is a different category altogether.

The tradition of arms, as a calling and a duty, is an integral part of the Indian civilization itself. A common fallacy, prejudiced to an error, is to convert this civilizational trait into somewhat simplistic caste patterns. Warfare, personal valour, and the codes of conduct in such circumstances were not the attributes of any one caste alone. 'Shakti', as a concept of power, its deification as a goddess, and its veneration is not by any one caste alone. Besides, through India's history, from the ancient to modern times arms have been taken up by all castes and classes. To carry a personal weapon was *de rigueur*, almost a dress code and this carried on well into the twentieth century. It is still so amongst many, not just the Sikhs. The disarming of India, a process imposed by a post-1857 imperial Britain, was not so much a measure for any pacification of India, as it was for attaining monopoly of the British state over the possession and use of arms. That immortal epic, Ramayana, which tells of struggle between good and evil, Ram and Ravana, illustrates the point; for the latter, Ravana, was a Brahmin (priestly caste), and his proficiency at arms has been lauded through centuries. So too the other great epic, Mahabharata, yet another account of warfare, in which too, many of various castes took up arms. In medieval times the great Rajput kingdom of Mewar had all castes fighting the invading Mughal arms shoulder to shoulder, Kshatriya, Brahmin, Vaishya and Shudra alike. That is why the coat-of-arms of Mewar has two figures – a Rajput and a Bhil (*dalit* or *adivasi* in today's parlance) – standing, puissant, supporting the shield of that ancient state. This tradition got sectionalized under the British, whose army, at least at first, was not simply of the conveniently designated 'martial classes' of India; for in reality there are no such classes – all sections of Indian society, except as explained in Chapter One, subscribe to the tradition of arms, of Shakti, and have, through the centuries, borne them with great individual valour and a highly developed sense of honour. Also, tenets like not striking at a fallen enemy, ceasing combat at sundown, of forgiving the defeated, of battle being confined to warring armies alone, not an entire society, as in today's 'total war' or, worse still, 'mutually assured destruction', were common societal traits. Deception though and the use of subterfuge and spies was very much a part of that overarching strategic culture, not really a component of the craft of war as such.

There are accounts of ancient battles, some as cited above in epic form; others, albeit partial and largely hagiographic in edicts and upon commemorative stone pillars that dot the country. Accounts remain of these valourous deeds in ballads and through the oral tradition. Deeply moving and stirring accounts of heroes of old who fought valiantly for a cause, and gave up their lives are an inherited asset of the country. In rural Indian society these ballads and tales, till recently (till the dawn of the television age, that is), were night-long performances, sometimes accompanied by drama and song. The week-long performance of that epic ballad 'Ramlila' is an example, as indeed is the dance form of Kerala, Kathakali, where, incidentally, an ancient martial art called Kalarippayat is still practised. This art, it is believed, gave birth to karate.

In weapons of war, till the advent of the British, and a slow and deliberate choking of most local crafts and skills by the occupying power, steel manufacture of quality, iron foundries, the fabrication of swords, knives and even guns was far superior to what Europe could then boast of. India could not have excelled in arts and crafts and architecture and lagged behind in weapons technology. It did not. Along with other crafts these great Indian skills were also destroyed, more particularly under British occupation. The deliberate choking of the great muslin of Dacca so that the mills of Lancashire could flourish is a case in point. Few, however, have reflected upon an attendant consequence of the disarming of India, post-1857: it was the destruction of Indian arms-making skills. Read, for instance what Philip Mason has to say about this in *A Matter of Honour:*

But, when pressed, any Englishman who knew India would admit that there were Indians whose personal courage could nowhere be surpassed. Nor was it a matter of personal prowess with weapons. All late-Victorian children had heard of Saladin, who had confounded Richard I of England by throwing up a silk cushion and slicing it in two with his scimitar while it was still in the air, a feat quite impossible for the Crusader with his straight ponderous two-handed cleaver of a sword. The tradition continued in India, where horsemen in late Mughal times spent many hours in exact training: swinging their horses in figures-of-eight that grew narrower and narrower till the horse was at such an angle that the rider could pick up a pistol from the ground; burnishing and sharpening swords so far superior to those of the British that English troopers would sometimes dismount and rearm themselves with the weapons of their opponents; exercising their bodies by rhythmic movements, by wrestling, by twanging the steel bow, which developed the muscles of chest, forearm and finger. Man for man, many eighteenth-century writers thought, the Indian trooper, in horsemanship and skill at arms, was the superior, and in personal courage the equal, of the British.[1]

We need to dwell just a bit longer in ancient India. The most detailed and the earliest account of warfare in that period is of Alexander's invasion of India. For our purpose, it is noteworthy for the details of battle formations and troop deployment that we obtain from it. We learn, for example, that when the Greeks marched into territories west of the river Indus they encountered local feudatories, not even the armies of the principal Indian ruler of the period, Chandragupta, and they were greatly impressed, for they found them 'far superior in the art of war' to the others they had so far encountered in their campaigns. On the east bank they were confronted by Poros, whom the Greeks called Pooros, of gigantic build and regal conduct; for even in defeat when queried by the victorious Alexander as to how he (Poros) ought to be treated, received a reply that still fills all Indian school textbooks: 'As one king treats another.' Soon after this, Alexander's troops mutinied and he turned homeward. But Poros' army and accounts of it are the first detailed description of the battle formations of ancient India.

There was a compact mass of two hundred war elephants in the centre, with chariots, cavalry and infantry. They held a strong defensive position on the left bank of the Hydaspes [Indus] and Alexander could not cross in the face of such opposition. After some days of feinting at different points, he left the bulk of his army demonstrating an intention to cross, while with only 11,000 of his best troops he made a secret night-march to the north, crossed the river and marched down the left bank. Poros had to change front to meet him but his forces were about four times as strong as those that Alexander had with him. The plan of the battle was simple; Alexander engaged the enemy on an extended front and, once they were committed, sent his cavalry on a wide outflanking movement and delivered a crushing charge on Poros's flank and rear. The elephants became unmanageable; Poros was seriously wounded, by no less than nine arrows, and the Indian losses are said to have been two-thirds of their total forces.[2]

Just two decades later, in 303 BC, when Selukos Nikator, the Conqueror, attempted to repeat the performance he was roundly defeated by Chandragupta Maurya, in a full-scale battle where, too, the elephant was the preponderant force. This victory, along with his court advisor Kautilya's treatise on warfare – two whole books – fixed the pattern of India's structure of forces for many centuries to come, remaining largely unaltered even after the early Muslim invasion of seventh century AD. The change came but only after Babur's invasion, and thereafter with the advent of the British.

It might be beneficial to spend some time with Kautilya and his treatise on war, on troops and on classical organization in ancient India.

Kautilya devotes a great deal of attention to war.

The Commander-in-Chief [he advises] will have

an Inspector-General for each of the four arms – elephants, chariots, cavalry and infantry; the functions of each arm are described, with the circumstances and the kind of country in which they will be found most useful and some indication of the kind of training they need.

It is at about this period that chariots go out of use. That great Cavalry Commander of the Greeks – Xenophon – had revolutionized the employment of the horse in war, through the invention of the foot stirrup. Riders could then rise and hurl or strike and also move more swiftly then chariots. And thus they, the chariots, went out of use in war.

But elephants are of great importance; they are the shock-troops, the tanks, the striking force in attack but also the core of the defence. And they are not only tanks but sappers, useful for crossing rivers and making earthworks; they prepare the roads and camps. They force entrances into impregnable places, quench fires, frighten the enemy. . . . But it is significant that while the functions of elephants in any army take up (in the translation I have used) a page of close print, the functions of infantry take up only one line: "At all times to carry all weapons to all places and to fight." These are the duties of infantry proper.[3]

Things do not appear to have changed much for the poor infantry in the past twenty-five centuries.

Chandragupta's empire was extremely efficient, and his army is believed to have included a high proportion of troops paid direct by the State and therefore more reliable than those of allies and vassals. In this it was exceptional; [as] it was far more usual for an Indian army to be a loose grouping of Chiefs seeking their own advantage.[4]

Our next halt is after traversing many centuries; we go directly to Babur's invasion in AD 1525. In the intervening eighteen centuries, the essentials and the principles of warfare and composition of forces remained largely unaltered. Standing armies in the Rajput period were small, and those too, really rather an exception, were meant primarily as bodyguards of the ruler, comprising mainly of feudal levies in which clan affiliations provided the cement of organization. Training was entirely personal, individual valour counted above all, and deployment in large numbers was always a response to the size of the challenge alone. Social standing was measured by the troops that could be summoned upon call.

In AD 1525, Babur, the founder of the Mughal Empire, swept down from Central Asia and, with no more than 12,000 men, defeated Ibrahim Lodi's 100,000 at the famous battleground of Panipat, north of Delhi, where so many battles have taken place. Lodi's force was defeated by almost exactly the same tactics that Alexander had employed against Poros: 'a strong defensive front with which the enemy became heavily involved, and then a swift cavalry movement right round the flank and a charge from the rear'.[5]

> The Mughals were nomadic horsemen, hardy and swift-moving; they kept a tradition, which lasted as long as the Empire, that the Emperor's sons must be born on a horse-blanket spread on the floor of a tent [so says history at least]. The formal wording of a petition to the Emperors had to begin with a reference to "the exalted stirrup" which the petitioner had succeeded in reaching. The court of the Mughal Emperor was always in theory a camp, and, conversely, whenever the army moved out to war, the whole apparatus of government must go too.[6]

Yet, the assimilative strength of India soon dissolved these differences and over time the invading Mughals adopted the very same elephant as the centre of their armies. But by then the Mughal empire had in reality become more of a Mughal-Rajput coalition.

Some more centuries go by. Aurangzeb – sixth in succession to Babur – was kept constantly occupied. An account of his army on the move is instructive of the change that a mere 170 odd years had brought about

> First [many accounts explain] came camels, bearing the treasure, one hundred loaded with gold and two hundred with silver; there was the Emperor's hunting establishment, with hawks and cheetahs; there were the official records, which could never be parted from the Emperor, and to carry them were eighty camels, thirty elephants and twenty carts. Fifty camels carried water for the Emperor's kitchen and another fifty the kitchen utensils and provisions; there were fifty milch-cows and a hundred cooks, each a specialist in one dish. Fifty camels and a hundred carts took the Emperor's wardrobe and that of his women; thirty elephants bore the women's jewellery and presents for successful commanders; next came the great mass of the cavalry, the main strength of the army proper; two thousand men with spades went before it to smooth the ground and one thousand after it; then came the elephants of the Emperor and his women. There was a rearguard of infantry.[7]

Poor infantry – always the same, no matter what the age and who the General. No doubt a great deal of this or such accounts are fanciful, but what they lack in accuracy they gain in flavour.

But pomp and luxury, as against fleetfootedness, had set in much earlier. Sir Thomas Roe, ambassador of James I of England to the court of Jehangir, Babur's great-grandson, wrote:

> I took a view of the Mogul's camp, which is one of the greatest wonders I ever beheld (and

chiefly for that I saw it set up and finished
in less than four hours), it being no less than
twenty English miles in compass . . . in the
middle, where the streets are orderly and tents
joined, there are all sort of shops and so regularly
disposed that every man knows wither to go
for what he wants.[8]

What about the command and control of such a
force? It comprised of 'a complicated system of ranks,
rewards and accounts'. The heart of it was the 'mansabdari'
system. This was both a recognition of social standing;
an obligation when called to provide a certain specified
number of troops, particularly for the cavalry; and a
right to draw from the imperial treasury. The lowest
mansabdar was a command of twenty; the highest for
anyone but the emperor and his immediate family, a
command of seven thousand, which, much later, was
bestowed on Dupleix.

Commanders in the higher ranks were of three
classes according to the proportion of horsemen.
They belonged to the first class if the whole
command was of horse, to the second class if
more than half, and to the third class if less
than half. This must not, however, be supposed
to imply that either the men or the horses
actually existed. "Lutfullah Khan Sadiqu, although
he held the rank of seven thousand, never entertained
seven asses, much less horses or riders on horses."
Dupleix's title 'haft-hazari', a seven-thousander,
constituted a rank and an entitlement to salary,
but again the salary would not, as a rule,
be drawn from the treasury.[9]

Mansab really means a rank, and what the Mughals
did was to recognize the existing Rajput system of
clan and tribal levies, transform and adopt them, and
also give it a monetary ingredient plus lend a certain
imperial, social cachet.

A form of reward and recognition with not all 'mansabdars' actually providing troops, being commanders or even fighters, ever. Not very dissimilar to the 'British colonels in the early eighteenth century who expected to make money out of their regiments'. The mansabdars drew from the imperial treasury what the rank of their mansabdari entitled them to, but only a fraction reached the troops.

> Mughal accountants seem to have been even more ingenious than [their counterparts today]: they stopped one day's pay in the month 'for the rising of the moon'. And it was normal practice to order that pay should be allowed only for ten months or for eight months in the year. It would be surprising if the mansabdars had kept their units always up to strength, but some extreme cases are mentioned; one officer in Bengal in the mid-eighteenth century, who was receiving pay for 1700 men, could not muster more than seventy or eighty. The Indian historian of events in Bengal at that time adds: 'Such are without exception all the armies and all the troops of India.'[10]

The Mughals introduced artillery.

The *Mir Atish* ("Lord of Fire"), the Master Gunner, was an important office-holder, and was responsible for the manufacture and supply of ordnance as well as being the artillery commander. Gunners, who were called *Golandaz* ("bringer of round-shot", a term used by the British until 1857), were paid directly by the State and for this reason were the most reliable part of the army. But they were extremely slow at loading and firing their guns,

which always had resounding names: "Zam Zama" (un-translatable); "Tiger Mouth", "Conqueror of the Army",

"Lord Champion", "Thunderer", "Fort-Demolisher", "Strength
of the Throne", etc., but they were all being prodigious
in size far too heavy to move. Once the cavalry got
past, there was nothing else to do but "abandon them".
And it was cavalry that was the bulk of the Mughal
Army, for 'it was the cavalry who enjoyed prestige as
warriors, gallant men with swagger and panache. The
infantry, on the other hand, were despised as drudges,
little more than watchmen to guard the baggage. Horsemanship
was highly esteemed and the standard achieved was
high. . . .

> A commander of cavalry would often bring with
> him his own retainers, mounted at his expense,
> though sometimes the trooper provided arms and
> equipment for himself. A man bringing such a
> troop on his own horses was a "*silladar*"; a
> man so mounted was a "*bargir*". Both these
> terms were used in the British service, and a
> remnant of the [Silladari] system existed until
> 1914.[11]

The Mughals had a system of recruitment by classes:

> For example, an officer from Iran should recruit
> not more than one-third Mughals; the rest must
> be Sayyads or Sheikhs. If Afghans were recruited,
> they should not be more than one-sixth of the
> force under a given officer, nor must Rajputs
> be more than one-seventh, except in the case
> of a Rajput officer, who might take Rajputs
> only.[12]

Doubtless, the successor British learnt their class
system of recruitment from these early examples. About
latter-day Mughal cavalry wrote Monstuart Elphinstone:

> They formed a cavalry . . . admirably fitted
> to prance in a procession and not ill-adapted
> to a charge in pitched battle, but not capable

for any long exertion and still less of any continuance of fatigue and hardship.

In a few generations, the Mughals had lost the 'hardiness, the simplicity and the mobility of the invaders' and had been transformed into the classical army of India: 'undisciplined horsemen surrounding a ponderous assembly of elephants'.[13] All they needed was military organization and political stability. How the echoes of history travel down the corridors of time.

As the Mughals declined there arose in the Deccan a new energy, a new force: it filled the vacuum, surged into the rapidly emptying North, 'looting and pillaging' as they went along and established the eponymous Maratha Confederacy. The rise of this power coincided with Aurangzeb's decline and was really also a reaction to the last of the great Mughal's tyrannical ways. The year is 1659; Shivaji has just assassinated Afzal Khan, one of Aurangzeb's Generals by employing Kautilya's concept of 'treacherous war'. Our preoccupation, however, is not with the history of this period; it is with the study of the military transformation that the Marathas brought about.

> The Maratha army at its best suggested the beginning of the kind of nation-state that grew up in Europe from Tudor times onward. There was nothing else like it in India before the rise of the Sikhs under Ranjit Singh. The Maratha power was swift in its growth because it was founded on new principles, but these were soon forgotten and both State and army began to revert to older ways; degeneracy and decay were well developed while the Maratha empire was still expanding.
>
> Maratha power may really be counted to begin . . . [with Shivaji, of] soaring ambition: he meant to establish himself against the Mughals as the independent chief of a Hindu empire based . . . [in the] north-western Deccan and the

Western Ghats [very largely today's Maharashtra. He epitomised the Maratha.] . . . Had Shivaji lived longer and had his principles been followed by his successors, the Maratha spirit would surely have grown into nationalism. It was based on the Hindu religion, the Marath[i] language and the Maharashtra country. . . .[14]

Shivaji died in 1680 but Maratha power continued to spread for the next century, although Shivaji's principles were increasingly neglected. By the end of the eighteenth century the Maratha cavalry had "watered their horses in the Indus", Calcutta had found it necessary to construct the Mahratta Ditch as a defence against their raids, they had defeated the Nizam and made him yield half his territory and they had carried their wars to the southern tip of the Indian peninsula.[15]

Arthur Wellesley and the battle of Assaye marks the beginning of their end. The year is 1803.
'Shivaji stands . . . as the outstanding leader produced by the sub-continent in two centuries.' Though there exist many accounts of Shivaji's military methods, just one would do for our purpose.

Discipline in Shivaji's army was rigid. No women were admitted. . . . Weight was kept down to the lowest limit possible, the men usually carrying several days' supply of food in their saddle-bags; often there were no tents even for Sivaji himself. Swift movement, surprise, ambush were what he sought. . . .

His men were hardy peasantry; 'little notice was taken of differences' between them and, 'shepherds, cowherds and the like', all joined. Shivaji sought to unify them under himself to reduce the strength of feudal allegiance and caste.

His infantry were mountaineers from the Ghats and in his early days there was none of that emphasis on cavalry that later became the rule. But his men had to be paid and it was part of Sivaji's system to pay as many as possible [directly] from the State treasury.

For this money was needed which they collected through war (and as they sought war their territories expanded).

[Though Shivaji himself] disliked indiscriminate looting as bad for discipline and there was great advantage in settling with a raja who would pay his protection-money annually without an expensive military operation to compel him. If he would not be compelled, loot belonged to the State and there were elaborate rules for the division of it.[16]

There was another major difference, with the Mughals that is, for, like the Rajputs,

Shivaji's men were Indians; they were not invaders. [But] otherwise they were not unlike Babur's invading force: they had the military virtues of discipline and fidelity; they could move fast and manoeuvre in the face of the enemy. But a decline began even with his immediate successor and it continued with increasing rapidity.

Soon enough the Maratha armies too began to be not much different from those of the Mughals. Silledari reappeared, management was thus made easier; 'as also court craft [which] went back to traditional courtiers; [thus the Peshwas] and slowly this army, too, lost its hardiness reverting to soft feudal indulgence'. There are many contemporary accounts of this period for the Europeans had begun to arrive; and they at least recorded all that they saw. Only one aspect, therefore, need detain us here: the various categories of cavalry troops.

The cream was the 'bargir', he who brought his own horse, but was paid directly by the state. Then the 'ekadar', who brought horse and equipment but was not paid directly; then the 'Silledars' who contracted to bring a certain numbers of horses with equipment and troops and received a proportion of the war booty in bulk payment. Then there was a fourth category, though not under Shivaji, the 'Pendharis', which the British simplified into 'Pindaris'.

These might be of any creed, speech or nation, and many were Muslims from the north. They were not paid; on the contrary, they engaged to give the state one-sixth of any booty they might take. They were, in short, licensed robbers and frequently made raids on their own account.[17]

In turn these Pindaris, after the Maratha decline, led to the short Pindari war; the detritus of the Pindaris becoming 'thugs', hence 'thugee' and its subsequent elimination by Sleeman. But we get far ahead of our times. Maratha infantry recruited all – 'Sikhs, Rajputs, Sindis and Baluchis; Arabs, Rohillas, Abyssinians and Portuguese.' Wages varied from Arab mercenaries earning fifteen rupees a month to six only for the Deccan recruit.

Shivaji's dream of a 'Hindu empire based on the Maharashtrian homeland' having been forgotten, the Marathas began to act in the name of the Mughal Emperor; alienating in the process their natural allies, the Rajputs, 'who found them even more rapacious than the Mughals'. To compensate, and to replace the loss of their native hardihood and vitality, they began recruiting French and other European mercenaries as higher commanders. This cost them their greatest asset, mobility, for as European drill replaced native agility Maratha armies became slow and unwieldy.

There is, however, one additional aspect of Maratha military thought which sets them apart entirely. After the great Chola dynasty, which largely for the protection of its trade had a fleet, the Marathas were the first to have a conscious, military naval presence. This, considering India's large coastline and extensive maritime trade (from ancient times), is a curious deficiency. And to an extent it persists. The Marathas were the first and perhaps the only to employ a navy; indeed, as the saying still goes 'Shivaji carried the capital of his empire on the high seas'.

Malgaonkar in his book on Kanhoji Angre, the Maratha admiral, gives an evocative description.

On 6 June, 1674, at a moment pronounced auspicious by the priest, Shivaji was enthroned at Raigad. For the first time in history, a Maratha was ruling in the land of the Marathas. No one remembered who the last Hindu King was, nor when and where he reigned; neither did they care, on that day. The proclamation made at the coronation described Shivaji's kingdom as "extending up to the limits of the ocean". [However] the Portuguese, in Goa, had already taken note of the growing power of Shivaji's fleet and signed a treaty of friendship with him. The Viceroy had sent his emissary to Shivaji with gifts and had undertaken to supply him with cannons at a fair price in return for a promise that he would not molest their ships.

At the time of his coronation, Shivaji had 57 major ships of war (excluding smaller craft) with a total fighting strength of over 5,000 men. Five years later, there were 66 major ships. Even his expedition to Karwar and Akola nine years earlier had been mounted with 85 assorted gallivants, each ranging from 30 to 150 tonnes, and three three-masted ghurabs, with a total fighting strength of 4,000 men – a formidable force even by today's standards.

Shivaji's fleet was barely five years – a building, raised from scratch. It was now being given its trial run; the ships and their commanders and

men were being put through their paces much
as they do with newly-fitted-outships to this day.
[This relates to an expedition to Karwar.] Then
. . . once again, in 1670, the fleet went out
to "show the flag", and caused the English at
Bombay many anxious moments. They had convinced
themselves that Shivaji was mounting a combined
operation against Surat. The fleet sailed past
Bombay . . . Shivaji was unquestionably the
first ruler in India to have realized the need
for protecting the coast. His ships gradually began
to patrol the coast in increasing numbers, "defying
the Portuguese, the Dutch, the Siddies, and the
English and (in all) twenty seven hostile powers;
living on the tributes offered by the people along
the cost and collecting for the King, ration .
. . gold . . . and other tributes. In this manner,
it soon came to be regarded as a formidable
fighting force, a veritable army upon the high
seas."[18]

Shivaji's Navy was distributed into different regional
commands and he could rely on a battery of experienced
naval commanders. There was, for example, his northern
command, though not exactly so designated.

Among the senior military commanders, was Siddoji
Gujjar, the newly-appointed Chief of the Maratha
Navy. The command of the coast fell to the
two Deputy Commanders: Kanhoji Angrey and Bhawanji
Mohitay. The Northern Command, with the remnants
of the fleet at Suvarna-durg and Gheria, came
to Kanhoji Angrey as an independent command.[19]

To this Kanhoji Angrey we shall be reverting shortly.
Malgaonkar proceeds: 'Shivaji, when he died, is said
to have left a fleet of "four to five hundred ships".[20]
This figure is on the high side and almost certainly
includes Shivaji's mercantile fleet. However, most historians
are agreed that 'Shivaji had built up a fleet of at

least two hundred fighting ships of various sizes'. And yet as for the army that he had built so too, for the navy: barely a decade after Shivaji's death of the 'magnificent fleet, now, only a shrivelled stump' remained.

The eight or ten ships that Kanhoji Angrey inherited could not have been anything more than a hotchpotch of patched-up gallivants and lesser vessels. It is possible that he may have had a battered old ghurab or two.

If, however, in the first years of the eighteenth century, any of the foreign powers along the coast of Konkan had been asked to nominate a common enemy, none of them would have picked out either the Moghuls or the Marathas. Their answer would have been the same: Kanhoji Angrey! . . . . To neutralise the man they chose to call a pirate, the British spent every year a sum equivalent to a million pounds at today's value. They dug a ditch around the town in Bombay as a protection against him, and then they erected a wall behind the ditch. They even joined hands with their bitterest rivals, the Portuguese, in an effort to destroy him. . . . The Portuguese made friends with him [Angre] and fought with him in turns, and all the while they secretly intrigued against him and helped his enemies. The Dutch lost an implausible number of men the only time they attacked one of his forts, and then they called up a squadron of warships all the way from Batavia in an effort to bring him to terms. . . . The British called him a land-shark who devoured everything on land as well as on water; they called him robber, pirate, villain, rebel, and sent emissaries to wait upon him with instructions to speak to him "civilly" and made a fabulous offer to buy him off. The Portuguese called him even worse names, and yet linked him to Barbarossa and sent him expensive presents. No ship could pass the Konkan waters singly, and not even warships were safe. They went in convoys, armed to the teeth, and a custom grew among the trading communities to present a purse of five hundred sovereigns to the captains of the escorting warships if they brought their convoys safely to port. . . . Whoever ruled the land, whoever lorded it over their trading settlements surrounded by ditches and walls, there were no two opinions as to who ruled the waters of the Konkan coast during the first years of the eighteenth century: Kanhoji Angrey.[21]

In the maritime sphere, Kanhoji Angrey had performed a miracle of even greater proportions than the transformation of the Maratha army. In the nine years since the command of the northern fleet had devolved upon him, he had built it up into a compact, powerful striking force of forty assorted vessels, already spoken of with awe and treated with respect along the coast. 'Angrey, a sevageee [Shivaji] pirate independent of the Raja', obviously troubled the early European powers greatly. In consequence the ships of the East India Company, although they were meant primarily as trading vessels, began to be armed just as powerfully as the ships of the British Navy. The Company thus began to maintain its own private navy, 'which, oddly enough, bore the same name as does our navy today: it was called the "Indian Navy" '.[22] And that is the distinction that set the Marathas apart, of which we have earlier spoken. The Indian Navy's origins can indeed be traced to that Maratha tradition.

THE SIKHS

If we do not spend a similar effort on the Sikhs it is not because they did not represent yet another step in the evolution of Indian military forces; they certainly did. In any event the Sikh faith was born to protect against Islamic onslaughts; which it survived despite having to bear direct onslaughts, almost similar to the experience of the Rajputs, based as both were largely in the north-west of India. Though Sikh principalities and kingdoms spawned, none achieved the historic greatness of either the Rajput kingdoms or of Shivaji. Besides, the Sikh faith is entirely egalitarian; it encourages and nurtures the spirit of the individual: 'make 125,000 out of one', was the inspiring call given by the tenth guru, Guru Gobind Singh. There are two other factors to consider. The Sikhs gave birth to just one great military commander, Ranjit Singh; and the rise of his kingdom coincided with, and therefore inevitably clashed with the rising British Empire.

Maharaja Ranjit Singh was the other great military commander of the subcontinent during the last two centuries. He learnt from the French and the British, closely studying their military methods and adapting them for his forces. But like the Rajput chieftains, the Mughal *mansabdars* or the Maratha feudatories of later years, the Sikhs too had their 'misals', clans, or septs, which jealously guarded their distinctiveness, though in times of need and when called by Ranjit Singh, answered with troops, horses, followers and arms. Under Ranjit Singh, however, there did come into existence a standing Sikh force. This force in fact became so potent that six years after the demise of Ranjit Singh in a period abounding in revolutions and assassinations, the regent mother became so afraid of the

restless and turbulent army and found their only hope of security in urging it on to challenge British supremacy. Either it would spend its energy in a career of conquest or it would be crushed in the conflict. So the Queen Mother authorised an invasion of the British territory and the army crossed the Sutlej, the boundary between the Sikh and British territories. Thereupon Lord Hardinge declared war in 1845.

There followed a series of engagements, culminating

in the Battle of Chillianwala in 1849.

The Sikhs fought with great courage and determination and repulsed a British brigade with fearful loss. They captured four guns and colours of three regiments but could not follow up their success. They abandoned their lines and retreated three miles in good order with the loss of 12 guns. The battle of Chillianwala is generally described as a drawn battle but the balance of success seems to have been in favour of the Sikhs.[23]

Subsequently, 'the brave Sikh soldiers were made into regiments with English officers, and formed, with the Gurkhas, some of the finest and best troops in India'.[24] 'By 1831, the Sikhs in the Punjab had an army of twenty thousand regular infantry and were able to defeat the British at Mudki in 1845. They were later defeated only because of dissension among rival Sikh leaders.[25] To study the methods of Ranjit Singh or that force however is to, in effect, move into the British period.

THE BRITISH PERIOD

When does this period begin? By the early eighteenth century, the Mughal Empire was in terminal decline. Embassies by Europeans had, however, been sent earlier and trading posts established. Vasco da Gama had after all 'discovered' the sea route to India almost two centuries earlier. But our concern is not so much with that as with identifying a conversion of trade into territory; for which the establishment of a force subject only to the Europeans' authority was the first requirement, indeed a vital instrument.

It was not for many years after its incorporation that the Company of Merchants of London trading into the East Indies found it necessary to employ military forces to protect its possessions and its interests, but guards of peons, undisciplined and armed after the native fashion, were enrolled in its factories, from the time when these were first established. These peons could hardly be regarded as soldiers, and were employed rather to add to the dignity of the Company's officials than for purposes of defence. . . . In 1662, King Charles II sent out a small force to defend Bombay, which was part of the dowry of his queen. . . . In 1668, when the king leased Bombay to the East India Company, its garrison consisted of twenty commissioned and non-commissioned officers, 124 privates and fifty-four Topasses or half-caste Portuguese and this force eventually became the nucleus of the Ist Bombay European Regiment. In 1711, the garrison of Madras consisted of 250 European soldiers and 200 Topasses. . . . [By] 1746 Captain Stringer Lawrence of the 14th Foot, the 'father of the Indian Army', [had] arrived at Fort St David, then temporarily the company's principal factor on the east coast, with the King's commission as Major, to command all the Company's troops in the East Indies. He embodied the Madras European Regiment and enlisted 2000 sepoys, and in 1748 various independent companies were embodied as a regiment, afterwards the Ist Madras Fusilliers, in which Robert Clive received his first commission as an ensign.[26]

If, therefore, a beginning is to be found of the Indian Army, it is this. As for the Navy the very act of trading,

of competition between European powers, of the rivalries and wars of Europe being so markedly with naval components, a continuous protective presence had always been there.

This, as we have seen earlier, when examining the

Marathas, was the beginning of the Indian Navy.

Clive's victory at Plassey [1757] and the deposition
of Siraj-ud-Daula, established the Company [EIC]
as the predominant authority in Bengal, and the
maintenance of its power required a respectable
military force.[27]

This got constituted. At this stage, however, the armies
of Bengal, Madras and Bombay developed independently.
The Company's behavior to its military forces was too
obviously that of a group of traders towards their servants.
To this Indian element of troops were slowly added European
troops, officers, men, complete complements of a full fledged
army. The trader was now a conqueror. 1857 provided
a serious check but also an opportune moment for
transformation. The entire corps of the Company's troops,
Indian and European, the latter now numbering over
15,000, were transferred to the service of the crown.

The corps of Bengal, Madras and Bombay artillery
and engineers were amalgamated with the Royal
Artillery and the Royal Engineers, and the European
infantry regiments, now including those raised
during the Mutiny, nine in number, became
regiments of the line, numbered from 101 to 109.[27]

And thus was born the British Indian army, formally
so.[28]

Self-defence, however, was not the whole story.

That every landowner or employer should
administer justice was the custom of the country
and it applied even among the servants of a
large household. As the Company grew, and the
number of its people increased, it became inevitable
that it should take its place as a part of Indian
society – indeed, of the Empire – like any other
chief or landowner. When, to give one example,
the emperor at Delhi sold to the East India

Company in Bengal the rights of a Zamindar
– who might very roughly be called Lord of the
manor – in three villages, they appointed one
of their number to act in this capacity. His
duties were twofold. He was the collector of revenues,
but also judge in "all matters both civil and
criminal, wherein the natives only, subjects of
the Mogul, are concerned. He tried in a summary
way . . ." He was exercising the ordinary rights
of a chief. He was an official of the Empire.
This meant he must have some force at his
disposal. And this, in a way they had not always
clearly understood, had been the case with all
the foreign settlements from the beginning.[29]

This is not simply a brief rendering of events in
those momentous centuries; it amounts to encapsulating
them, in the process scarcely doing them justice. The
reason is not indifference, it is to examine more closely
the various aspects of a virtual military revolution
that took place in India during the British period. This
revolution was, of course, a revolution of transferred
thoughts from Europe to Asia, particularly India; its
many components, however, stand so distinctly apart
that they must be highlighted. After all both the Mughals
and the British were alien conquering forces; both had
a major concern with internal order; how then did
the British build and export 'surplus military power'
throughout their reign, but not the Mughals? Is it
because the Mughals settled, became Indian but not
so the British? Stephen Rosen has an explanation to
offer.

How could the British conquer and then maintain
internal order within India – and afterward export
surplus military power from India – as early
as 1800? What changed? Both British and Mughal
political systems represented empires in which
a religiously distinct foreign military elite claimed
to rule an enormous indigenous population without

political institutions that allowed for mass political participation and representation or persuasion and compulsion. But as early as 1789, Lord Cornwallis asked for and received sepoys, native Indian soldiers trained and deployed under British command, who would volunteer to serve in Sumatra. The Governor General of the East India Company (EIC) in Calcutta, Richard Wellesley, responded to the news that the French army had established itself in Egypt and might be headed for India by writing the EIC Board of Control back in London that "if the French should be established in Egypt, it might be advisable to consider whether an expedition might be fitted out from India to cooperate by way of the Red Sea with any attempt which might be undertaken from the Mediterranean". If Wellesley was ordered by England to dispatch such an expedition, that order 'will be executed with alacrity and diligence, by not only me, but by the whole army in India'. Troops from India did arrive in Cairo in 1801. . . . Sepoys from India were sent as well to Sri Lanka and Aden. . . . in order to maintain control, it became within two generations a limited exporter of military power.[30]

What had happened? Was it greater ruthlessness in putting down the 'native', far worse than what India had ever experienced? Rosen quotes a commander serving under Warren Hastings writing during one of his marches that 'there are destroyed upwards of a thousand villages. Had not rain etc. prevented us, which occasioned our return, we should have done very considerable more damage'.[31] It was then not technological superiority either, we have already examined that.

Amongst the many other causes Stephen Rosen offers one:

The key to understanding the military revolution which took place in India in the eighteenth century and which gave the European-trained and European-led armies their great advantage over the existing Indian armies is understanding the military revolution that took place in Europe beginning in the sixteenth century. Historians of this revolution in offensive land warfare have noted the massive increase in the power of infantry troops, with or without firearms, when they were kept under discipline for periods of time long enough to train them to act in unison under the command of their leader on the battle field and who would remain loyal to their military unit and to their comrades even under enemy attack. Infantrymen so disciplined and trained could withstand cavalry attacks even if they were armed only with pikes. When armed with muskets, the effect of massed, coordinated musket fire wielded by units, which could have some men fire in unison while others reloaded their weapons and which could maneuvers as to bring that massed fire power to bear on a series of targets in different locations on the battle field, was devastating on armies not so trained and disciplined. The military parade ground exercises now useful primarily for ceremonial performances had their origins in one of the most significant revolutions in human organization. Close-order drill and maneuvers were a self-conscious revival in Europe of the practices of the Roman legions. . . . The power of the new military system was that its intense training could take men from disparate groups and even nations and mould them into a fighting force. Properly done, the military revolution could be applied to [any] groups of people. . . . In short, it could be and was applied in India.[32]

The British, however, were not the first to do so; the French were: they had raised 'four-five native Indian infantry companies in 1746' and provided military training to 'ten thousand infantry serving the king of Travancore in 1755'. But even before the British and the French, the Maratha army based in the southwestern area of India had begun to adopt European military practices. 'By the second half of the seventeenth century, the Maratha army was the dominant military power in those parts of India not under Mughal control.'[33] But this we have already examined, and though training was certainly a factor of significance it can scarcely account for every aspect.

Two other reasons are cited.

One was within the military – professionalization of logistics. Together with the development of militarily powerful infantry units, the mobility of the EIC army gave it the power to defeat any other regular army in India but also the power to defeat irregular, guerrilla forces that continued to fight the British after the regular armies had been defeated. The other factor was EIC agricultural policy, which led to, in the language of modern counterinsurgency, the pacification of the Indian countryside.[34]

Both are of compelling significance and have already been referred to earlier. The concept of having all the requirements of troops under command being met from one's own resources, and professionalizing logistics instead of living off the countryside was without doubt a major factor, it imparted great flexibility to deployment, and also much greater mobility.

Arthur Wellesley's letters during his campaigns against Tipu Sultan and then the Marathas at the end of the eighteenth century and the beginning of the nineteenth are obsessed with the problem of obtaining supplies, particularly grain.

He took immense pride in obtaining grain for his army of thirty thousand without upsetting the prices in local markets, flying into a fury when his pursuit of a band of Maratha guerrillas was delayed because grain had not been stockpiled and packed so as to make possible his rapid mounted movement. After successfully hunting down and killing the head of the Maratha guerrillas, he immediately ordered that the newly established garrisons be stockpiled with grain so as to make possible the sustained military control of the areas to which other guerrillas were expected to return. Observing this performance, Lord Mornington wrote to Wellesley, "we have now proved (a perfect novelty in India) that we can hunt down the lightest footed and most rapid armies as well as we can destroy heavy groups and storm strong fortifications".[35]

The other was the disarming of India, which Rosen calls 'pacification of the countryside'. The British forcefully acquired a monopoly over weapons and in exchange of this enforced disarmament offered security against attack, personal, local or any other

Quasi-military forces, localised military clans led by chiefs called poligars and large nomadic groups of Hindu mendicants, the Sanyasi, who were armed .and who extracted resources from the villages through which they passed, were also a threat to the British monopoly of force.[36]

These too were disarmed, as were the larger forces. In turn this 'pacification' released the troops from other duties, and thus generated a surplus of military power available to the British.

But there were some other causes of significance. A sense of territoriality and geography was one. This, as already noted, was largely absent culturally in India; it was introduced as a military factor. It had several components: survey, for example; or detailed mapmaking (astonishing that no authentic geographical map of the pre-British period exists), and finally with this 'revolution of logistics' was introduced large-scale road-building –

not in today's freeway sense – more as a clearing of routes of passage, to facilitate movement of large bodies of troops.

And yet it does not explain all. Why did the Indians fight for and along with the British? The relationship was not of equals, it was that of the conquering and the conquered. Yet, for well on two and a half centuries, the Indians not only fought with the British, they fought as volunteers – there simply was no conscription, or forced enrolment at any stage. On the contrary, service in the Army, the British Indian Army, that is, was turned into and remained all through the British period, a matter of high honour, conferring great prestige on the volunteer. Why? And why is that not so now in independent India? What did the British do which India is failing to do for itself?

Does a possible, even a half answer lie in what Philip Mason suggests?

> What made Indian soldiers give their lives for a flag they could hardly call their own? National pride did not play much part till late in their long history. It was · only in the Second World War that it appeared and then only occasionally. When it did, it was a two-edged sword: pride in the regiment, in the division, yes, that was something on which everyone could agree, but pride in a nation that was not yet a nation produced very mixed feelings. Officers and men could not share it in the same spirit . . . it explains nothing to say simply that they were "mercenary". Men may came to the colours for pay but it is not for pay that they earn the Victoria Cross.[37]

And here Mason cites just one amongst many such instances from the glorious annals of the Indian Army.

Take, for example, the affair at Koregaum on New Year's Day, 1818. Captain Staunton, of the

Bombay Army, received orders on New Year's Eve to bring the troops under his command to reinforce Colonel Burr, 41 miles away, whose two battalions were in danger of being cut off by the larger forces of the Peshwa, the Maratha chief. Staunton marched at eight o'clock that evening. He had some 500 sepoys, that is, privates, of the Bombay Army (the 2nd Battalion of the Ist Bombay Regiment, later the 2nd Battalion, 4th Bombay Grenadiers), 250 newly raised auxiliary horse (who eventually became the Poona Horse), and a party of the Madras Artillery. There were two six-pounder guns with 24 European gunners and some Indian drivers and gun lascars, the whole artillery contingent probably numbering about 100 men, the entire force being less than 900. They marched all night, covering 27 miles, and at about ten in the morning on New Year's Day were preparing to halt for rest during the heat of the day, when they came suddenly in view of the Peshwa's main army. This consisted of about 20,000 horse and 8,000 infantry. The village of Koregaum, with stone-built houses and enclosures, was close at hand, and Staunton at once saw that his best move was to take up a defensive position in the village. But the enemy were equally quick and dispatched three columns of their best Arab troops, each column about a thousand-strong, to prevent him.

Neither side was able to occupy the whole village before the other, and there developed a battle, house to house and hand to hand . . . About nine o'clock that night, twenty-five hours after their march had begun, Staunton's force cleared the village of the enemy and were able to get water. . . .

[They] brought away colours, guns and wounded and marched for the nearest garrison town, where they arrived forty-eight hours after they had left their own station. During that time they

had had no food and had been constantly marching
or fighting. For nearly twelve hours of fighting
they had been without water. [They] lost 50
men killed and 105 wounded out of fewer than
500. Of the 250 auxiliary horse, ninety were
killed, wounded or missing. But, before reaching
the town where they might expect rest, they
halted to dress their ranks and marched in
with drums beating and colours flying. . . .

   Their general wrote, after Koregaum, of
the sepoys' "most noble devotion and most
romantic bravery under pressure of thirst and
hunger almost beyond human endurance." Why
did they give such service? . . .

   [This cannot] be answered by a simple yes
or no. If you could answer . . . every answer
would involve some exception or qualification –
you might have some idea of what went to
make up the spirit that, at its best, animated
this unusual army.[38]

THE TWENTIETH CENTURY

The three armies of East India Company were incorporated into the crown (1858) and amalgamated only
by 1895. By then

   the Indian army was a highly professional army,
   the men serving for twenty-one years and both
   officers and men being more likely than in the
   British army to have had some experience of
   active service. It was an army designed to keep
   the peace in India and to be able to dispatch
   a temporary force to the Persian Gulf, Malaya,
   Hong Kong or China; it was strong enough to
   deal with 'the minor danger' – that is, attack
   by any Asian power then envisaged – and to
   provide against the 'major danger' a delaying
   screen that would give time for reinforcements

to come from England. The 'major danger' was defined as a European power, and in the nineteenth century this meant Russia.[39]

But the Indian army at the turn of the century was not designed for contribution to a world war lasting four years. Much of the organization for this had to be improvised while the war was in progress.

Between the First and Second World Wars the first task was to complete the transformation from a professional army designed for a local task into a modern army, capable of rapid expansion in war and of meeting a first-class power. This involved reorganization, rearming, the revision of all training, the substitution of tanks for cavalry, of engines for mules, bullocks, camels and elephants. It meant foreseeing the importance of air power.[40]

This was a major transformation, for it was in essence the first step in converting

an army which had established foreign rule over the whole of India into a national army which would be the instrument of an independent state.[41]

To this challenging task the ruling British brought hesitation and tentativeness, the Indians part indifference, part incomprehension and in part suspicion. For there was truth in the charge made by Indian leaders that Indian soldiers still thought of themselves as the favoured servants of a foreign power. Almost until the end, there were some British officers who could think of Indian national leaders only as 'disloyal'.[42]

It is in this backdrop that 1947 and independence arrived, and with it came the partition. But before that a brief outline of the Indianizing process.

INDIANIZATION

It is rather a misnomer, this 'Indianization'. The Indian Army, whether as a force of the East India Company or in the subsequently evolved forms was always almost wholly Indian: in manpower, in recruitment, in habits and in conduct. The number of British was always a small fraction, and that too only officers. There are many reason why the British resisted opening this up until the last, not really till the Second World War. But these reasons need not detain us; they were after all the inevitable consequence of colonialism.

Race, language, religion, amongst other aspects, separated the British officers from the Indian men. How then did they function? It was through a unique innovation, wholly Indian, born partly of pragmatism but more as a direct descendant of an earlier system; and this was the office known as a Viceroy's Commissioned Officer (VCO). This functionary, now called Junior Commissioned Officer (JCO) (to be distinguished from the much later Indian Commissioned Officer, ICO) was the conduit, the connecting link that bridged the divide. The VCO was directly in charge of a body of troops; he was answerable for their discipline, welfare, leave, complaints, problems at home, even promotion and recognition. Seldom could an ordinary Indian soldier hope to rise having fallen foul of his VCO. And this VCO, conceptually and effectively, was the direct descendant (altered no doubt, but only in progression) of the basic idea of mansabdari and silledari discussed earlier. The British, as they replaced the Mughals, improved upon the inherited mansabdari/ silledari systems, adapted them and innovatively discovered the VCO. It is significant that this practice was unique to the Indian Army alone. Neither the Navy nor the Air Force felt the need, ever, having in any case evolved in a staggered time frame. It is both curious and telling that till date this rank continues, not just in India but in the armies of Pakistan and Bangladesh too. In that sense the Indian Army was an Indianized army always, from its inception.

The quest and the problem both centred upon Indianizing the officer component of this Army which is what we focus upon now.
Though some 700 Indians were granted commissions in the Medical Service during the First World War, the officer ranks remained largely closed to Indians. In 1918, ten places were reserved for Indians at the Royal Military College at Sandhurst. In consequence, and as the freedom movement gathered momentum in the 1920s and 1930s, one issue dominated the military debate in India – that of Indianization.

This could hardly be discussed without questioning the fundamental purpose of the Indian Army, or the future of the colonial state which it defended. The officer corps could not be Indianised without transforming the Army from a colonial garrison into an embryonic, national defence force of an independent country struggling to be born. In the early 1920s, the recruitment, equipment, and organisation of the Indian Army faithfully reflected its colonial role.

The British began the 1920s by making some very limited concessions which did not affect the regular forces. An Indian Territorial Force was set up in 1920, as a 'safety valve'. In March 1921, the Legislative Assembly passed a resolution demanding rapid Indianization of the Army and greater facilities for obtaining King's Commissions. It proposed

that the King-Emperor's Indian subjects should be freely admitted to all arms of His Majesty's military, naval and air forces in India, and that every encouragement should be given Indians – including the educated middle classes – to enter the commissioned ranks of the army.[43]

The Assembly also wanted a quarter of all new King's Commissions to be reserved for Indians, pending the creation of an 'Indian Sandhurst'. This resolution was moved by Sir P. S. Sivaswamy Aiyer, a leading moderate interested in military affairs. The passage of this resolution, its watering down, the amendments that were made to it and the many examinations and scrutinies of it would be too tedious an exercise. Having survived many committees of examination, the first under General Henry Rawlinson, then Commander-in-Chief, and the 17 February 1923 announcement of the 'eight-unit' scheme, which aimed at giving 'Indians a fair opportunity of proving that units officered by Indians will be efficient in every way'; the resolution saw the establishing of the Second Committee. In February 1925, this was set up, a committee under Sir Andrew Skeen to discuss the issue of establishing an 'Indian Sandhurst'. This included many distinguished Indians of the time including Pandit Motilal Nehru and M. A. Jinnah. The Skeen proposals were sent to the British Cabinet which, in turn, set up a committee under Lord Balfour. This committee rejected the Skeen proposals partly because they placed British officers under the command of Indians.

Meanwhile, in May 1931, the Government of India set up an expert committee to work out the details of an Indian Sandhurst. It published its report in September. The plans of the expert committee were adopted more or less completely. The Indian Military Academy (IMA) – as it was known – opened at Dehradun on 10 December 1932. And thus India could now, finally, train its own officers.

At the inauguration of the IMA, Field Marshal Chetwode stated that which has remained as a kind of exhortatory reminder to successive generations of young men marching into responsibility:

Three principles must guide an officer of a national army, and they are: First, the safety, honour, and welfare of your country come first, always and every time. Second, the honour, welfare, and comfort of the men you command come next. Third, your own ease, comfort and safety come   last,   always   and   every   time.

PARTITION

The partition of the armed forces in 1947 could not have come at a worse time for India. The Indian armed forces had just returned from assignments abroad during the Second World War, and upon return demobilization had followed. The tenfold expansion of the Army for the war – two million all ranks – was reduced to 400,000 personnel in less than two years, by June 1947.

On 3 June 1947, the new Viceroy of India, Lord Louis Mountbatten, announced the partition of India; this to be achieved within just 75 days. By 15 August, the Indian and Pakistani governments were to control their own administrative machinery and armed forces. For implementation a Partition Council was established, but only by 26 June. Thus, four days later, when this Council announced the guidelines for the division of the armed forces, just about 45 days were left in which to complete the task. This responsibility was entrusted to the Armed Forces Reconstitution Committee (AFRC), chaired by Field Marshal Sir Claude Auchinleck, then the Commander-in-Chief in India. It also included two future Chiefs of the Indian Army – Cariappa and Thimayya. The actual process, however, of splitting up began only in the third week of July, when all departments of the Indian Government were bifurcated under the two heads of India and Pakistan. The Defence Department suffered the same fate. That which had taken two and a half centuries to construct was to be dismantled within three weeks!

At a fairly early stage it was agreed that the reconstitution of the armed forces was to be carried out on the basis of territorial considerations, not communal. In effect, however, the division of personnel would not take place on the basis of religion alone, and not on geographical grounds at all. Military personnel were given the choice of leaving the services or volunteering for either the Indian or Pakistani armed forces, with the proviso that this would not be applicable to Hindus and Muslims serving in the Indian and Pakistani armed forces, respectively. Whereas equipment and movable stores were to be divided largely in proportion to the respective strengths of the armed forces, the technical training establishments were to be allocated on the basis of geographical location (they could hardly be physically relocated). By 15 August 1947, they were to be reorganized into two independent armed forces: of India and of Pakistan.

The Army in India had comprised of British troops from Britain and the regular Indian Army. The former consisted mostly of units of the fighting arms, who were turned over regularly: fresh units from Britain replacing those that had done their Indian tour of duty. The overall ratio of such troops to the Indian element was roughly 1 : 2; but they were not maintained as a separate force. After the partition plan was launched, these troops were removed from Indian formations and grouped separately. On 7 August 1948 they started leaving India. The last British unit to leave the Indian shores was in February 1948. The send-off was a military ceremonial. From 1748, and the establishing of 1st Madras Fusiliers of Stringer Lawrence, two centuries had gone by.

The order of battle of this partitioned Indian Army consisted of the 4th, 5th, 7th and 10th Infantry Divisions, the Ist Armoured Division and the 2nd Airborne Division. The composition of the pre-partition army was such that a division of it was inevitably to lead to severe disruption and dislocation. There were only a few single-class regiments like the Maratha Light Infantry, the Dogra Regiment or the Garhwal Rifles, or purely non-Muslim ones like the Kumaon Regiment. In the rest of the army, the Hindus, Muslims, and Sikhs served and fought together. In the services, the units were usually mixed, without any consideration of class, region or religion. In the fighting arms, however, the sub-units in a regiment or battalion were usually formed on a class basis, each unit comprising two or more classes, except in the single-class regiments. For example, of the four rifle companies in one battalion, two might consist of Punjabi Muslims, one of Sikhs, and another of Dogras. Another battalion might have two companies of Rajputs and two of Punjabi Muslims. However, there were no all-Muslim units.

Out of a 400,000-strong army, the Indian Army got some 260,000 all ranks, and the rest became part of the Pakistan Army, in a rough division of 2 : 1. Of the 21 regiments of cavalry, 19 regiments of infantry (excluding the 10 regiments of Gorkhas), and the 28 regiments of artillery, India was allocated 14 regiments of cavalry, 11 regiments of infantry and 18½ regiments of artillery. The Indian Army was also allocated 61 Engineer units, organized into the Madras, Bengal, and Bombay Engineer Groups.

In the sphere of Indian Muslim sub-units, however, mistakes were made by the Army sub-committee of the AFRC. It had assumed, for planning purposes, that the majority of Indian Muslim personnel would opt for Pakistan, and had already allotted Indian Muslim sub-units to Pakistan even before the concerned Record Offices could process individual options. This was both untidy and cruel but perhaps inevitable when dividing an almost half-million-strong standing force, jealous of its particularities and traditions, of a history won through valour and sacrifice spanning centuries, in the course of just 21 days!

Of the ten Gorkha regiments, it was agreed amongst India, Nepal and Britain that 6 were to remain with the Indian Army and four were to be allotted to Britain.

In view of the disparity in size between India and Pakistan, the two countries shared assets in the proportion of 64 : 36, which roughly paralleled their respective sizes and populations. Of the important fixed installations. Pakistan got the Staff College at Quetta, the Royal Indian Army Service Corps School at Kakul, and a number of regimental training centres; India the others.

INTEGRATION OF STATE FORCES

The consequences of partition were manifold. For the armed forces they posed mainly three immediate challenges: of a physical separation of units on the basis of religion, and this went down to Company/Squadron levels; a proper division of the military assets of an undivided India between the partitioned countries of India and Pakistan; and thirdly, of integrating divided units, as also the forces transferring to the union of India from princely states. Whereas the other two aspects have often been examined, not so (at least not so frequently) the question of state forces of princely India.

Ian Copland has authored perhaps the most detailed and objective study of the subject. He does not examine the aspect of state forces as such but offers a wealth of connected data.

What were the many challenges faced in reorganizing the state forces?

> First and foremost, . . . was the sheer scale of the task . . . the princely states numbered – if one counts all the non-jurisdictionary estates which abounded in Kathiawar and Central India – around 600. And collectively they comprised a major slice of the pre-1947 Indian bodypolitic – two-fifths of the area and one-third of the population of the erstwhile Indian Empire excluding Burma. Moreover, many of them were considerable countries in their own right. Kashmir, with an area of 84,000 square miles, was bigger than France; Travancore, with a population in 1921 of over 5 million, had more inhabitants than Portugal or Austria; from the pokey recesses of his Peshi Office, Nizam Osman Ali of Hyderabad presided over a kingdom whose income and expenditure in 1947-48 rivalled Belgium's and exceeded that of twenty member states of the United Stations. On the face of it, the project appeared to call for the re-constitution –in some form – of

the modern political histories of several hundreds of separate principalities scattered across a large part of the subcontinent.[44]

What was the military record and potential of these forces from 'two fifths of the area and one third of the population'; also what had been their record?

> . . . these State Forces had helped the British Indian Army, in the two great wars, and even earlier as during the Boxer Rebellion. Some dozen regiments of states' Imperial Service Troops saw service in France or the Middle East, (in WW I) while the maharajas of Bikaner, Nawanagar and Idar, the raja of Akalkot and the nawabs of Loharu and Sachin all spent time at the battlefront. As well, the states gave generously of money and munitions. Tiny Sangli donated Rs. 75,000 directly to war funds and invested five lakhs in war bonds; Nawanagar contributed the equivalent of half a year's revenue from the public fisc and the jam saheb another pounds 21,000 out of his own pocket; Bikaner in 1916 gave the equivalent of his "entire Privy Purse allowance for one year"; Rewa offered his entire hoard of jewels. At the same time the rulers helped out on the propaganda front, lending their names to recruitment drives and weighing in on the government's side. . . . For instance, in 1914 Hardinge asked the nizam as the de facto leader of India's Sunni Muslim community to try to get his co-religionists to ignore the fatwa issued by the Ottoman khalif calling for a holy war; Osman Ali obliged with a formal proclamation of his own urging them to fight instead on the Allied side.[45]

And Jodhpur Lancers distinguished itself at Haifa, capturing the city through a cavalry charge. They, along with the Lancers of Hyderabad and Mysore, stand immortalized on the entrance of Teen Murti (literally three statues of these three Lancers) Bhawan, which earlier housed the Commander-in-Chief, India and upon partition became the official residence of the first Indian Prime Minister, Pandit Nehru.

During the Second World War

Travancore built at its own expense a patrol boat for the Indian navy; Bhopal spent its entire stock of US securities on the purchase of American fighter planes; Jodhpur contributed money for a Halifax bomber; Kashmir donated eighteen field ambulances; Hyderabad, determined that in this as in all things it should be the premier performer, paid for no less than three squadrons of warplanes. Altogether, the cost of war materials provided by the states down to 1945 exceeded pounds 5 million. In addition, the states made numerous direct grants of cash and gave generously of their land, buildings and work forces for war purposes, Mysore handing over all state-owned buildings in Bangalore for the use of the army, Nawanagar starting a torpedo training school, Gwalior converting its Hattersley Mills in Bombay to the production of webbing for parachutes and Bikaner building a military hospital. By 1945 Hyderabad had spent Rs. 5.27 crores on war-related projects, Bhopal over 2 crores. Again, [they] made an important indirect contribution to the war effort by actively promoting it among their subjects. By the end of 1944 over 300,000 men from 59 states had signed up for military service and 15,000 more for war-related jobs in industry – a higher per-capita response than that of any of the provinces except for the Punjab – while some Rs. 180 million had been contributed by the states' people in subscriptions to government war bonds and securities and through donations to the viceroy's War Purposes Fund – again, a result that put British India to shame.[46]

The question was not simply of numbers, though that in itself was significant enough. In 1947 'even a moderately small state like Junagadh had about 2,400 men under arms, while at the top end of the scale Hyderabad could put a full division into the field'. It was more a question of the potential. After all, upon partition, Hyderabad, which had the capacity put out a serious

> bid to lease or buy Goa from the Portuguese for use as a duty-free port; . . . and asked British air chief marshal Sir Christopher Courtney for advice on the creation of a modern air force. While Bhopal investigated the purchase of Mistri Airlines as a state carrier and explored with the Quaid-i-Azam the possibility of the north-western states forming some sort of confederation in association with Pakistan.[47]

Of course, with the benefit of hindsight it is tempting to say that the states here were clutching at straws; however, initially at least, the responses to these overtures gave them reason to hope.

> If the Americans reacted coolly, France and several Arab countries gave strong signals that they were willing to consider diplomatic ties with such states as did not accede to India or Pakistan; Courtney and for that matter the joint chiefs-of-staff warmly welcomed the nizam's request for assistance as affording a golden opportunity for the United Kingdom to retain a "strong foothold" in southern India; and even within the cabinet voices were heard to argue that Travancore's pleas for diplomatic recognition should be heeded in view of the state's importance as the United Kingdom's major source of monazite, a basic ingredient of the fissionable mineral thorium.[48]

The task, however, was handled with ease, despatch

and without any complications – the exception being Hyderabad whose integration, through a police action, is not relevant here. The Indian Army established a committee, officers were deputed to visit the various states and offer absorption in the Army of the Union of India. Simultaneously, demobilization was also carried out of surplus or unabsorbable units. That all this was achieved with fluency was largely on account of the prevailing political atmosphere. The absorption of manpower provided no major hurdles, for in any event not only did the State Forces have skilled and well-trained elements (at least the larger ones did), they came largely from those very rural backgrounds as did the basic stock of the Indian Army.

ARMY IN INDEPENDENT INDIA: ETHOS AND ORGANIZATION

Here our concern alters in substance. It no longer suffices to narrate the course of events. A bland enumeration of the statistics of growth, inevitable as India grew in its independence, will simply not do. Our enquiry is into the fundamentals that governed this growth.

The very first need then was the obvious enough establishment of an Indian Ministry of Defence, on Indian soil, in Indian hands, for India, at last, after centuries of servitude. Was it preceded, accompanied, or even followed by investing this ministry with a comprehensive strategic doctrine for an independent India; or a policy for the security of this new state, an ancient nation? Thereafter, what innovative thought was given to defining the interrelationship between this new ministry and the old inherited service headquarters of the armed forces? We are concerned here not so much with the minute and the day to day, as with the overarching principles, the thought process. If these were either insufficiently clear, or limited, or even faulty, then inevitably adverse consequences would follow. Even as we view this from the better illuminated stance of hindsight we find that the instruments then designed have had a crippling effect; that they were not the correct answers, and were an inadequate preparation for the challenges that then lay ahead. This is one aspect of our enquiry; the second, being the vital ingredient of strategic policy. Did independent India and its political leadership, then or later or ever, undertake a definition and enunciation of it? Or did it simply put aside the responsibility as too inconvenient? Because the consequences of that are being faced, rather have already been faced, by succeeding generations; free India continues to pay a price. Our concern thereafter is with the challenge inherent in the two acts: of partition and of attaining independence; thereafter of reorganization, reform, and most importantly of infusing the armed forces of independent India with the ethos and spirit of the freedom movement. The expansion and growth of the armed forces was implicit in the management of the security environment of an emergent India. And as with the passage of time the environs altered so did the challenges; but did the response meet the demands of change? The phases of this period, not necessarily in any hierarchical sense of importance, were

• the immediate aftermaths of partition and independence;
• 1947 and the first conflict over Jammu & Kashmir;
• the occupation of Tibet, conflict over the high Himalayas and the border wars with China 1962; thereafter 1965, the second war with Pakistan; then 1971, the emergence of Bangladesh and the third conflict; and
• the decade of the eighties and the challenges of insurgency including the IPKF experiment.

Integral to all this was the aspect of a weapons and equipment policy, of indigenization and productionizing the intellect of India through defence research and development; the challenge of moulding India's armed forces as a befitting instrument of state in the service of the nation's interests. Did the Indian political leadership, during all these years, take any initiative for clearly enunciating the national goals, core aims and vital national interests in the pursuance of which, or for the protection of which, no matter what the price, the nation, through the instrumentality of its armed forces, would undertake to pay any price? These questions we now attempt to answer in the succeeding paragraphs, and in Chapters Three and Four.

A full-fledged Defence Ministry for the political leadership of independent India was a new and unusual experience. India was used to the presence and functioning of a Defence Department and also a Defence Member of the Viceroy's Council, but as for executive authority in defence matters that had always been the prerogative of the India Office and Whitehall. The demands of the Second World War, particularly the Burma theatre, had then necessitated changes, also a great deal of flexibility in operational matters but not so far as policy determination went. This new experience of a defence ministry was also combined with a partitioning of the country. Understandably, the political leadership remained more engaged with the immediate aftermath of partition rather than with formulating policies and struggling with strategic concepts. Besides, there had been scant preparation for it. The Congress, as the spearhead of the movement, had given hardly any thought to what a divided India's defence requirements would be.

There were some additional, attendant difficulties, not simply operational or administrative; they arose from the fundamentals of approach. We have already examined how Gandhi's pacifism and non-violence as a creed has influenced independent India's strategic culture. This had a more direct and a far more telling, even if unobtrusive, influence on the fledgling Ministry of Defence. The environment in which it had to operate, accompanied by the benumbing violence of partition, was influenced also by sentiments like 'India is a peace-loving country', 'we shun war', 'pacifism is our credo', and sentiments of that ilk. Despite partition, and on account of Pandit Nehru's early enunciation of the country's foreign policy, India deluded itself into thinking that simply because it bore no enmity against another, therefore, none harboured any designs against it either. Naive credulity replaced statecraft.

There was one other aspect. Indian independence had been achieved after a long and dramatic struggle against imperialism. Thus, deservingly, India became the standard bearer of anti-colonialism; inevitably then to India passed the flag of the entire colonized world seeking their respective spaces under the sun. In consequence, India joined the ranks of 'leaders', not simply of the Third World but as a spokesman of the 'poor of the world' as well. In any event anti-colonialism, South-South unity and its obverse and implicit the North-South confrontation, or invocations of the kind that the 'socialist bloc is the natural ally of the Third World', etc. became standardized as the icons of independent India's foreign policy. (Astonishing that they still hold sway.) This had a drag, a deleterious consequence for emergent India's defence policy. A 'poor nation' mentality came to infuse the entire thinking process, not simply of the political class but also of the administering civil service. In turn, this led to sentiments like 'India is a poor country, it cannot afford to waste scarce resources on luxuries like defence', etc. Various instances can be cited in support of this: like the early debates about defence versus development; the employment of the armed forces in seemingly developmental efforts like building housing for soldiers by soldiers instead of emphasizing and training for greater combat effectiveness. But it was not simply defence expenditure that had been relegated in importance, the defence forces too had begun to be treated as almost a superfluity.

All this, combined with an absence of strategic culture, lack of commitment to territory and a somewhat naive and idealistic approach to the country's security, thus became the ethos in which the new Ministry of Defence began addressing itself to its responsibilities. Not that it got much time or leisure to reflect on these issues. Within months of independence problems of integration of princely states and issues like Hyderabad were confronting India. There was then the question of the accession of Jammu & Kashmir, and also the first invasion of it by Pakistani raiders. This last, however, is the subject of enquiry for the next chapter.

What we are engaged in is an examination of the early philosophy that governed the subsequent evolution of the armed forces of India. Here exemplifying that old adage about physical versus the moral was the approach of independent India's political leadership to the pay, allowances and status of the armed forces, their officers and other ranks. As a British Indian Army, Navy or Air Force, the status and emoluments of all those that served in them were markedly better than in any other service. This was by design; the armed forces had to be conferred a status befitting their role as the principal arm of the imperial power. They simply had to be available and ready in fine fettle largely for maintaining internal order. Therefore, whenever these forces came into conflict with the dynamics of the freedom movement, or its leadership, the personnel of the Army particularly were seen only as extensions of British interest. Those that cooperated with the British during the latter part of their empire in India were, almost all of them – irrespective of their calling – often pejoratively referred to as 'toadys'.

Regrettably, even after independence the approach of the new ruling political class to the entire personnel of the armed forces was coloured by the same prejudice. A distance separated those that had fought for freedom and those that had instead fought for the ruler. A condescending distrust was the consequence; the anglicization of the forces grated the homespun political leadership, and in turn the forces continued to distance themselves from the new political class. This was not either a happy or an auspicious augury. This is altogether more surprising, and less comprehensible when examined against the readiness with which the administrative class of India – 'the steel frame' – the civil service under the new Home Minister, was almost immediately accepted and utilized as a fit instrument for the new nation's new endeavours; not so, however, the Army, the Navy or the Air Force. There was for this a second cause as well. The Commander-in-Chief, India, during the entire period of British viceroyalty was always, in terms of protocol, the second most important figure, only after the British Viceroy. Such a situation, of course, could not continue. There had to be a bringing down, in terms of importance, it was not simply a question of protocol. To a combination of these two was then added a third factor, a more operational and administrative aspect.

Based on the recommendations of Lord Ismay, and upon the advice of the first Governor General, Lord Mountbatten, as part of the process of a reorganization of independent India's armed forces, service headquarters opted to function distinctly apart and separately from the Defence Ministry. This was a grave error with lasting consequences. Behind such a decision lay two main causes. The first, along with a desire to distance the armed forces from the political centre of power, was the inherently apolitical nature of the services themselves. When, therefore, the then Commanders-in-Chief of the Army, Navy and the Air Force were asked their opinion, they opted for the more familiar functioning mode of a theatre command. In any event the Second World War could only have been managed in a largely decentralized form through various theatres of operation. India was the headquarters, in that sense, of not simply the South Asia Command but the entire theatre of conflict. For this purpose, theatre commanders functioned largely autonomously and separately from the direct chain of command of the then political leadership. A simple translation of this concept, as the answer to independent India's reforms was an error. The causes outlined cannot by themselves provide sufficient grounds for the arrangement that came into being. It is because of this system that independent India's decision-making apparatus in matters of defence is today, possibly, the most cumbersome, time-consuming, bureaucratic and expensive.

There was an element of unstated apprehension too, which over time only got cemented as in Pakistan democracy was easily brushed aside and repeated coups followed. Apprehensions about a similar denouement in India only confirmed early prejudices. In consequence, a system got devised that today requires every possible need of the armed forces to travel to the Ministry of Defence from services headquarters where it is examined afresh, then scrutinized inhouse from the financial angle, only whereafter the 'elephantine file' makes its way to the Cabinet; whereafter, again for a second financial scrutiny and only then finally, and hopefully, a decision is taken, even if it be a severely truncated one from the original requirement. Time wasted by this overelaborate procedure is incalculable in terms of efficiency, of meeting defence requirements timely, as also of the attendant morale frustrations of the services headquarters. Inevitably thereafter, financial proposals, simply by this process of a timelag balloon hopelessly out of the original estimates and their implementation stretches to an extent where the functional efficiency of the armed forces is severely affected. As there is no horizontal integration between the service headquarters and the Defence Ministry, and as early prejudices have now got layered over by bureaucratic oneupmanship, a combative mentality has grown between the service headquarters and the Ministry. Such an attitude has its own damaging consequences; the Defence Ministry, in effect, becomes the principal destroyer of the cutting edge of the military's morale; ironic considering that the very reverse of it is their responsibility. The sword arm of the state gets blunted by the state itself. So marked is resistance then to change here, and so deep the mutual suspicions, inertia and antipathy that all efforts at reforming the system have always floundered against a rock of ossified thought.

This has had another, obvious enough, consequence: an institutionalizing of policymaking during the past 50 years has simply not taken place. The country has deluded itself into thinking that a vast and ever-growing ministry is the proper alternative for such an institutional mechanism. Occasionally, half-hearted and half-digested thoughts like policy planning cells, etc. have been set up but as the spirit is wanting, the functioning of such cells has scarcely had any effect on real policymaking; it has at best been marginal, at the worst inconsequential.

Just as independent India inherited no institutional mechanism for policymaking and as there had been no accompanying thought which could be dignified by the term of strategic doctrine, not only were vital national interests never defined, even essential administrative and elementary steps by way of precaution were not taken. Thus, independent India failed to evaluate for itself what the strategic consequences of partition were going to be. The imperial power had always conceived of the defence of India starting from well beyond the geographical territories of the Empire. Thus, for the British, the Indian Ocean was important not simply as the arena on which floated British trade but as also vital for a country with as wide and long a peninsula jutting into the ocean as India has. India's long coastline and a strategic positioning – from the southern fringes of Asia, to the East coast of Africa, the northern shores of Australia and lying as it does between the chokepoints of the Suez Canal in the West and the Straits of Malacca in the East – compel attention – not of the Indian political-military class though. In consequence the Indian Navy has remained a coastal protection force. Indian air power and its rapid advancement during the Second World War remained largely an opportunity not taken. This new element of war, air, had in any case largely sidestepped this theatre of war with the exception of air transportation support provided by Dakotas for personal and supply lifts through air strips constructed with US help, and used for engagement by the latter against selected Japanese targets. Yet again, therefore, and also on account of an absence of thought by the Indian political leadership, the Indian Air Force at independence remained, not as a new element in the triad of forces, but really as a supporting arm for the Army.

For this last, and to even these tasks were brought two other major deficiencies, both of which have contributed to afflicting Indian defence policymaking with all kinds of problems in the last 50 years. Despite the bastion of the Himalayas, for the British, a landward protection of their empire involved a military concept of Central Asia. It is not necessary for us to recount in any detail all the efforts that were made under that evocative phrase, 'the great game'.

What is truly astounding is that for independent India's political leadership, particularly Pandit Nehru, who was not simply a student of history but had a sense of it, the Central Asian factor was completely absent. It was forgotten that forces from Central Asia had repeatedly invaded India during the past many centuries and had altered the course of its history. Upon partition, and perhaps on account of the then Soviet empire stretching over Central Asia, no such thought ever troubled the Indian political class. In consequence India's entire policy towards Afghanistan remained ill-conceived, ill-executed and confined to mostly treating Afghanistan as a counterpoise between India and the new state of Pakistan. That this was a profound error got dramatically established in the last two decades of independence, after the Soviet invasion of Afghanistan and of all the subsequent events that then followed: the withdrawal of the Soviet Union; its collapse as an imperial power in Central Asia; extension of other nations' interests into Afghanistan and its descent into the worst kind of tribal anarchy. Just as there was an absence of Central Asian thought, the presence of the high Himalayas deluded our political leadership into a false sense of security. It was astonishing that whereas developments in Nepal could deeply trouble Pandit Nehru, persuading him to intervene in a most marked manner; yet just another step away, developments in Tibet resulted in no other reaction than one of quiet and timid acquiescence. This too can be attributed to that second failing: absence of a strategic concept about the role and place of the high Himalayas in the geopolitics of the South Asian subcontinent.

After 1948, the Army comfortably slid into a period of golden cantonment soldiering, with occasional confusion about building houses; thus dawned sterile debates like defence versus development. This had to result in 1962, when Panchsheel died a premature and violent death upon the bleak heights of the Aksai Chin. The short interruption of 1965 followed. But an expansion was the consequence: of a largely plains force into a two-front Army; one for the Himalayas and the other one for the plains. Inevitably, therefore, the Army virtually doubled in the process. Its employment became as diverse as from the frozen and stormy glaciers of Siachen to the hot and humid jungles of the North-East, the deep south, to the desert of Rajasthan and the estuarine wastes of Kutch. In the process it developed an expertise greater than that of any other army in the world, particularly about combat in both high altitude and extreme cold; a combination that has not been matched by any other army in the world.

As exhaustive and detailed a tabulation of the armed forces of India as is possible is at the end of this chapter. From a small 7 division force that the Army was in 1947, in the intervening 50 years it has quadrupled; from just about a quarter of a million in 1947, the Army alone is today more than a million strong. And as the manpower strength has grown so have all other equipment and support requirements. That all this is not most cost-effective is something that has been examined separately. A caution, however, is needed about manpower policies. For a volunteer army, 50 years after independence, to have critical shortages (reportedly 13,000) in the sword-edge middle ranks of Captains and Majors, and similar shortages in the Air Force is a serious reminder of significant failures in managing men. The Parliament has taken note of this; it has also noted the fall in numbers and standards, both, of young men volunteering for commission by opting for training in the many more training academies that now offer such an option. This is the moral coefficient of the physical side of this army and it is a cause for serious anxiety, at least so it is stated.[49]

An account of the management of the various conflicts

is the subject of our enquiry in the following chapter. Details of budgets and force profiles are in Chapter Four. Here, what remains are the aspects of weapons and equipment, defence research and development, and that great success story, the Border Roads Organization (BRO). These follow, but only after the Navy and the Air Force.

THE INDIAN NAVY[50]

The partition and reconstitution of the Navy was the responsibility of the naval sub-committee of the AFRC. One of the first recommendations of the naval sub-committee was that ships should be allocated on the basis of the actual needs of the two dominions, that is India and Pakistan, rather than the estimated strengths of their naval personnel. In this sense, the Chairman of the Partition Council, Lord Mountbatten, felt that naval reconstitution was made on 'common sense lines'. This was quite different from the division of assets carried out for the Army and Air Force, which was based on the numerical strengths of the respective armed forces. The prospective addition of the cruiser 'Achilles' to the Indian Navy was taken into account while dividing the RIN (Royal Indian Navy).

The naval sub-committee unanimously allocated 33 ships to the Indian Navy and 16 ships to Pakistan (in the rough proportion of 2 : 1). Since India had a considerably larger maritime trade, and a much longer coastline, it was given four of the six sloops; in addition, it was granted two frigates, twelve fleet and four motor minesweepers, four trawlers, four harbour defence motor launches, a corvette, a survey ship, a motor launch, and a number of small landing craft. The Pakistani Navy, meanwhile, was allocated two sloops, two frigates, four fleet minesweepers, two trawlers and four harbour defence motor launches. On 18 November 1947, the AFRC recommended the complete demilitarization of the sloop 'Hindustan'; and then its transfer to the Pakistani

Navy as a training ship.

The Navy's technical training establishments were divided between India and Pakistan on the basis of geographical location. As a result, the three major training establishments located in Karachi were allocated to the Pakistani Navy. The Indian Navy, meanwhile, was given the less important training institutions. The naval sub-committee unanimously recommended the adoption of certain principles for the distribution of movable assets such as reserves of arms, ammunition, equipment, clothing, vehicles and stores of all kinds.

In July and August 1947 the division of naval personnel on the basis of 'territorial considerations' took place. While 538 officers and 4,121 ratings volunteered to serve the Indian Navy, some 3,580 men (including 3,400 ratings) opted for Pakistan.

For the Navy of independent India the principal challenges were three: what was to be its role and function; how was it be equipped for that role; and thirdly, where was it to find the Senior Commanders for it, as they had been almost entirely British. All the other factors, attitudinal and of resource priorities remaining exactly the same; the Indian Navy's evolution was retarded by the last: an absence of senior officers. And as the Ministry of Defence provided no conceptual direction, the British actually determined what the Indian Navy was all about till well into the fifties. Let us see how.

Within ten days of Independence, the British Chief of the Indian Navy, Rear Admiral J. T. S. Hall prepared an expansion plan for it. This ten-year plan (1948-1958) attempted to combine the protection of merchant shipping as the primary task, with India's aspiration to 'a position of strength, pre-eminence, and leadership among the nations of South-East Asia'. Clearly another early priority was the expansion of training facilities, to replace what had gone to Karachi. This plan, in terms of warships, aimed for a naval force which would include two Light Fleet Aircraft Carriers, three cruisers, eight destroyers and four submarines before the end of the decade. While the development of the air arm was scheduled for consideration only after four years, the deployment of a cruiser and procurement of three destroyers were given priority. A subsequent expansion plan formulated by Hall's successor, Vice Admiral Parry, in 1948 was not markedly different; this involved the expansion of the Indian Navy to a carrier task force comprising two carriers, three cruisers, and appropriate destroyers, an escort force of frigates and destroyers, and a small submarine service by the end of 1958. But there was, at least on paper, a difference. Whereas the British Indian Government had envisaged the Indian Navy as only a local defence force, the Hall and Parry plans did conceptualize a role of protecting India's sealanes of communication in the Indian Ocean; not independently to start with; however, in the long term an independent naval capability was to come eventually.

A successful implementation of the Parry expansion plan rested on two premises: funding and an ability to acquire relatively sophisticated warships, obviously from foreign sources for India had none of her own. It was thus a virtual non-starter, abandoned even before its launch. This was followed in 1954 by a ten-year comprehensive 'naval replacement' programme, formu- lated by the new British Chief of the Indian Navy, Vice Admiral Mark Pizey. The Pizey plan recommended the acquisition of smaller, though faster, warships with modern armament and equipment. Most of the aged second- hand ships were to be replaced by new anti-submarine and anti-aircraft frigates, and coastal and inshore minesweepers. This plan also envisaged increasing dockyard and training facilities for the Navy.

In this plan was a major reassessment of the future role and composition of the Indian Navy. The emphasis shifted from the development of a naval force capable of air, surface and sub-surface operations to one devoted primarily to defensive anti-submarine warfare (ASW). Much more significantly, this plan was hardly for India, it echoed the British Admiralty's desired role for the Indian Navy, and in defence of the Commonwealth.

The basic assumption was that the Indian Navy's vessels were to deal with a Soviet and/or Chinese threat in the form of submarines, or mines dropped from aircraft, and if India implied so, it was unlikely that their sale by Britain would be refused. The execution of these operations was assumed on the basis of a global war between the United States and its allies (including the British Commonwealth), and the military forces of the Soviet Union and China. It was felt that since most of India's maritime trade was carried on western bloc ships, the Indian Navy would join western naval forces during a global war.

This was clearly spelt out in a 'Strictly Personal' letter from Lord Mountbatten to L. J. Callaghan, the Parliamentary Secretary, dated 31 August 1951.

> When I was in India I did everything in my power to try and get them to build up a Navy which would be of some use to the allied effort in that part or the world in the event of a world war. The fact that Nehru is doing all in his power to hold the balance and prevent the war from breaking out has made people mis-understand the fundamental position, which is that there can be no question of India fighting on the wrong side in the war, if it comes. She may not join at once but if the war becomes really world wide I do not see how she can really keep out and I think that everybody in India realises that she will eventually be fighting on our side. Their contribution therefore can make a considerable difference to us, since they have good naval bases at Bombay, Cochin, Vizagapatnam, etc. All of which would be at our disposal and, of course, their inexhaustible supply of manpower which is exceptionally quick to learn and fearless in battle.[51]

The astonishing thing about this letter is not Mountbatten's presumptuousness, which after all was but a personality trait. It is the confidence with which India's security interests, and thus responses, were dovetailed with those of the allies; proof of the absence then of sufficient thought on the subject by the Indian political leadership; the dependence on British equipment and doctrines; and finally, and most disturbingly Mountbatten's continuing role (four years after independence) as a factor that continued to influence India's defence policies: the Indian Navy in this instance; and Kashmir, as we shall see later.

Such an enunciation of Indian naval doctrine, and a neglect of planning for limited war (against Pakistan) soon came in for criticism. The issue focused on the question of submarines. It was apparently felt that a Pakistani naval threat, if and when it materializes, would take the form of surface and air forces, not that of submarines. In this regard, the then Minister for Defence Organization, Mahavir Tyagi, correctly questioned the Navy's stress on ASW. He complained to Pizey that,

> As there is no submarine threat in the Indian Ocean, and as it would take a long time for the same to develop, would Naval Headquarters not like to reconsider the proportion in which we are ordering Anti-Aircraft to Anti-Submarine frigates?[52]

Indian naval officers also questioned Mountbatten on the advisability of procuring anti-submarine ships for the Navy. He remained unfazed and during his tour of India in 1956, as the First Sea Lord, he somewhat patronizingly expressed confidence in the Indian naval doctrine, and said that he 'could not recommend a switching over of the present (warship) building programme'.

Due to this misplaced emphasis on defensive ASW operations in a global war, planning for a limited war involving only India's interests was neglected. The deployment of new frigates and minesweepers was not intended for hostilities against Pakistan. These ships were not perceived to be 'of great use to either India or Pakistan', when therefore,

Pakistan began to expand its surface naval force in the mid-1950s, tension arose between the contradictory goals of Indian naval planning and of a global and limited war. The dominance, or at least precedence, of British interests over India's is revealed by another letter to the new British Chief of the Indian Navy, Vice Admiral S. H. Carlill, on 16 May 1956, again from Lord Mountbatten, who wrote:

> From conversations between Katari and William Carne, it is clear that he is worried as to whether the Indian Navy is getting good value in buying Type 14 frigates. Katari kept on remarking that if a convoy is escorted by nothing but Type 14s there is no reason why submarines should not surface and finish off the escorts by gunfire; if, on the other hand the escorts were to contain one or more larger frigates, presumably the Senior Officer would be in the larger Frigate and would not wish to detach himself to go and engage a submarine, possibly at some distance form the convoy. . . .
>
> I saw Katari on Whit Sunday and had a very satisfactory general talk. He certainly does not like having the frigates without any worthwhile gun armament and I think would prefer that no more should be ordered. As I know the background of all this is the "surface threat" from a certain quarter I will go into this with the Controller on my return from my visit to the Home Fleet and write to you again.[53]

Eventually the Indian Navy acquiesced, accepting an ASW doctrine in planning for global warfare. The British Admiralty, however, refused to provide it with the arms critical for the task – the submarines themselves. The Indian Government had agreed with the policy, but for an entirely different set of reasons. While the Indian Government's opposition to the acquisition of armed submarines lay primarily on grounds of cost, and the aspiration of an offensive naval policy, the British Admiralty stressed only the latter aspect by commenting upon the implications of Indian submarine operations in the Indian Ocean. Thus went the reasoning: since first-generation submarines in a Navy were known to be more efficient in anti-ship roles than in ASW operations, they were not perceived as being effective in enhancing the Indian Navy's latter missions, which for India were primary. More important, Indian sub-surface anti-ship operations, in a worst-case scenario, could prove a nuisance to western merchant shipping too, certainly in the Indian Ocean. And finally, the establishment of a submarine force in the Indian Navy would result in an entirely new dimension of warfare between the Indian and Pakistani navies. In view of these considerations an internal British Admiralty memorandum was to note that submarines 'for use against surface ships had no role to play in Commonwealth defence planning'.[54]

This account has been given in some detail to emphasize the absence of a coherent Indian naval doctrine; continued interference by Mountbatten, his access (direct and secret) to the then chiefs of Indian Naval Staff, well into the mid-fifties; and the acquiescence of the Indian political leadership to foreign interference in the nation's defence policy; and all this well after independence.

When it came to arms acquisition the situation was worse. The Indian Navy, predictably, faced difficulties in the acquisition of certain warships from Britain. While the Parry plan was acceptable, in principle, to the Indian Government, it was not to the Admiralty in London. It expressed views divergent to those stated by Parry, particularly over the future role and composition of the Indian Navy. They (the British) were, therefore, extremely reluctant to provide the needed warships. In its formal response to the Indian naval expansion plan, the Admiralty simply snubbed Parry. The British First Sea Lord, Admiral of the Fleet Lord Fraser, bluntly reminded Parry that the primary function of the Indian Navy was simply the 'protection of the coastline and harbours of India', and stated that he 'was a little surprised to see that you had not made provision for minesweepers'.[55]

Parry's proposals for the development of Indian naval aviation came in for even more acidulous scorn. The Admiralty held that ship-based naval aviation had absolutely no role to play in the Indian Navy (even as part of an anti-submarine force). Unresponsive to Parry's first annual report to the Admiralty, its Director of Plans felt that

> no opportunity should be lost in persuading the RIN to . . . build a Navy capable of carrying out its primary function, which must be the protection of India's coast line and harbours.

The British Vice Chief of Naval Staff also brusquely noted that Parry's ideas were 'incapable of implementation from this country for many a long day'.[56]

However, once the Indian Navy's plans began to conform to those of the British Admiralty, by virtue of the Pizey plans, the attitude of the Admiralty altered rapidly and dramatically. The Admiralty agreed, in principle, to supply an aircraft carrier (in terms of its ASW functions) to India. In early 1955, a British Admiralty report, written for the specific purpose of briefing Prime Minister Nehru on the subject, emphasized such a requirement. Based entirely on a global war scenario, thereby again stressing the desired role of the Indian Navy, and omitting any awkward reference to Pakistan, it stated that India's sealanes of communication would be threatened even in the case of Indian neutrality. For the defence of Indian maritime trade, therefore, it recommended the purchase of three Light Fleet Aircraft Carriers, two squadrons of long-range maritime aircraft, and a frontline strength of some 150 aircraft. In order to persuade the Indian Government to expand its naval ASW force, Lord Mountbatten even counselled Nehru on the prestige value of a carrier in the Indian Navy.[57] This, well into the mid-fifties.

Consequently, in May 1956, the Indian Government

finally decided to place an order for an aircraft carrier with Britain. This was largely a result of its perceived role in warfare, and its value in terms of prestige. An Indian naval team subsequently visited Britain to inspect the 16,000 ton carrier on offer, HMS Hercules. Although its keel had been laid in October 1943, its construction was brought to a halt some three years later when it was only three-quarters complete. The Indian delegation's recommendations to the British Admiralty included the provision of a long-stroke catapult for the carrier (to augment the variety of carrier-operated aircraft, and subsequently their roles). The British Admiralty, however, expressed its inability to comply with this request. Although the official explanation related to a 'very grave shortage of design staff', the actual reason was different: it was the apprehension of '. . . the employment of "Hercules" in a role other than that of an escort carrier for which . . . she is primarily suited'. Indian naval officers were unhappy with this decision and pressed the British Admiralty to accept the suggested modifications. On this issue, Lord Mountbatten expressed annoyance with Indian Naval Headquarters, and warned Vice Admiral Carlill,

> If the Indians insist on running at the full speed of a Fleet Carrier before they can even walk with an escort carrier I prophecy they never will have a Fleet Air Arm . . . this is it; you either take what amounts to the limit of our offer or give up the contest.[58]

The Navy eventually (and yet again) bowed to pressure from Lord Mountbatten and the British Admiralty, and in January 1957 the Indian Cabinet agreed to recondition the 'Hercules' (minus the long-stroke catapult) at the Harland and Wolff shipyard in Belfast, Northern Ireland, UK. Some four years later it was commissioned into the Navy as INS Vikrant.

There is another aspect that we need to reflect upon. The Indian Navy's umbilical cord with the Royal

Navy remained uncut for too long some think. For example, the relationship between the British Chiefs of the Indian Navy and Lord Mountbatten, who was in service with the Royal Navy in Malta and England, was invariably that of colleagues; the former more often than not looking to the latter for advice and encouragement. A special case was that of the acquisition of the second cruiser for the Indian Navy. Although the 1947 and 1948 plan papers had recommended two cruisers, only one had been acquired by the Indian Navy, and that in 1948. Since the acquisition of the second cruiser was envisaged in 1952, negotiations with the Admiralty were begun at the end of 1949. The Admiralty favoured the sale of another cruiser to India in terms of its role in coastal defence, and the sea training of junior officers and ratings. As a result, negotiations were virtually concluded by the summer of 1950. In view of the Korean war, however, the Admiralty halted the transfer of all naval vessels, including that of the cruiser, to India.

In order to enlist help in the matter, Vice Admiral Parry wrote a personal and confidential letter to Lord Mountbatten on 2 January 1951, emphasizing the seriousness of the situation. He stated,

> If the question (of the cruiser) has to be shelved very much longer we shall have to make some rather drastic decisions. We have trained practically everybody needed for the extra ship and these people must be employed somewhere. In addition we have our usual flow of young officers and ratings who urgently need training afloat; and without the second cruiser it will mean turning "Delhi" into a training ship, which will obviously very seriously interfere with our fleet training and will in effect mean we will not have an efficient squadron ready for emergencies. We might also have to seriously curtail our recruiting programme and possibly our entry of officers as well.[59]

During the Prime Minister's Conference in London in 1951, Prime Minister Nehru met the First Sea Lord at a small dinner, and brought up the issue. He followed it up with a personal letter written directly to Prime Minister C. R. Attlee on 28 January 1951, in which he stated,

I am taking the liberty of writing to you personally on this (acquisition of the cruiser) subject to request you to help us in getting the "Jamaica" (cruiser). You have a great Navy with a very large number of Cruisers; we have only a small and young Navy to which the addition of the "Jamaica" would make a very great difference. I hope that you will help us in this matter.[60]

Notwithstanding this appeal, the transfer of the second cruiser to India did not take place for another three years. During this period the roles of the major players got reversed.

The Indian Government now appeared reluctant to accept the second cruiser, whereas the Admiralty was keen to part with one as by then the Korean war had come to an end. This resistance of the Indian side was finally overcome not by the British Government, the Admiralty, Lord Mountbatten, or Vice Admiral Pizey, C-in-C, Indian Navy, but by Lady Edwina Mountbatten. Vice Admiral Pizey's personal and private letter to Lord Mountbatten, written on 23 March 1954, makes this quite apparent. He writes,

Edwina has been wonderfully helpful, as indeed she always is, and it was mainly due to a "whisper" in the right direction that we managed to speed up the government's acceptance of the second cruiser. It really was becoming a farce because despite the fact that the P.M. had decided, as soon as the offer was made, to accept it immediately, the lower levels of Defence and Finance started making extremely, and quite unnecessarily, heavy weather, including a desire to send a team of naval "experts" from India to examine the ship before recommending acceptance. Of course I rather naturally blew up, and it was at this stage that Edwina dropped the necessary pennies! You must get her to expand on this because the speed with which things happened over a certain weekend was really quite remarkable![61]

Not surprisingly, the Indian Navy's second cruiser, commissioned as INS Mysore, arrived just over two years later, in 1956. This example is cited for highlighting the obvious enough aspect of British interest being subserved by an Indian Chief of the Naval Staff – and only because he was on loan from the Royal Navy. These early experiences have had lasting consequences for an evolution of the Indian Navy as an integrated and well-equipped force.

Besides, since those early years of double loyalties, and perhaps as a direct consequence of them the Indian Navy has in effect remained largely a coastal protection navy. This is despite the two wars of 1965 and 1971 that it has fought; also the expansion (relative); the accretion of additional naval commands, as separately explained; its expansion as a two-sea Navy (Arabian and Bay of Bengal); the establishment of a separate Coast Guard and the expansion of the Indian Navy's commercial responsibilities by the discovery of exploitable hydrocarbon reserves along the coastal shelf of India and the definition of India's EEZ.

1958-1965
A good ten years after independence, in April 1958, the first Indian naval officer, Vice Admiral R. D. Katari, took over as the Chief of Naval Staff. Nonetheless, a few British naval officers remained; the last leaving only in the early 1960s. Katari's appointment did not result in any significant change in naval policy or doctrine. Funding had already been allocated for the purchase of the aircraft carrier "Hercules", as well as the eight

frigates. Additional funding could not be provided for other naval vessels, such as submarines. Moreover, in the late 1950s, the Indian Government did not commit itself to the acquisition of submarines, although it accepted the naval case for three submarines, though only 'in principle'. During this period naval planning for a limited war against Pakistan took on greater importance, yet the Navy continued to emphasize an Anti-Submarine Warfare (ASW) doctrine for global warfare.

Whereas the Navy played a support role (with the loss of lives) during the liberation of Goa in 1961, essentially involving the disabling of a Portuguese frigate and gaining control of Anjidev island, it had obviously no role to play in the 1962 Sino-Indian conflict. Although the strengthening of the Indian armed forces assumed top priority in the wake of that war, the Navy was denied additional funding as it had not participated in the military action. Nonetheless, this conflict forced the government to seriously plan to acquire armed submarines.

During the 1965 Indo-Pakistan war, the government even forbade the Navy to initiate any offensive action against Pakistani forces at sea or operate beyond a given range, except in pursuit of Pakistani naval ships, notwithstanding a Pakistani naval attack on Dwarka. The range of permissible naval operations was confined to within 200 nautical miles of Bombay, or south of the parallel of Porbandar. This appears to have been due to the Government's attempt to limit the scope of the war, and a lack of confidence in the Navy: this last a consequence of early confusion and neglect.

1965-1980

In the wake of the 1965 Indo-Pakistan war, the Navy was provided additional funding for limited expansion, as part of the overall strengthening of the armed forces. Significantly, it decided to acquire armed submarines from the erstwhile Soviet Union, in view of the denial of boats from both the United States as well as the UK. This major arms deal, moreover, severed the last remaining link between the Indian Navy and the Royal

Navy, in terms of the supply of British naval weapon systems. The Navy's first submarine, 'Kalvari', arrived at Vishakapatnam in July 1968. In March that year, the serving CNS, Vice Admiral A. K. Chatterji, was appointed the first four-star Admiral. Naval operations during the 1971 Indo-Pakistani war, in both the Bay of Bengal and the Arabian Sea, vindicated the Navy's role in Indian security policy.

In this period, the expansion of the Navy included the acquisition of the last four of the eight submarines ordered, a number of small frigates, a few corvettes, missile boats and auxiliary vessels; three maritime reconnaissance (MR) aircraft, and five helicopters. Significantly all these weapon systems originated from the erstwhile Soviet Union. The only naval weaponry acquired from Britain was ten Sea King ASW helicopters. In addition, the Navy also commissioned five Nilgiri-class frigates, a landing craft, and three seaward defence boats from local shipyards. The Navy also ordered three Kashin 11-class destroyers and three II-38 MR planes from the erstwhile Soviet Union during this period.

1980-1991
The eighties demonstrated significant progress in the modernization and expansion of the Indian naval forces: from 32 principal combatants in the early 1980s, to 44 by the end of the decade. The acquisition of a second aircraft carrier, 'Hermes', from the UK, the three-year lease of a nuclear-powered submarine from the erstwhile Soviet Union, and the indigenous construction of modern frigates in Indian shipyards, were part of that design by which the Navy sought to defend India's maritime interests. These warships and aircraft not only enhanced the reach of the Navy, but bolstered its combat and power projection capabilities in the Indian Ocean too. In effect, the nature and the scale of the naval expansion indicated the maintenance of a medium-sized balanced blue-water fleet. The Navy also played a crucial role in support of military operations in Sri Lanka (1987-90), and was part of the force that suppressed an attempted

coup in the Maldives (1988).

1991-1998

Unfortunately, the eighties established no pattern, they were an aberration. For in the subsequent decade, the 1990s, we witness a major setback to the modernization and expansion plans of the Navy, due partly to the disintegration of the erstwhile Soviet Union. This gravely disrupted the transfer of spare parts and sophisticated arms to the Navy during the period 1990-95. Suitable alternatives could have been explored (Indonesia acquired 39 warships during the period) but our leadership remained content with talking of "more with less". The severity of this crisis can be gauged from the extent of dependence on Soviet supplies. In early 1995, for example, 25 of the Navy's 40 principal combatants (nearly two-third) were of Soviet origin, as were 15 conventional submarines, and 10 surface combatants. The Indian Navy's story is of one dependence – formerly on the British – to another, the Soviet variety. It is in itself comment enough on the management of India's defence policies during the past fifty years. In the absence of a coherent sustained doctrine, the self reliance thus far generated has been at best marginal.

Today, the Indian Navy faces a crisis in terms of its rapidly declining force levels, lack of sufficient funding, and limited warship construction programmes, all of which directly affect its operational preparedness. This decrease in the force levels of principal combatants since 1995 has repercussions that will extend to at least the next 25 years. Besides, and in addition, during this next quarter century, the Navy is also expected to decommission as many as 12 principal combatants. Even after accounting for the commissioning of warships from Russia, already in the pipeline, and indigenous sources, the net consequence will be a massive reduction in principal combatants, from 40 in 1995 to 32 in 2000, and 28 in 2005. The aircraft carrier force and the submarines arm will be the worst hit. In terms of current policy, this deplorable state of affairs is due, almost entirely, to a lack of decision-making by successive governments. It scarcely needs underlining thereafter that an absence of a timely decision is a decision in itself, it does not make the problem go away. That in short is the story of the Indian Navy during the period 1947-97.

AIR FORCE[62]

At the time of Independence, the ten squadrons of the RIAF (Royal Indian Air Force), the youngest of the three armed services, were also equally abruptly divided. In view of the respective numerical strength of personnel opting for the Indian and Pakistani air forces, India sought an allocation of eight squadrons, thus two went to Pakistan. As Pakistan required, a viable transport capability, therefore, an additional half of such a squadron was also allotted. Consequently the newly formed IAF (Indian Air Force) started its life with six fighter squadrons (Nos. 3, 4, 7, 8 and 10 equipped with Hawker Tempest Mk.11s, and No. 2 with Supermarine Spitfires Mk VIII), and half a squadron (No. 12) of C-47 Dakota transport planes, along with an Air Observation Patrol (AOP) unit. Meanwhile, as already outlined, Pakistan was allocated two fighter squadrons and half a transport squadron of C-47 Dakotas.

Several important training establishments and air stations, such as Karachi, Risalpur, Peshawar, Kohat and Lahore, obviously remained in Pakistan. So did the only repair and maintenance workshop, located at Drigh Road, Karachi. Meanwhile, India possessed an initial flying training base at Ambala, two airmen training schools in the South – one for some technical trades at Tambaram and the other for non-technical trades at Coimbatore, and two Equipment Depots, one each at Bombay and Avadi in Madras.

The air as the third element came to India at just about the time that the First World War was ending. It was rudimentary, experimental, and largely British dominated. Thus, for the entire period between the two wars, air power in India comprised almost entirely of the Royal Air Force (RAF). The Indian Air Force, with the Royal affixed (thus RIAF), was born on 1 April 1932 when No. 1 Squadron was raised at Karachi. In any event the bulk of the air force (RAF) in India since the early 1920s was deployed in the North-Western Frontier Province (NWFP), with the specific role of 'air control' of the tribesmen, also to provide air support to the army's ground columns engaged in similar tasks. This was entirely in line with what we have earlier observed: a preoccupation with maintaining internal order. It is not at all surprising then to find that this first operational formation of the RIAF was designated as an 'Army Cooperation' squadron. And both, this first designation and an early definition of its role, have had a lasting consequence, that which has not entirely worn off. What the IAF is actually for remains unanswered. Is it for support to the ground troops, or (is it) an agency of defence and offence in itself? There was yet another, a more fundamental, strategic logic behind this designation and assignment of role.

British strategy (in the shape of the policies of the East India Company) from the early eighteenth century onwards was centred on retaining the dominant component of military power directly with them as perhaps it would be in the case of any conquering power. And this not only in terms of actual command, but also in access to and manning of the weapons systems themselves. Thus artillery was limited to the British troops in the eighteenth century, and horse artillery remained the exclusive preserve of the British even during the nineteenth century, largely, with 'native' troops being allowed to provide manual labour alone. The Court of Directors of the East India Company (which was the management board ruling India directly till 1858), in fact, reiterated and specified the broad policy on this issue after the Mutiny.

The weapons and equipment of the Indian troops, according to this policy (crafted in 1857 while

the British still had to regain control of India)
were to be superior to those of the likely enemy
of the British, but were to be inferior to those
of the British troops of the East India Company.
The forces, in any case, were to be officered
exclusively by the British.[63]

That is why this newly created IAF was restricted
to support roles, while the RAF in India was assigned
independent and strategic roles of fighter defences and
independent bombing. The eight operational units of
IAF raised after No. 1 Squadron were all Coastal Defence
Flights. The Second World War was to change all this
but even then not entirely, for the fundamentals remained
unaltered. The expansion of the IAF, necessitated by
the Second World War, remained within the broad strategic
policy of an earlier century. This 1941 plan, for air
power for the defence of India, visualized a total of 10
squadrons of IAF and 20 of RAF, for an undivided India.
But the critical element was that all ten IAF squadrons
were to be tactical army support only (in those years
essentially consisting of artillery spotting and visual
reconnaissance), while the RAF would consist of fighter
and bomber squadrons.

The Second World War, its impact especially in the
Asia Pacific Theatre after Pearl Harbour, the fall of
Singapore and reverses in Europe altered many of these
assumptions. The war effort in Europe, an obvious priority,
left little 'surplus' for the defence of India. The British
were increasingly compelled to rely on Indian resources.
That is why an expansion of the IAF was now inevitable.
But the prejudices of the earlier years remained; and
even under the pressure of direct threat to the defence
of India (which constituted a key source of strength
for Imperial defence), the British policy of retaining
the strategic elements of military power with British
forces continued. Thus, while the strength of IAF was
built up to nine squadrons, all of them were assigned
only to a basic army cooperation role.

This experience of the Second World War has left

its impact on the doctrine and employment of air power in independent India. And we need to examine that here. Firstly, the extent of resources invested in air power during the war led to doubts whether similar employment was feasible for an independent India with no such availability, and severely competing priorities, given the consequences of partition and a division of assets. In any event air power, by definition, generally operates at 'higher' levels of technology; this is the nature of this third military element of war. Inevitably, therefore, air power capabilities, almost always, remain sub-optimal in any country. India at independence could not be different.

Secondly, post-war Europe, especially the UK, adopted a philosophy that in a nuclear age there would neither be the time nor the resources for conducting such prolonged battles as had characterized the employment of air power during the Second World War; whether in the struggle for air superiority or in strategic bombing campaigns. Air power could now, the argument went, do the task much faster and with much less force, armed as they would be with nuclear weapons. Conventional air power in a nuclear age was interpreted as primarily for a role supportive of the land forces. The IAF had grown up with British traditions, and almost all military strategic literature was derived from British-American sources. Besides, the IAF had been raised only for a tactical role. As it emerged in independent India, the weight of prevalent strategic thought dominated and kept the IAF's thinking slotted essentially on those very channels.

Thirdly, upon independence, the seniormost Indian officers in the IAF, like their counterparts in the Army and Navy, had barely 15 years of service, and almost none had any experience of higher command. Their experience was limited to operating as a tactical air force, in support of the army, in the Burma Campaign.

Fourthly, for a country where continental defence dominated thinking, and the land forces naturally assumed higher priority, lower priority for an air force, except where it directly provided support to the land forces, was inevitable.

Fifthly, since the strategic and independent role had been retained by the RAF (or shared by the US Army/Air Forces in India), equipment and infrastructure in India was designed to meet those tactical objectives only. Under the circumstances it appears almost a miracle that a large section of the IAF leadership, in fact, even thought about or actually believed in an independent and strategic role for independent India's air power.

Concurrently, other developments were to shape thinking about the role and employment of air power. What had characterized the use of air power in the Second World War was largely a denial of the adversary's economic infrastructure, strategic bombing, fire-bombing of cities like Coventry, Dresden and Tokyo, plus its employment as the carrier of atomic/nuclear weapons. The Indian political leadership remained ignorant of and uninvolved with these larger aspects. Their experience was limited to a desultory Japanese bombing of Madras (where at most a few small bombs were dropped while the fleet sailed north in the Bay of Bengal). Even this had resulted in a near total evacuation of the city. Bombing from carriers had also occurred on Vishakapatnam and Kakinada, while later, land-based Japanese bombers from Akyab had bombed Calcutta, Chittagong, and Cox's Bazaar. Even though these bombings were elementary compared to the bombing in Europe, this was about the sum of the experience that Indian leadership could muster. Is it any wonder, therefore, that a proper grasp of the employment of this arm remains almost pre-Second World War, conceptually?

Given the circumstances, the policies that evolved about air power in independent India were confused. This conceptual fogginess has continued, surprisingly within the IAF too. The dichotomy has revolved essentially around two connected aspects. One is whether the IAF should function as a strategic component of national air power or should it remain what the British had designed it for, a tactical air force? The other examines the role (appropriate for India) in terms of air power being strategically defensive or offensive. But for independent India resources were the final determinant. The Indian Air Force could only be that which the Indian purse could afford.

Resources available for defence were low (are always so) constituting a mere 1.6 per cent of the GDP during the first fifteen years. (This is examined in detail separately in Chapter Four.) But, as observed earlier, air power, by definition being technology driven, needed much higher per unit allocations. For India, thus, acquisition of military hardware had to be within this major constraint. When, therefore, the air force was expanded from 10 to 25 squadron force in the 1950s, it had to make do with a great deal of older, low performance aircraft and equipment. The importance of the 1950s, however, lies more in the conceptual base that determined decisions on force structures.

In the mid-1950s, the IAF set about seeking an indigenously designed and produced multirole combat aircraft. This search resulted in the HF-24 Marut. The IAF was one of the few air forces that correctly then laid stress on a conventional multirole aircraft, the other notable one being the US Air Force. The British at about the same time came to a different conclusion, that missiles rather than manned combat aircraft would be the requirement of the future. This had long-term consequences for their domestic fighter aircraft industry; it lost out in the ultimate. The IAF's design got defeated differently, by a pincer of technology capability limitations, and bureaucratic incomprehension of aircraft design; above all, by the new challenges from across the Northern frontiers, and the 1962 Sino-Indian war.

This war with China had long-term effects. From that time, Soviet equipment (accepted reluctantly by the IAF after successive attempts at sourcing from the United States failed) became the dominant component. This had deep and long-term implications for self-reliance. But the doctrinal impact deserves more attention. Contrary to the advocates of conventional wisdom, Soviet equipment, for a variety of reasons which need not distract us, was then heavily weighted in favour of defence, till at least the early eighties. Their reliance on ground-based air defences, short-range low-endurance fighter aircraft with low payloads, and relatively simple weapon aiming and delivery systems, all pointed to a priority for a tactical defensive role for such equipment. Of course the USSR relied upon (as did the West) its nuclear arsenal for the strategic and offensive role. India did not imbibe any Soviet doctrinal beliefs and there was no contact between the military training institutions of the two countries till the 1990s. But the limitations of design and capability of equipment carried their own consequences. This infusion of Soviet systems into the IAF resulted in reinforcing an existing defensive and tactical orientation. On the other hand, with internal pressures for a more offence-oriented and a proactive role, air power provided the impetus for further expanding this envelope of dependence upon Soviet-designed equipment. And thus followed 'improvisation', as almost a hardy standby for absence and shortages, becoming almost a standard of equipment policy. This was so in the Army, Navy and the Air Force, where the example of MiG-21 truly illustrates the process. This aircraft was subjected to various modifications of the original design thus enhancing the performance envelope of the aircraft from a purely high-altitude interceptor to a multirole combat aircraft. The basic design limitations, however, could not increase its combat radius beyond the tactical battlefields, thus improvisation resulted, at best, in a compromise.

Two questions arise here relevant to all the three Services and their evolution. First, if the tactical employment of a weapon's system is dictated by its technology what happens to the tactical doctrines (which in India were almost entirely British) of a country when it becomes technology dependent (which in the present instance we were on the Soviets)? Can the marriage of the two be improvised? And that is where the second query lies. If a country only improvises an equipment programme will its defence policy not then also be a mere improvisation?

The Government then imposed a ceiling on the number of combat squadrons the Air Force could have. This was based not on any empirical study of cost-effectiveness or operational needs/task-based calculations, it appears more to have been a consequence of bureaucratic convenience; not perhaps, dissimilar to independent India imposing ceilings on land, income, family, etc. The IAF had sought to increase the force levels from a 25-squadron force of the late 1950s, to an ultimate 65-squadron force, as a long-term force structure, with the additional responsibility of defending the country's northern borders. In 1961, the Government agreed, but again typically through a bureaucratic compromise of sanctioning a 45-squadron force (35 combat and 10 transport). This was obviously meant to be an interim level because training during the 1960s was geared to cater for a force no larger than a 45-squadron force. But the interim, as happens with most governments, became the permanent, as a fixed ceiling. The actual needs then were, and remain, greater but to little avail. In turn the IAF sought to compensate this limitation on firepower by opting for surface-to-air missiles. It is instructive that these missile units were initially meant for a defence of cities, especially the national capital. There being no indigenous missile programme in the country they were sought to be acquired from abroad. And, of course, the USSR was the choice; but be it said that they too relied heavily on SAMs. The strategic concept lost to bureaucratic strategies, and as always the cost of acquisition overrode the cost of operations.

To conceptual confusion, between 'favourable air situation' and 'air superiority' has been added the universal phenomenon of inter-service rivalry. Naturally, therefore, the Indian Army consistently advocates only a tactical role for the Indian Air Force. Inter-service cooperation not having evolved, and India being yet far removed from combined force commands, only well-informed and able governance could have provided the leadership. That, as we have observed, has not contributed meaningfully to independent India's security challenges.

Principally, this problem arises from a lack of understanding of the attributes and capabilities of air power, and the inherent logic of its optimum employment. The Army has not fully grasped the value and appropriate employment of air power primarily because the Air Force itself has been ambivalent in its doctrines. The Air Force, internally not clear about its own role and priorities, tends to accommodate the Army's perceptions which, in turn, treat combat air power more as aerial artillery rather than as a component of that military triad of land, air, sea power.

Independent India accorded high priority to self-reliance in defence. In the early years, the search was for self-sufficiency. But this was progressively modified to self-reliance, especially where it concerned the Air Force. For a country that had been systematically deindustrialized for more than two centuries before independence, the challenge of self-reliance, in high-technology systems, was a formidable task.

Diversification of the sources of equipment was seen as an integral part of this self-reliance strategy. Naturally, all equipment until then was British, up to that time. India sought to purchase suitable equipment from the United States, but not with any great success. The only option was to diversify to European sources, since Soviet equipment was then not considered as suitable. This self-reliance had two integrals: either licensed production in India, or direct purchase with licence to manufacture indigenously. To those priorities only the USSR was in sympathy. Thus, to other factors was also added this, and an equipment-dependency linkage with the USSR got established. It certainly provided an answer, but in the short term only. For this the Soviet linkage, enfeebled; it allowed defence equipment to be progressively purchased on long-term credits, and with rupee payments. More important, the Soviets agreed to licence the manufacture of such equipment in India. The result was substantive growth of self-reliance but based on Soviet licence. This built up an extensive capability in production techniques and technology. But these two factors combined to relegate the key pillar of self-reliance, and indigenous design and development till the early 1980s. The result has been a thirty-year gap between attempts to design an indigenous combat aircraft (from the HF-24 Marut in the 1950s to the LCA in the 1980s). Technology, meanwhile, has advanced as never before. The current 10-year self-reliance initiative of the Government seeks to increase the indigenous content from the existing 30 per cent to about 70 per cent by AD 2005.

The men behind the machines are the crucial factor, more so for an air force. Pilot training, for example, has been the subject of frequent experimentation over the years. More often than not, training patterns have been altered to fit in with the near permanent shortage of appropriate equipment. The case of the lead-in fighter trainer (called the AJT, Advance Jet Trainer in officialese) is symptomatic. The Vampire aircraft, which had served in this role from 1954 to 1972, were to be replaced by the indigenously designed HF-24 Marut trainer/fighter combination. But this was not done and the Vampires were scrapped in the early 1980s, although most were then still fully airworthy. It was only in 1983 that the IAF evolved an ASR (Air Staff Requirement) for an AJT, essentially because the LaFontaine Committee set up to look into a high accident rate had strongly proposed the provision of an appropriate training aircraft. Yet, 14 years later, even a decision on what aircraft to provide has not been taken, and nor has any effort been made to design and develop an indigenous alternative, with or without foreign collaboration. But training syllabic have been modified to cater for failures of planning!

While the number of aircraft will reduce in future, the number of operational pilots, especially combat pilots, had started to reduce much earlier more than a decade back. By the beginning of the 1990s, shortages of fighter pilots in operational squadrons had come down to the 50 per cent level. The situation has improved since then, but at a cost. What is perhaps more important is the issue of leadership. The IAF, as it reduces in size and goes in for more sophisticated aircraft, will have to rely on its younger air crew for combat performance. Morale and motivation, therefore, will need to be paid special attention for this elite group which for decades have been treated as just another, and in some respects less important, component. Above all, leadership will need to provide a clearer and more appropriate doctrinal direction than what has been in vogue in the past.

The IAF is a large and a professional force. But as reflected in its performance, in internal budget battles and the wider political debate, it does not seem to have developed an air doctrine that articulates the importance of air power for the defence of India. Land oriented thinking continues to dominate in spite of the demonstration of air power in the Gulf War. Nor has the IAF developed and publicized a concept for the greater employment of air power in the defence of India.

RESEARCH AND DEVELOPMENT[64]

The Defence Research and Development Organization (DRDO) was established in 1958 by amalgamating the Defence Science Organization and some of the technical development establishments. A separate Department of Defence Research and Development was formed in 1980 which operates now through a network of some 50 laboratories/establishments. This Department is engaged in pursuit of self-reliance in critical technologies of relevance to national security. It formulates and executes programmes of scientific research, design and development leading to induction of state-of-the-art weapons, platforms and other equipments required by the armed forces. It functions under the control of the Scientific Adviser to the Raksha Mantri who is also Secretary, Defence Research and Development.

The research and development activities of the department cover important demarcated disciplines like aeronautics, missiles, electronics and instrumentation, combat vehicles, engineering system sciences including advanced computing, life sciences including high-altitude agriculture, physiology, food technology and nuclear medicine and allied sciences. In addition, the Department also assists the Services by rendering technical advice regarding formulation of requirements, evaluation of systems to be acquired, fire and explosive safety and mathematical/ statistical analysis of operational problems. The DRDO has registered significant achievements in its various activities. The notable developmental successes of the Department include the surface-to-surface missile, Prithvi, the state-of-the-art main battle tank, Arjun, flight simulators for aircraft, pilotless target aircraft (PTA), balloon barrage system, parallel supercomputers Pace-plus, etc. The weapons and ammunition developed by the organization and productionized by production agencies include the Indian field gun, INSAS rifle 5.56 mm, charge line mine clearing for safe passage of vehicles in a battlefield, illuminating ammunition for enhancing night-field fighting capability, cluster weapon system for fighter aircraft, new generation bombs for high-speed aircraft, naval mines and 105 mm PSAPDS. Multi-barrel rocket system Pinaka is getting ready for trials by the Army. In the area of electronics and instrumentation, amongst the significant developments are low-level tracking radar Indra I, Indra II, for Army and Air Force, lightweight field artillery radar, battlefield surveillance radar, secondary surveillance radar, automatic electronic switch, avalanche victim detector, tidex, EW systems, night vision devices and secured telephone (Sectel). Some of the development successes in the area of engineering systems are bridge-layer tank Kartik, military bridging systems, various types of shelter, crash fire tenders, rapid intervention vehicle. In the area of naval systems and materials, the Organization has developed an advanced ship sonar system, marine acoustic research ship, Sagardhwani, underwater anti-fouling paints, torpedoes, naval simulators and jackal steels. Submarine sonar and weapon control system, Panchendriya, is getting ready for harbour/sea trials. The indigenous Light Combat Aircraft (LCA) is in the first flight trial preparation stage. The remotely piloted vehicle, Falcon, has successfully undergone developmental flight trials.

India's Integrated Guided Missile Development Programme (IGMDP) comprises four missile systems: Prithvi, surface-to-surface tactical battlefield missile; Akash, medium-range surface-to-air missile; Trishul, short-range surface-to-air missile; and Nag, third-generation anti-tank missile. Trishul is getting ready for user trials. Akash and Nag are in advanced stages of development. This programme includes a development of the intermediate-range ballistic missile, Agni.

The Department has developed and preserved convenience foods for the armed forces. It is vigorously pursuing the goal of technological self-reliance in defence systems through a 10-year national self-reliance mission. State-of-the-art technologies developed for missile programme, LCA and other high technology systems are being channellized to make available bio-medical equipment at a much less cost.

NOTES

1. Philip Mason, *A Matter of Honour* (Jonathan Cape Ltd, London, 1974) p. 40.
2. Ibid., p. 41.
3. Ibid., p. 42.
4. Ibid., p. 44.
5. Ibid., p. 44.
6. Ibid., p. 45.
7. Ibid., p. 45.
8. Ibid., p. 45.
9. Ibid., p. 46.
10. Ibid., p. 46.
11. Ibid., p. 48.
12. Ibid., p. 48.
13. Ibid., p. 49.
14. Ibid., p. 50.
15. Ibid., p. 51.
16. Ibid., p. 52.
17. Manohar Malgonkar, *Kanhoji Angrey: The Maratha Admiral* (1669-1729) (Asia Publishing House, New Delhi, 1959) pp. 29-54.
18. Ibid., pp. 17, 18.
19. Ibid., p. 61.
20. Ibid., p. 62.
21. Ibid., p. 7.
22. Ibid., p. 8.
23. Professor L. Mukherjee, *History of India* (details not available).
24. E. Marsden, *History of India* (details not available).
25. Stephen Peter Rosen, op. cit.
26. H. H. Dodwell, *The Cambridge History of India*, Vol. VI: *The Indian*

Empire and *The Last Phase* (New Delhi: S. Chand & Company, 1969), p. 153.
27. Ibid., p. 155.
28. H. H. Dodwell, op. cit., p. 395.
29. Philip Mason, op. cit., p. 30.
30. Stephen Peter Rosen, op. cit., p. 164.
31. Ibid., p. 165.
32. Ibid., p. 173.
33. Ibid., p. 174.
34. Ibid., p. 180.
35. Antony Brett-James, *A Selection of His Wartime Letters 1794-1815* (London: Macmillan, 1961) pp. 22, 37, 38, 41, 42, 44.
36. Philip Mason, op. cit., p. 15.
37. Ibid., p. 15.
38. Ibid., p. 17.
39. Ibid., p. 25.
40. Ibid., p. 25.
41. Ibid., p. 25.
42. Ibid., p. 25.
43. Legislative Assembly Records (1921).
44. Ian Copland, *The Princes of India in the Endgame of Empire, (1917-1947)*, (Cambridge: Cambridge University Press, 1997) p. 8.
45. Ibid., p. 33.
46. Ibid., p. 186.
47. Ibid., p. 251.
48. Ibid., p. 252.
49. Estimates Committee of Parliament Report (New Delhi: Lok Sabha Secretariat, 1992).
50. Contributed by Rahul Roy Choudhry.
51. Letter from Lord Mountbatten to L. J. Callaghan, the Parliament Secretary dated 31 August 1951 (MBI/G24, HMSO Copyright Office, Norwich).
52. Ibid.
53. Ibid.
54. Ibid.
55. Ibid.
56. Contributed by Rahul Roy Choudhry.
57. Ibid.
58. Ibid.
59. Ibid.
60. Ibid.
61. Ibid.
62. Contributed by Air Commodore Jasjit Singh, VrC, Director, IDSA, New Delhi.
63. Ibid.
64. Research, Reference and Training Division, *India 1996: A Reference Annual* (New Delhi: Publications Division, Ministry of Information & Broadcasting, Government of India, May 1997).

3

Independent India's Military Operations

MAJOR MILITARY OPERATIONS (1947-97)

A. Inter-State Wars
   1947-48   The First Indo-Pak Conflict
   1962   Sino-Indian Border War
   1965   The Second Indo-Pak War
   1971   The Third Indo-Pak War: Creation of Bangladesh

B. Other Internal Military Operations
   1947   Punjab Boundary Force
   1947   Junagarh deployment
   1948   Hyderabad police action
   1961   Liberation of Goa
   1984   Operation Bluestar

C. Counter-Insurgency Operations
   1954-74   Anti-insurgency operations in Nagaland
   1965-67   Anti-insurgency operations in Mizoram
   1971   Anti-insurgency operations in Tripura and
Mizoram
   1985-90   Anti-terrorist deployments in Punjab
   1989-   Anti-terrorist deployments in Jammu & Kashmir
   1991   Anti-insurgency operation in Assam:
              Operation Rhino

D. Other Minor Operations

1965   Rann of Kutch operations
1967   Sino-Indian skirmishes at Nathu La, Sikkim

MAJOR PEACEKEEPING OPERATIONS (1947-97)

A. Bilateral Peacekeeping

1950   To help deal with the Rana uprisings in Nepal
1971   In aid of civil government in Sri Lanka
1987-90   Indian Peacekeeping Force in Sri Lanka
1988   Operation Cactus in the Maldives

B. UN Peace Enforcement Operations

1961-63   UN Peacekeeping in Congo/Zaire
1993-94   UN Observers Group to
            overlook elections in Cambodia
1994   UN Assistance Mission in Rwanda II
1995   UN Peacekeeping in Somalia
1992-95   UN Peacekeeping in Angola

C. UN Peacekeeping Operations

1953   Korean Armistice Agreement
1956   UN Force in Egypt
1958   Observer Group in Lebanon
1988-91   UN Iraq-Iran Military Group
1989   UN Angola Verification Mission
1992-95   UN Military team for Mozambique

There are three broad operational and definitional categories that emerge: major military operations, as inter-state wars and as counter-insurgency operations within the country; UN-sponsored operations of both peacekeeping and peace-enforcing; and the third, of bilateral military assistance, for example, in Nepal or in Sri Lanka.

The accompanying chart is a convenient broad chronological guide to facilitate understanding. It would be absurd to simply add the numbers of operations engaged in, principally by the Army, and on that basis assess the challenges confronted. There is a straight-line arithmetical deduction however: 32 military operations of consequence in a period of 50 years. That would test the national military capabilities of any country, and, of course, India was tested repeatedly. It is also not as if these challenges came sequentially; conveniently spaced in time gaps of roughly two years between one and the other, so that if nothing else, the nation could recover its breath, as it were.

A remarkable aspect is that all these challenges were met without compromising the routine democratic processes of the land. Of course, economic activity suffered particularly as a consequence of 1962, or in 1971-72; but a recovery followed too, not dramatically but surely thus demonstrating India's great resilience. The growth was only checked, not permanently crippled. It is difficult to find another example of a newly independent nation addressing itself to such tasks and succeeding in finding an answer: not a perfect answer, of course, not perhaps entirely satisfactory but certainly adequate enough. In 1947, India was independent; it had a new government, but no experience. It is the people that had stamina, a resilient tolerance born of long experience and of centuries of trial.

These extraordinary challenges were met even as aid to civil authority made its demands, as in India it does, or all the in-house and routine responsibilities that all militaries have like training, re-equipping, modernizing, expansion; these were all, of course, undertaken concurrently. Do we grant a fitness certificate, therefore? Not really, for the independent state of India was hesitantly and inexpertly steered, it survived, though not on account of any able captaincy; just resilience and survivability. That is why there is scant satisfaction to be derived from this straight-line tally of numbers, for these are not all success stories. What would be a fair summation is that India – typically, in a near unique Indian way – bumbled its way through. In the process, of course, many mistakes were made: national interests were often not subserved, quite often not even properly assessed; but bungle through we nevertheless did. The legacy thus bequeathed at the end of this half century is full of the unresolved, the carried-forward additional and accumulated consequences of mistakes made.

More elaboration is necessary here. We have arrived at this focus on managing conflict through an inquiry on the strategic culture of India, and a survey of the evolution of its armed forces. No good ever came of ignoring the financial aspect of things, which we undertake as an examination of the budgetary and comparative force levels (Chapter Four). There is a need, therefore, to explain what we attempt here. It is to assess the landmark operations of the last 50 years. This is not a chapter on campaign studies, or even a purely military analysis, it is an attempt at broadly surveying the higher direction of conflict in independent India.

The absence of a proper concept of Central Asia and of the Himalayan bastion, or the delusive sense of protection that this latter provided has already been referred to. Central Asia and forces emerging from that region have, through centuries, altered the course of Indian history. We have seen how a proper historical sense, a sense of geography, indeed even of territory afflicts India's strategic thinking. Has this shortcoming persisted during these last five decades? The Himalayan bastions have provided the entire subcontinent with a natural protection. Did this result in any obvious blind spots in our thinking? Independent India's response to questions posed by an occupation of Tibet in the fifties, and then some three decades later the occupation of Afghanistan – posing similar queries all over again – gives rise to doubts about our sense of statecraft, the directness of its vision or even purpose. In this context, one other factor of historic continuity, and lasting consequence, needs to be mentioned.

This subcontinent has an inherent equilibrium, provided by its common historical evolution and by the very geography of the region. The presence of a foreign force in this subcontinent – through invitation, or involuntary acceptance, or worse in acquiescence, and worse still despite our resistance – has a consequence that is always and inevitably profoundly unsettling. This is a historically established fact. The natural balance of the subcontinent when disturbed remains so disturbed until an answer is found for the foreign body. We shall be addressing ourselves to this aspect too.

If we take into account the central relevance of geography as a factor in strategic thinking, and if a kind of strategic unity of Europe be a given, or the Americas be valued as a geographical unit, then in like manner South Asia too is a geographically delineated and distinctly apart strategic unity. The Imperial British understood and recognized this: that the separate and sovereign components that comprise this subcontinent have a strategic oneness. It was upon such a conceptual wholeness and clarity that they based their policy structures. The British have withdrawn but they have not in the process taken away with them the older and more lasting geostrategic verities of India. That is why the present exclusions from the purely political definitions of South Asia, if for example Tibet, Afghanistan or Myanmar are strategically unsound, exemplifying an assertion of political geography over the strategic. Conversely, even if South Asia is generally delineated as at present even then, so far as India's strategic interests go, this region has to be considered as one and as inclusive of the nations mentioned, otherwise our strategic thought would be fractured, neither subserving adequately our national interests nor enabling us to meet the challenges that the nations of this region, individually or severally, could face. Principally on account of an irrefutable dictum, the geographic territorial boundaries and the strategic frontiers of India do not match.

In our evaluation of forces we have seen how air power in India is relatively a new entrant both conceptually and in fact. We have also seen how till almost the late fifties the idea of naval power, despite an ancient and continuing naval tradition, was almost totally lost by India. At the level of policy formulation – strategically – these two aspects shall have to be examined against the management of the conflicts proper. Has air power grown at the same pace as say, for example, land power? Was this air power utilized as an available resource of the state when confronted by a challenge? As for naval power, the very structure of the subcontinent makes it an ocean to which it has given a name; which though not proprietary nomenclature, is yet of significance. None of the littoral states have demonstrated any proper grasp of the concept or utilization of this power, not even those that have a significant coastline. India, of course, has not met this challenge adequately at all, as we have already seen in an earlier chapter. But neither has Pakistan, nor, of course, and understandably Bangladesh, or even Myanmar or Sri Lanka either. Our inquiry, however, is not focused on these countries. We shall in this chapter be addressing ourselves only to the management of India's challenges and whether naval power played a role, and if it did how effectively or otherwise did it do so.

The Indian forces employed under UN aegis were not all simply peacekeeping forces, there were some like the earlier Korean armistice force which was partly peacekeeping, as a kind of buffer between combating forces, but it was also partly peace-enforcing. It is in this period, 1961-63, that the UN force in Congo, of which the Indian contingent was a principal component, was first involved in a major peace-enforcing role. This phrase had, however, till then not gained currency and no distinction was made between peacekeeping and peace-enforcing. In contrast whenever Indian troops were employed bilaterally, once in Nepal, twice in Sri Lanka and once in the Maldives, it invariably involved a kind of combat operation and an enforcement of order through the use of India's military force. This distinction has to be made because the challenge posed to Indian political and military leadership was, on these bilateral military assistance occasions, entirely different. Yet again we are faced by the same question: during such engagements was India's decision-making and employment of force marked by any sense of higher strategic direction and national purpose or was it mere ad hocism, a reactive intervention? If there was a higher purpose, what is the balance sheet at the end?

In this chapter we have delineated all the military operations, peacekeeping and otherwise. However, as our inquiry is not about the purely military conduct of a particular campaign, we are concerned with examining the higher direction of the employment of state power, in pursuit of a national goal or purpose. It is this criterion alone that we shall apply. The military management of a particular campaign is, obviously enough, important but that is not the centre of focus of our study. Besides, numerous accounts, even if only unofficial, already exist of most of the major campaigns of India. There is need here, however, to re-emphasize a very big lacuna; an absence of the official history of any of these campaigns except the first Jammu & Kashmir operations of 1948, which apparently took 30 years to write and another ten to publish in 1988. Unquestionably this particular absence is yet another illustration of a lack of any historic sense, combined with an entirely inexplicable tendency of not releasing official history timely. It is a comment on the leadership of independent India that half a century down the line, when about 32 major operations have taken place, official history exists of only one of them. For a reviewer then of the events of these past 50 years, this becomes a major difficulty: on what is one to rely? There exist no official accounts against which personal accounts can be weighed; more importantly there are simply no benchmarks against which an assessment of the higher direction of war can be objectively conducted.

TIBET AND AFGHANISTAN

Soon after the revolution the newly engaged People's Republic of China began to assert its suzerainty over Tibet. This takes us back to 1950. For a newly independent India, this was a major issue. Tibet posed questions of lasting consequence and substance to the early political leadership of independent India. Because these were not addressed satisfactorily they have continued to bedevil the country's security situation for all the succeeding decades. Indo-Tibet linkages are ancient and many-faceted; one central aspect of it being that Tibet is amongst the last remaining islands of Buddhist thought; hence of a distinctive civilization, connecting that land and its people to India civilizationally, culturally and emotionally. There was then the aspect of Tibet having been an independent country, to which had been extended British imperial authority only in the early years of the twentieth century. This notwithstanding, India's military involvements with that country go back even further, to Dogra General Zorawar Singh's expedition to Tibet for example. Tibet adjoins not simply the Indian state of Jammu & Kashmir in the North – indeed Aksai Chin plateau and its large Buddhist population is also (even though only occasionally now) referred to as Little Tibet – but also other states of the Indian Union. Had national security consideration aspects predominated, and had a realistic geostrategic sense about the region taken priority over emotional anti-imperialism, then Pandit Nehru could have more readily assessed that for an independent India to have an independent Tibet, as a buffer between it and an emerging China, was not simply a wise precaution, it was a policy imperative. This is altogether more inexplicable when one examines the rapidity with which Nehru reacted to events in Nepal in the mid-fifties, forcefully intervening there to restore the Nepalese monarchy. Nepal and Tibet were both Himalayan kingdoms, both were of vital strategic importance to India, and they were both afflicted, almost simultaneously, whether externally or internally, and yet India and its political leadership reacted differently.

Much further to the West at the other end of the Himalayan bastion, lying at the foot of that great knot of the Pamirs and the Hindukush, Afghanistan, almost three decades later, posed questions that, from India's perspectives, were almost exactly the same. Only the participants were different. How was India to react in the face of a Soviet occupation of that country early in 1980? That soon after partition a strategic sense of the importance of Afghanistan was absent has been earlier observed upon; as also the fact that so far as the British empire and its presence in India was concerned, control over Afghanistan was one of the principal planks for protecting their empire. What this recognized was a continuing historical and geostrategic reality; that routes of ingress into the south Asian landmass lie essentially through Afghanistan. Besides, before its conversion to Islam, Afghanistan had been a part of the empire of the Kushans, and it had also been a Buddhist land. The Mughals consistently mounted forays into Afghanistan, as they too recognized the vital need of protecting this northern frontier, for in that lay the protection of their own throne in Agra and Delhi. The Sikh kingdom under Maharaja Ranjit Singh spread all the way up to Kabul, and this was not to extract revenge for that great plunder and defilement of the Golden Temple at Amritsar by Ahmed Shah Abdali. For centuries Afghanistan has had a central place in the overall strategic unity of South Asia. For the Indian political leadership to, therefore, have reacted as they did in 1980 was yet another illustration of an absence of integrated strategic thinking. The consequences were almost instantaneous and directly experienced. In the decade of the eighties India had to undergo a flooding of the subcontinent by all kinds of lethal small arms, and a great rise in the illegal narcotics trade. That the security interests of India are inextricably linked with what happens in Afghanistan is tellingly illustrated by the presence not simply of surplus or 'excess' Afghan arms finding their way into the Indian state of Jammu & Kashmir, but indeed even of Afghan mercenaries beginning to operate in the Kashmir Valley: admittedly a far more salubrious alternative anyway to the bleak hazards of the mountains west of the Khyber.

Paradoxically, even as we neglected the import of events in Tibet and Afghanistan, simultaneously we remained dependent on the illusive protective ability of the high Himalayas. This was an inaccurate and insufficient understanding of both the reality of modern warfare, advancements in it and a questionable thesis about the impermeability of the Himalayas. It is because a proper assessment of the military aspect of the Himalayas was not conducted, therefore, that independent India now has to deploy large numbers of troops there; in possibly the most forbidding of terrains and the most inhospitable of climates – from the glacial wastes of Siachen in the north to the mist-clad, dank and forested slopes of the lower Himalayas at that trijunction between China, Myanmar and India in the South-East. Enormous resources, both financial as also human, have gone into this endeavour, particularly in the post-1962 period. Has the Indian political leadership correctly understood all the lessons that events in Tibet, Afghanistan or Himalayas teach. Does it now, in consequence, approach its responsibility for the security of India in a more mature and measured manner? It has not, it does not.

COUNTER-INSURGENCY OPERATIONS

As the accompanying chart shows, in the past 50 years India has been engaged in significant anti-insurgency operations starting with Nagaland around the mid-fifties, and then in yet another state of the North-East, Mizoram, in Jammu & Kashmir, Punjab, and when insurgency spread to the valley of Brahmaputra, in the state of Assam as well. It is not our purpose to examine the socio-political genesis of these major challenges to the authority of the Indian state. Our concern is with the handling of them, this challenging responsibility, by the political leadership.

An attempt to discern the underlying pattern of these five major insurgencies reveals that each of them flared along the geographical and political extremities of the country. A geographical distancing of these far-flung states of the Indian Union has had consequences born not simply of the distance alone; the relatively lower contribution to the arithmetic of India's parliament is another reason. Consequently, the importance and the say of these states in the political calculus of the power play at the centre is less. This, in part, was compensated for by the international factor, which then had predictable consequences. In the ultimate a geographical distancing combined with diminished political importance resulted in an emotional separateness. Then the substance of an ameliorative grievance redressal policy was replaced by fashionable and oft-repeated phrases, like join the 'mainstream of national life' or exhortatory and obtrusive hoardings of the 'India is one from Kanyakumari to Kashmir' variety hardly add to any sense of belonging. To this is added another, a further separating thesis; that the so disaffected are altogether a different people, a race apart, or, as in the case of Jammu & Kashmir, inspired by the same divisive logic that led to the creation of Pakistan, another region. Insurgency in India, wherever it has occurred, has initially had its genesis in a mishandling of the situation by the political leadership alone. Each of the five instances, therefore, that we have cited finds its roots in precisely that early wrong. Political insensitivity to the just needs and demands of the people; their yearning to be masters of their own political and economic destiny; the failure of the Central Government to at first understand this thirst, thereafter to respond to it but always too late and even then mostly with too little, and that too, only grudgingly has always caused deep alienation.

Into these troubled waters we find, as of routine, inevitable intervention from nations and forces outside of India, to support the insurgency within. The nature, thereafter, of the conflict becomes one of externally aided and abetted revolt against the Indian Union. And herein lie the seeds of a proxy or a covert or clandestine war. Unquestionably, geographic contiguity plays a significant role. That is why the early Naga insurgency received overt and covert military and other variety of assistance from the People's Republic of China. Similarly, the adjacency of Assam with Bangladesh, the social and ethnic problems of Assam arising out of living next to a dominating Bengali culture, and the factor of Islam has resulted in the United Liberation Front of Assam (ULFA) receiving not simply shelter but also assistance from pockets within Bangladesh. A similar insurgency, in Assam again, of the Bodo tribes finds shelter in adjoining Bhutan. Insurgency in the Kashmir Valley is fuelled from Pakistan, and principally through Pakistan-occupied Kashmir, which extends not just other variety of support. It covers using the media as a weapon in this new form of warfare. Thus, both television and radio broadcasts today are the newest weapons that come to the aid of insurgency. With television reaching almost every rural hamlet across the length and breadth of India, at a particularly virulent phase of insurgency in the Kashmir Valley, scenes of the break up of Soviet Union and of the Intefada movement in Palestine inspired the local population, no doubt falsely, but they did delude themselves into thinking that what was happening in the former USSR could well happen in India too, or that Islamic revolutions are best if they emulate the Intefada. How much has Pan-Islamism as a factor aided and continues to encourage insurgency in the Kashmir Valley is yet to be fully documented.

Along with the Government mishandling the situation, as is evident, in all the five major insurgencies that we have examined, there is an even more worrisome aspect: that of the Government of the day in search of short-term political gains actually unleashes those very political forces which eventually change into near uncontrollable revolutions against the state. Punjab, in that sense, is almost a classic example of short-sighted governmental policy converting one of the most prosperous states of India into, at one time, among the most troubled. The genesis of the Punjab trouble can safely be traced back to the late Mrs Gandhi's efforts in finding a political counter to the political and social domination of the Punjab by Shiromani Akali Dal. That she, therefore, engaged forces like the late Sant Jarnail

Singh Bhindranwale, is by now sufficiently well established. It is tragic that the very forces that she unleashed ultimately devoured not simply her political policy, but most sadly took her own life as well. As our focus is not an examination of the insurgency proper in the Punjab, we shall not dwell long on this other than to emphasize one other aspect: the exploitation of India's difficulties by Pakistan. It would have been surprising if Pakistan had actually not done so. After all, troubles in the Punjab were the direct consequence of misgovernance and mishandling by the Central Government in Delhi, and when an adversary is found to be tottering, it calls for more than human goodness to act in a restrained manner. In accordance, therefore, with the pattern that we have already spoken of, the Punjab insurgency too received significant military and other assistance from Pakistan.

After the Nagaland and Mizoram insurgencies the rest of India remained largely free of the ailment till about the decade of the eighties. This decade was, however, in every sense arguably the most profligate decade of independent India's first half century. This was the decade when the situation was mishandled by Mrs Gandhi as Prime Minister followed subsequently by her son, Rajiv Gandhi. This mishandling resulted in the spread of insurgency in the otherwise peaceful and tranquil valley of Brahmaputra, of the state of Assam and thereafter the valley of Jhelum in Kashmir was set aflame by their political shortsightedness. Punjab too followed the same pattern, and most tragically and with very significant consequences it was during this period that encouragement was given to the Liberation Tigers of Tamil Eelam (LTTE), indeed even training, monetary and arms assistance was given to them by the same two Prime Ministers. Again the consequences were tragic and there was another demonic initiation, the first human bomb was employed for political assassination, the tragic victim of which foul deed was Rajiv Gandhi.

If a military method and pattern is to be found in the countering of these insurgencies, then notwithstanding the occasional alarms about human rights violations what is most significant is the restraint with which the Indian Army has operated in all these regions. No anti-personnel mines were ever employed at any time. The force employed has always been the minimum; air power was used only once in Nagaland and, thereafter, only for lifting of troops or supplies, and all military operations have always been under civil control. This persuades the conclusion that India developed its own counter-insurgency methods; which were much more humane methods in response to the challenge posed by each of these insurgencies.

We now undertake an examination of the four inter-state wars and only one of the major bilateral peacekeeping roles that India undertook during the last 50 years. These are the First Indo-Pak War of 1948, the Sino-Indian War of 1962, the Second Indo-Pak War of 1965, and the Third Indo-Pak War of 1971 for the liberation of Bangladesh, and the Indian Peacekeeping Operations in Sri Lanka during the period 1987-90. As has already been explained, our study will not examine the conduct of the military operations proper. We will attempt to discern the accompanying policy of the Government of India, the national aims that were to be subserved and the strategic or higher direction of the conflict itself.

THE FIRST INDO-PAK WAR, 1948

Early on the morning of 22 October 1947, barely two months after Independence, the first military raid on India occurred. The main column of the raiders from Pakistan crossed the frontier of the state of Jammu & Kashmir from Garhi Habibullah and attacked Muzaffarabad. The raiders met with little or no resistance, pressed on and entered Baramula on the evening of 26 October 1974. Officially, it was on 24 October 1947, that the Pakistan Army Headquarters informed New Delhi that around 5,000 tribesmen had attacked and captured Muzaffarabad and Domel and were approaching Srinagar. The same evening at around 11 p.m. Maharaja Hari Singh of Jammu & Kashmir sent an urgent request that Indian troops be sent to Kashmir to save it from the invaders. On consideration by the Defence Committee of the Indian Cabinet no locus standi for interfering in the crisis was found. This was followed by visits to Srinagar by high-ranking Indian officials. The Instrument of Accession to India was signed by the Maharaja on 26 October 1947. Immediately thereupon Jammu & Kashmir legally and constitutionally became an integral part of India, therefore, defending it became the responsibility of the new Indian Government. Accordingly, beginning from the morning of 27 October 1947, Indian troops began to be flown into Srinagar. By early November Indian troops had consolidated their positions and began mopping-up operations with air transport support.

Even as these military operations were going on, Prime Minister Jawaharlal Nehru made efforts through diplomatic channels to persuade Pakistan to cease all further assistance to the raiders in Jammu & Kashmir. Failing to receive any positive response from Pakistan, the Government of India, on 1 January 1948, brought to the notice of the UN Security Council that, due to the operations being carried on against the Indian state of Jammu & Kashmir by nationals of Pakistan, a situation had arisen that could lead to an international conflict. This did actually result: the whole of the Indo-Pak boundary in Jammu & Kashmir became a conflict zone in which the combatants were no longer the raiders and regular Indian soldiers; the two armies fought small tactical battles against each other all along the border.

In the meantime the UN Security Council had passed a resolution, made recommendations and established terms for a cease-fire, a plebiscite and for establishing a commission of five members to proceed to the Indian subcontinent to place its good offices at the disposal of the two governments with a view to facilitating the restoration of peace. The commission reached in July 1948. On 13 August 1948, the Commission adopted a resolution providing for a cease-fire, a truce agreement, and consultations for a plebiscite after the Truce Agreement was concluded. The cease-fire became effective from the midnight of 1-2 January 1949 and an agreement on the cease-fire line was signed in Karachi on 27 July 1949.

What national goals and objectives did independent India's political-military leadership pursue during this conflict? What ought they to have been? Did the British military command have prior information about the opening phase of the conflict – at least the raid proper? Could they have forestalled this military conflict, as it began barely two months after Independence? After all, in both India and in Pakistan they were in positions of decisive authority, and in consultation with their counterparts in the other capital, and they were also keeping in touch with Lord Mountbatten on almost a daily basis. These are only some of the queries that arise.

About premeditation and prior information we have two versions. This first is from a reproduction of the relevant portions of an account quoted by Lieutenant General Chibber:

Jinnah, whose exact responsibility[1] for launching the tribal invasion will probably never be known, . . . realised that he had to do something, and gave orders through the Defence Ministry in Karachi for regular Pakistan troops to be moved into Kashmir. The order reached Douglas Gracey[2] on 26th October in Rawalpindi, where he was acting Commander in Chief (Pakistan) in the temporary absence of Frank Messervy (who was then) in the U.K. Gracey, realising the implications of complying with Jinnah's order, replied that he was not prepared to issue any such instructions without the approval of Auchinleck, the Supreme Commander. He then, with great difficulty, got through to the Auk in Delhi, and persuaded him to fly to Lahore, where Jinnah was staying with Mudie, the provincial Governor, to explain the consequences of executing the order. Auchinleck arrived in Lahore on the morning of 27th October; he told Jinnah that to send Pakistan troops into Kashmir, now that the State had acceded to India, would constitute an act of invasion. In such circumstances, he, the Supreme Commander, would have no option but to order automatically and immediately the withdrawal of every British officer serving with the Pakistan army. Since such action would have made it quite impossible to reform and reorganise the Pakistan army, which depended to a far greater extent than the Indian, on retaining the services of British officers, Jinnah, reluctantly accepted the Supreme Commander's decision.[3]

.   .   .

Late Major General Akbar Khan, who led the Pakistani forces in the invasion under the pseudonym General Tariq has (subsequently) revealed in his article published in Defence Journal Karachi in September 1983 how he was asked to prepare a plan to help the people of Kashmir in September, 1947, and he wrote the plan called "armed Revolt in Kashmir".[4]

There is reason, therefore, to believe that prior knowledge of the conflict existed with the British on both sides of the boundary. It is doubtful that they could have prevented it. In any event such authority as they possessed or such influence as they could bring to bear was employed. On this, however, there were severe constraints of both time and circumstance, and there was the very real limitation of the very transience of their status, for in their respective appointments was an in-built temporariness, they were all on the way out.

In the conduct proper of the military operations it is noteworthy that there did exist a Defence Committee of the Indian Cabinet. It was almost a direct descendant of the wartime Defence Committee of the Viceroy, but at least it was there, which is more than what we witness in later years. And it deliberated upon situations, to it were presented plans by the Service Chiefs which were then examined and discussed; alternatives were explored even if somewhat inexpertly by the then political leadership and there existed an institutional formality about decision-making. This is in striking contrast to the subsequent institutional atrophy.

Notwithstanding this Defence Committee of the Cabinet, at no stage did any deeper strategic analysis of the vital nature of the whole state of Jammu & Kashmir ever take place. The approach was limited and purely military; and in that too it consisted only of containing and repulsing the invading force. Battles and engagements were entirely tactical; seldom was there an operation at a level above that of a battalion, most were even smaller. The experience of the Indian commanders in the field during the Second World War was in any event restricted to just that level. The high strategic aims cited then and repeated to date involve territorial inviolability of the frontiers of India – an obvious enough choice – and to assert the vital importance of this state as a pointer to the secular principles of the Republic. These two aspects are unexceptionable but they are not a full statement of the case. They omit all the other crucial geostrategic factors almost entirely: the origins of the five great rivers of the Punjab from domineering heights in the high Himalayas; the fact that only a third of the state – principally the Srinagar Valley which, in fact, is but a tiny fraction of the entire territory of the State – are followers of Islam; the vast Buddhist stretches of Ladakh; that a severance of the region was militarily and in all other respects inconceivable; and so much else besides. Because of this strategic limitedness (not simply) in an enunciation of the case then, India's position even 50 years later, remains extremely limited, definitionally. There was not, at any stage during the operation of 1948, any examination of the potential for difficulties ahead as, for example, when a communist China emerged. The whole question of this state, and of an invasion of it in terms of international relations was confined to and by a reference to the UN.

The military goals set were extremely limited: repulse the invader about sums up the objectives as fairly and as accurately as possible. The operations were limited to the tactical; the strategic objective of denying routes of ingress, denying lines of communications and supply were not even examined. Hence, air power was not offensively employed; bridges and road arteries reaching into Jammu & Kashmir were left entirely untouched. To pulverize the adversary's capacity to strike again was not spelt out as a military task; a simple pushing back of the Pakistani military became the goal. Inevitably, thereafter, the cease-fire line proper, when agreed to, followed no military logic, not even convenience, and displayed no strategic sense of geography either. It conceded to the invader whatever territory was not recovered; more damagingly a delineation proper of this line (the CFL), leave alone being strategically sound made little scant tactical sense either. It followed no natural geographical feature – defensive or otherwise; it accounted for no military logic, even a militarily sound delineation on the ground. This first Indo-Pak war of 1948 did not resolve the issue – militarily or internationally; in fact it bred even more confusion.

THE SINO-INDIAN BORDER WAR, 1962

On 8 September 1962, about 600 Chinese soldiers crossed the McMahon Line along the Thagla Ridge area and came down to the Dhola border post of India. Between 8 September and 20 October, there was intermittent firing from both sides with India then primarily engaged in reinforcing its positions in the North-Eastern Frontier Province. On 20 October 1962 the invasion proper started with the Chinese striking against Indian positions near Dhola and Khinzemane, following which the Chinese developed a two-pronged attack on Tawang, one from Boomla in the north and the other from the west where Chinese troops were pursuing the Indian troops retreating from Nyamkachu (near Dhola post). There was

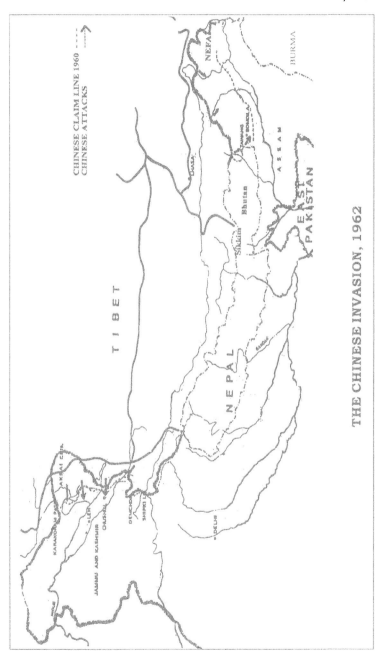

THE CHINESE INVASION, 1962

then a lull in the fighting for the next few days. The battle, however, was resumed on 14 November 1962. It had also by then spread to the East in the Walong sector and in the North to Ladakh where Chushul and Rezeng La were invested heavily by the Chinese. By 20 November 1962, the Chinese had overrun practically the entire Kameng Division and virtually destroyed the 4 Infantry Division of India. The Walong sector saw more equal and hence inconclusive battles. In Ladakh no such military hesitation was witnessed as demonstrated in the North-East. There were fierce localized battles, particularly at Rezeng La. On 21 November 1962 Beijing radio announced a cease-fire unilaterally.

Background
The Sino-Indian border war of 1962 demonstrates two major failures: one of India's foreign policy particularly towards the People's Republic of China; and the other of the country's defence policy. This failure to manage the border conflict properly resulted in a humiliating military reverse. In Chapter One, we have examined Nehru's own explanation for the entire episode. Those percepts need to be examined in some detail now.

A review of the ups and downs of India-China relations would show that the oscillations were not brought about by any major bilateral problems alone between the two countries. India was prompt in recognizing the People's Republic and became a vigorous spokesman for its seating in the UN; yet, because of China's ideological predilections – which were then parallel to the reserve of Stalin's Russia – bilateral relations remained tepid, also potentially antagonistic. India's independent role in international politics, especially in Korea and in the Indo-China Conference in Geneva (1954) brought prestige to India and some warmth in Sino-Indian relations, to which was added depth by a bilateral agreement. This 1954 Agreement on Tibet, in which India recognized that country as an autonomous region of China and gave up the right to station Indian army units in Yatung and Gyantse, rationalized arrangements for border trade and pilgrimages, surrendered Indian control over the post and telegraph administration of Tibet, and a variety of other inherited rights. This Agreement was signed on 29 April 1954, a good four years after the Chinese entry into Tibet, indicating a deliberate decision. It was through this Agreement that the five principles of co-existence were also first enunciated.

The period, 1954-58, was a curious phase; it was of mutual affirmation of 'indestructible friendship' between the two countries. This was symbolized by the slogan 'Hindi-Chini Bhai-Bhai' (Indians and Chinese are brothers). Notwithstanding the ideological divergence and the known differences on the interpretations of the common border, relations remained harmonious between the two governments with an emphasis on a common approach to international politics. Nehru, with his faith in post-Imperial Asian harmony, was the spokesman for a new China, notably at Bandung (1955). However, even during this period, on the border and in the implementation of the Tibet Agreement, there were already difficulties. The potential of the situation and the illogicality of some of the stances began to assert themselves, but all these were either minimized, suppressed or brushed away. This was a period of make-believe; 'good relations' was the cherished goal.

The first crisis occurred in 1959. It was unexpected on both sides. Indian public opinion had not been aroused much at the reports of the Khampa revolt – underway since 1956 – but it became assertively sympathetic after the Dalai Lama's dramatic escape. Then followed reports on the plight of the Tibetans, who by then were also streaming into India. Reactions in India, in the Parliament, press and through public debate were of concern and sympathy. China's accusations that the disaffection in Tibet was due to subversion by India (bourgeois reactionaries) flattered the capabilities of the Indian intelligence agencies to ignite and sustain such a revolt deep inside Tibet. Whether the civil government in India, and Nehru personally, were aware of the CIA/ Taiwan involvement in air-dropping to help anti-China elements is uncertain but it is now known that the CIA activities also started in 1956.

This Tibetan disaffection was entirely due to a failure of China's Tibet policy; that is why disaffection in Tibet persists when not even China accuses the CIA or India of fomenting it. A propagandist defence of this exposed failure was compounded by China bracketing Nehru, by name, with the 'revolt in Tibet and Nehru's philosophy'.[5] For the Indian political-military class this ought to have been a signal like many others which had by now begun to surface: border violations by China, India's restrained objections to them, the less than satisfactory response from China, and in turn India not publicly saying so; India was in fact conveying a message other than the one actually intended. That even in Zhou Enlai's first reply to Nehru in January 1959, China did not specify China's own notions of the common boundary ought to have been analysed, for this omission was in itself a significant statement.

The two governments had divergent rationales in fostering the psychological and concrete manifestation of their friendly relations. Both, for their own reasons, seemed to be reluctant to probe and thus risk exposing the ambiguities both inherent and of interpretation. At all events Nehru's India did not foresee the explosive potential of this divergence in the interpretation of a common boundary. The strategic choice here for India was stark: if India accepted the logic of the situation it would have to take adequate measures; and for that if resources were scarce they would have to be sought; and if that were done alliances would follow, as a matter of course. Non-alignment would have to be abandoned. Are we then to conclude that a safeguarding of a principle of foreign policy, non-alignment, took precedence over safeguarding Indian territory, as also – as subsequent events demonstrated, Indian prestige? There is evidence for such a conclusion.

Yet again, the conceptual framework of India's China policy has to be traced to Nehru's intellectual genealogy. Not only was Nehru committed to nationalism against all manifestations of imperialism, but influenced – in the thirties – by Fabian philosophy; he believed in democratic-socialism against a free market philosophy. This developed into a deep faith that socialism's priority was always for building an egalitarian and socially just society. This required peace, and so he concluded that there was no likelihood of socialist Russia or communist China turning belligerent or expansionist. Nehru's attitude to China also reflected his conviction that the relations between independent countries in Asia would be harmonious and peaceful once European imperialism had been compelled to withdraw. This half-reason and half-hope remained even after 1959. The downturn came in this very year, in the wake of the revolt in Tibet and some border incidents. Even when the political climate had changed sharply, more so after the Forward Policy (1961 and 1962) and right up to September 1962, Nehru, like Krishna Menon, did not expect a military conflict with China.

Along with inhabiting a make-believe world, the other striking feature of this post-1959 phase was the aspect of intelligence. Numerous accounts exist, written principally by the participants themselves, though there is not only no official history of the period. Even an investigatory report on the conflict prepared by Lieutenant General Henderson Brooks has not yet been made public. That is why it is bewildering how Nehru could continue to inform the Indian Parliament and thus the people that nothing 'very serious'[6] need be apprehended. It is entirely beyond understanding. To say later that 'We were living in an artificial atmosphere of our own creation' is a comment not on Nehru alone; it is a comment upon the entire military-political class of the period, for they were part of this 'artificial' world, indeed they had helped create it.

What then was this 'artificial' world? A component of it was the aspect of civil-military relations. Kavic in his pioneering study comments,

One of the major facts which emerges is the

mutual distrust and even contempt between top civilians (politicians and bureaucrats) on the one hand, and the military, on the other. Where Nehru is concerned, it is difficult to speak of any contempt given his unique status in Indian politics. But there is no doubt that amongst the military leaders there was a certain degree of mistrust even towards him, or at least a feeling that he did not fully understand the needs of the armed forces and tended to identify with the civilian position on defense and strategy. This feeling was probably more pervasive after 1957 when Krishna Menon, an intimate of Nehru's, was appointed Minister of Defense. The failure of the military leadership can only in part be rationalised by the earlier Thimayya episode . . . [which] increased Nehru's tendency to perceive military officers as hostile to his policies and to depend more and more on Menon and his group of proteges. In turn this resulted in a crisis of "confidence and growing mistrust between the professional military and the civilians. Officers in senior army posts were replaced either with those whose loyalties were tied to the senior politicians and bureaucrats in the Ministry of Defense, the Ministry of External Affairs (MEA) and the Prime Minister's Office, or by officers who did not dare to stand up for their convictions.". . . In any event "Nehru tended to accept the evaluations presented to him by the civilian echelons, even concerning differences of opinion pertaining to strictly military matters. When in October 1962 Thapar (not too forcefully) tried to convince Nehru that the army could not carry out Operation Leghorn, Nehru rejected the claim by arguing that he had information that indicated that the Chinese would not strike back." [In consequence] majority of senior staff officers . . . ceased [taking] into account the real military situation, and insisted on their own optimistic evaluations, creating a deepening rift between them and senior field officers.[7]

Various commentators have subsequently judged that India's forward policy, announced as such in 1961, and involving a more assertive manning of the borders, was the spark that ignited the conflict. Whether the military significance of this was assessed or not, given the atmosphere that then prevailed it would be astonishing if it were even discussed.

Thus the army's demand to deploy and concentrate available military forces on the likely three axes of invasion was ignored, and the politicians' demand to distribute the forces along the McMahon Line was given preference so that Nehru could claim in Parliament that the army was positioned all along the McMahon Line. As a result, air force headquarters was also under pressure to exaggerate its ability to provide the necessary logistic aid to the force thus spread out.[8]

A thesis was propounded that China would not attack India, even when confronted, for that had been the Chinese response so far. The question 'What if the PLA behaves differently' had never been asked, as Nehru was to admit later in Parliament. This was not a query of a routine tactical nature, not befitting a government to be seized of. Its significance was strategic, for on this response of the Chinese hinged the future of Sino-Indian relations. This was an institutional failure, not of the Prime Minister alone. Nehru decided, others agreed, disagreeing only on 'the most efficient ways to arrive at the predetermined operational decisions made by Nehru'.[9] And who were these that even bothered to disagree? 'The inner circle.'

This inner circle around Nehru had a number of common traits. Most of the permanent members of this group were intellectuals, very articulate, open-minded, or at least defined by Nehru as such. Most were Hindu, and they all had a British education. Some had long experience in the British Indian civil service. They had years of experience in working with Nehru, and all expressed in one way or another their complete identification with his [world view]. Most, if not all, revered him as a man and as statesman, as the one and only representative of the true India. The group even had a kind of "whip", who kept members in line whenever necessary. This was, of course, the man closest to Nehru, personally and ideologically – Krishna Menon. None of the members of this group had an independent power base; was dependent on Nehru, but this situation gave them more power than their formal role or position ever could. This power derived from the recognition by other organizations and people of their close contact with Nehru.[10]

Moreover, to its participants, this group of people seemed to have all the necessary ingredients and personnel for efficient evaluations, both intellectually and functionally. It even appeared to 'debate' constructively, but, as we have seen, all this was a thin disguise for a predetermined operational consensus. And their failure was all the greater for not assessing, perhaps not even enquiring, as to what was then happening within the People's Republic.

By the early 1960s, Mao had begun to speculate about the implications of Soviet revisionism for Chinese domestic politics. The Hungarian revolt and Soviet response had precipitated a rectification campaign in China. But China faced, in the same period another challenging issue, the Taiwan straits crisis of 1958. Unlike the Korean War, in this instance, there was no direct threat to the PRC "but by bombarding Quemoy (Jinmen) from August 1958, Mao was better able to whip up fervour,"[11] informs MacFarqualer.

The Sino-Indian border conflict coincided also with the Cuban Missile Crisis. This event, or its foreshadow influenced the decision making of both the superpowers – the US and the USSR; it certainly influenced the attitude of PRC, of USSR about the disputed border, and of the USA in what its responses would or could be.[12]

As to whether the Indian political-military decision ever took this into account is not clear from any contemporary records.

It is difficult also to assess Indian strategic thinking in respect of three other critical aspects of the entire unfolding situation: of the position of Mao himself within the Chinese hierarchy in the period; the economic situation in PRC following repeated famines; and the deepening of the Sino-Soviet rift. These three were in addition to the Cuban, Taiwanese and the Tibetan border issue. In no account so far has any light been shed on this aspect: did Indian planners or the political leadership ever examine the larger global strategic aspect of the timing of the Sino-Indian border question? There is reason to believe that they remained innocent of most such concerns.

R. MacFarqualer has shared an interesting analysis.

Khrushchev's restraint in the Sino-Soviet dispute in the summer and early autumn of 1962, his modest tilt to Beijing and away from New Delhi, and his cordial treatment of Ambassador Liu Xiao, probably had less to do with a change of heart on the Sino-Indian border issue and more to do with his anticipated confrontation with the United States. Khrushchev needed to face Kennedy with a united communist bloc behind him. The Chinese had not wanted a two front war in the summer of 1962; Khrushchev did not want to have to confront both America and China in the autumn.

Khrushchev anticipated provoking this confrontation in early November, after America's mid-term congressional elections.

At that point, he would reveal to Kennedy that the Russians had placed nuclear missiles in Cuba. If Chinese "militancy" in its relations with India could in part be attributed to Nehru's forward policy in the Himalayas, equally Beijing's renewal of the Sino-Soviet polemics in the autumn of 1962 could in part be attributed to Khrushchev's "forward" policy in the Caribbean, which led to the Cuban missile crisis.[13]

A chronology of this period 'illustrates the overlapping development of the crises in the Caribbean and on the Himalayas'.[14]

THE HIMALAYAS AND THE CARIBBEAN CRISES
CRISES TIMETABLES, 1962

October	Himalayas	Caribbean
14	Khrushchev pledges support for China	US discovers missile silos on Cuba
20	First Chinese attack Khrushchev letter to Nehru	
22		Kennedy reveals Soviet missiles, demands removal, imposes naval quarantine
24	China proposes talks	Soviet ships halt *en route* Cuba
25	*Pravda* editorial tilts to China	
26		First ship stopped by US Navy
27	First Chinese offensive ends	
28		Khrushchev agrees to remove missiles

November

Early   Moscow resumes neutrality
5-14   Chinese criticized at Bulgarian Party Congress
14   Indian attack; Soviet ambassador conveys good wishes to Nehru (Before 21st: MiG-21 sales confirmed)
16   Second Chinese attack
21   Chinese cease-fire

December

1   Chinese withdrawal commences

In the Sino-Indian war of 1962 the biggest of Nehru's failures, however, in the field of national security was not, as conventional wisdom has it,

> his inadequate appreciation of the Chinese threat, or his inadequate support to defence preparedness, or his forward policy, it was his failure to consult the Air Force in October-November 1962 and commit it to battle. There was a corresponding failure on the part of the Chiefs of Staff, and especially the Army Chief, who thought of a war against China as a strictly land war, wholly within the Army's responsibility, the Air Force having nothing to do with it beyond dropping supplies to forward troops . . . there is no evidence that he thought of taking advantage of the Chinese difficulties in matching our air effort over Arunachal or even Southern Tibet.[15]

This war was obviously a severe setback not for Nehru alone but for India. Internal polity, international prestige and standing, the morale of the military and the economy all suffered. And in the aftermath of this humiliating defeat, notwithstanding his principles on propriety and accountability, not once did Nehru offer to resign.

India is still to recover from the psychological consequences of this war. In 1964 China conducted its first nuclear explosion, soon overtaking India in this field as well.

Economically it now weighs as the heavier force. From the early fifties, when Indian policy 'helped' an emerging China, to now when the century ends, a relationship of equals no longer obtains. Clearly India's management of Sino-Indian relations has been a failure and the nation continues to pay the price.

THE SECOND INDO-PAK WAR, 1965

Background
The genesis of the second Indo-Pak war of 1965 lay in three separate events: the first Indo-Pak war of 1948 which resulted in a UN-sponsored cease-fire and a militarily unsound 'cease-fire line'. Large parts of the Indian state of Jammu & Kashmir became Pakistan-Occupied Kashmir. The issue was shelved, not resolved.

The second event was the 1954 Sino-Indian Agreement over Tibet. From this originated India's conceding Chinese suzerainty over Tibet, a country which adjoins the Ladakh region of Jammu & Kashmir in India. Almost immediately, the People's Republic of China began a major road construction programme, for the only alignment that was possible was through Indian Ladakh, over its Aksai Chin plateau. In time this incursion resulted in the Sino-India border war of 1962. Independent India suffered its first major military reverse. In 1964, Pandit Nehru died, not in the fullness of his years with glorious national and international achievements crowning the end; it was a sad and broken departure. India too was dispirited: the military humiliation of 1962 was followed by what was felt by a large number of Indians as their personal loss (in Nehru's death). Militarily, India was still adjusting; its economy was not sustaining the new needs. Politically, there was a new prime minister in office, a diminutive, homespun kind of a person, in marked contrast to that internationally renowned, and for most Indians the heroic figure of Pandit Nehru.

In Pakistan too there had been changes of significance. Democracy had received the first setback in that country.

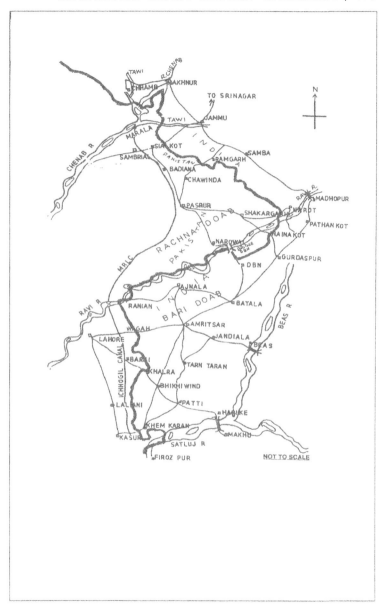

THE WESTERN SECTOR, 1965

In 1965 Field Marshal Ayub Khan was the President of Pakistan, with Zulfikar Ali Bhutto as his assertive foreign minister. For the establishment in Pakistan, it appeared that in all respects India, in 1965, was a disoriented and dispirited nation. Thus, if the situation was to be exploited to Pakistan's advantage, a 'final solution' to the Kashmir question had to be sought militarily. There was another, a connected but purely military calculation: the pattern of Indian responses to hostile military action had revealed that whenever attacked India reacted, but only to repel the aggressor, and at the point of aggression only. Thus, if Kashmir was to be taken by force then a popular uprising would have to be simulated there; a kind of a rebel government established in a part of it. Pakistan would then move, upon invitation, to its assistance and the Indian counter would be contained by severing the road links between Jammu & Kashmir and the rest of India. There are reasons to believe that whereas Field Marshal Ayub Khan appreciated the strategic enfeeblement of India, he was not convinced that if pressed India would not widen the options and counterattack at a time and upon a ground of its own choosing. It is in this broad strategic backdrop that the second Indo-Pak war occurred – as unnecessary as the first, and in the ultimate providing just as few answers as the first.

But first there was an interregnum. This was the Kutch episode. A wholly contrived affair; it was more a Pakistani reconnaissance in force; of Indian military responses; of the attitude and approach of the new and unknown Indian leadership, to test their will and to assess them; also, and more importantly, to distract attention from the real aim: the valley of Kashmir. And, therefore, in these estuarine wastes of the Rann of Kutch was contrived a border dispute of an entirely inconsequential nature, and around this battle positions were drawn, posts were occupied and evacuated, fire exchanged and angry pronouncements flew about the two capitals. A phoney and unnecessary conflict. This was in April 1965. Two months later followed the Commonwealth

Prime Ministers' Conference, during which this august assembly found welcome distraction from their other high responsibilities by arranging a 'cease-fire'. The issue of this hitherto entirely unknown part of the Indian landscape was then referred to international arbitration. This was an error, for this amounted to repeating earlier such mistakes: of internationalizing bilateral disputes.

But this was not the end of Pakistan's ambitions, it was only Phase I, a beginning. Soon Pakistan, under a grand plan of sending thousands of armed guerrillas to 'liberate' Kashmir, launched the second phase. From July 1965 Pakistan began sending a mixture of military personnel out of uniform and others as infiltrators, under two groups named the Salaudin force and the Ghaznavi force. Here, the focus is not on this effort aimed at inciting rebellion and insurgency; rather it is on India's assessment of Pakistani intentions. By August 1965 most of these infiltrators had been rounded up. Phase II had failed just as much as the first (Kutch reconnaissance) had succeeded, at least up to a point. Then came the gamble – Phase III. President Ayub Khan decided to bring his regular armed forces into action. On 1 September 1965, a Pakistani attack in brigade strength supported by 90 tanks was launched over the international boundary, in southern Jammu & Kashmir. It was done with international finesse, for though the attack was not over any cease-fire line, it was on the Indian state of Jammu & Kashmir. The aim of this offensive was to capture the township of Akhnur, on river Chenab, thus severing the road link Jammu-Rajauri-Poonch.

India decided to use its Air Force – the first such employment since 1947. The employment, however, was limited to the sector and was almost entirely supportive of the land forces. Pakistan captured the tactically important Jaurian by 5 September 1965. A day later, on 6 September 1965, Indian troops crossed the international boundary in the Punjab. That evening dusk raids were carried out by the Pakistan Air Force (PAF) on a number of forward Indian airfields. Each nation accused the other of being the aggressor. In the meantime diplomatic activities had also commenced and the UN Secretary General, U Thant, had already appealed for cessation of hostilities. This was on 2 September 1965; followed by two Security Council Resolutions to the same effect on 3 and 6 September 1965. India had already declared that it was ready for a cease-fire provided Pakistan withdrew. It was only on 22 September that Foreign Minister Bhutto responded to another UN Security Council resolution, of 20 September 1965 and announced Pakistan's acceptance of the cease-fire proposal. Thus stopped this 22-day war on 23 September 1965.

The three-week-long, somewhat inconclusive war, was marked by some significant departures from the past. At the same time it established a kind of a pattern of conflict between India and Pakistan that was not, in essentials, broken at least in the western sector even in the Third Indo-Pakistan war of 1971. 1965 was the year in which for the first time the international boundary between India and Pakistan was crossed offensively. Though the genesis of the war, as of the earlier conflict of 1948, lay in the disputations over the Indian state of Jammu & Kashmir, hostilities had remained confined to that state alone. On this occasion both India and Pakistan broke from the past. All the three Services were employed, though in very limited roles as such with even more limited tasks. Yet again the United Nations stepped in and stopped the conflict.

War on the ground having started as a reconnaissance in force early in 1965 in Kutch, it had moved to that centre of the conflict Jammu & Kashmir by stages, by the beginning of August. The inherent logic of conflicts acquiring an autonomy of their own began thereafter to assert itself and barely a month later manoeuvres and skirmishes converted themselves into a full-fledged three-services war.

The Indian Army's drive across the Punjab border on the Amritsar-Wagah-Lahore axis achieved strategic surprise. India demonstrated action on its earlier warning that should Pakistan continue to push towards the strategically important road axis of Pathankot-Jammu-Srinagar, then the country retained its right to react at a time and place of its choosing. The surprise achieved despite that early warning demonstrated Pakistan's complacence, and a misreading of Indian responses. Pakistan was caught off-balance; its forces, particularly armour, concentrated much further north were found to be in a deployment of near total imbalance. Within 24 hours of crossing the border, advance elements of the Indian Army's drive were on the outskirts of Lahore, which then lay virtually undefended. Thus, it was not any stout defending of their positions that checked the advancing Indian forces. It was a lack of prepared contingency planning, an absence of the spirit to exploit success, and a lack of vigorous execution of plans that resulted in converting what would have been a significant military victory into what became almost a disorderly withdrawal, and then simply a slugging match of attrition. The Indian Army's thrust was not led by any definable goals. In this sector, therefore, their fall-back battles were mostly around that manmade obstacle of a waterway called the Ichhogil Canal. Just as the Indian offensive ran out of steam, so did the Pakistani counter-attack, a little further to the south in the Punjab in the Khemkaran sector. Here, in a battle, substantial casualties were caused to the Pakistan Army and unacceptable tank losses. It is in this context that there was a major intelligence failure on the part of the Indian political-military leadership. All Indian planning had hitherto been based on an assessment which showed Pakistan in possession of only one armoured division. A tactical and intelligence surprise was thus sprung upon India by this thrust of the Pakistani armour towards the heart of Indian Punjab at Khemkaran.

Further to the north, India had launched its major armour thrust towards Sialkot, as the terrain here permits the employment of larger bodies of armoured formations. The ground itself thus robs the offensive of any element of strategic surprise. Even though Indian troops moved well into Pakistani territory, the three-week-long battles here again were more battles of attrition than of manoeuvre and gain of territory. With the crossing of the international boundary in Punjab, pressure had almost instantly been eased on the vital road link Pathankot-Jammu-Srinagar and the Pakistani offensive towards Akhnoor had stopped after the capture of Jaurian.

In the Kashmir Valley, Indian troops by now having acquired much greater expertise in warfare in such areas, displayed commendably greater abilities; operations being marked by an identifiable goal of correcting military anomalies of the cease-fire line. Therefore, even though there were scarcely any battles of more than a battalion strength, there were some in this area of up to a brigade level, particularly that operation which resulted in the capture of the important Haji Pir Pass.

Other than this, the only other area of operation of the Indian Army was much further to the south along the Rajasthan-Sind border, where largely because the entire Rajasthan sector was treated as a subsidiary sector, neither was any great military effort involved nor expended.

The employment of the Indian Army was marked by a certain tentativeness, lack of a surety in command and a firmness in the conduct of operations. Additionally, the military commanders displayed little understanding of deploying and commanding troops in anything above a brigade strength. In the higher direction of war, a significant intelligence failure is cited. When cease-fire came the ammunition reserves of the Pakistani forces had been depleted to barely a few days' capability. India thus lost an opportunity of a striking military victory.

The employment of air and naval power was even more limited. Indian air strikes were carried out against airfields and other strategic objects, though almost all of military nature, in Pakistan. The attrition rate of the Indian Air Force was high. Equipment capability disparities were obviously corrected at a very early stage by a better tactical employment of the Indian Air Force. The Navy's role was limited to neutralizing the one known Pakistani submarine and keeping the Karachi harbour largely inoperational. But it was forbidden to go north of the Dwarka latitude. It is significant that there was scarcely any military activity of the Army, Navy or the Air Force in the Eastern wing and even though there was some redeployment of the Indian Army along the then East Pakistan border, war did not spread to this region at all. So far as India was concerned the inhibiting factor remained the presence of Chinese troops in the vicinity of the Himalayan borders and the by then well-established Sino-Pak cooperation.

The cease-fire was followed by a conference in Tashkent in the opening months of 1966, out of which an agreement followed. This Tashkent Declaration and announcement of good intentions was the consequence of a major Soviet diplomatic initiative in South Asia. The USA provided more than tacit consent to such a Soviet initiative. That the two superpowers, at the height of the cold war, could agree to such a Soviet initiative and that the US consented to an enhancement of Soviet prestige and consequent influence in the region is only one part of the significance of this event. The other, and, from the Indian viewpoint more important, is the entry into South Asian affairs, this time on invitation of a foreign power – the USSR.

This extraneous influence was eventually to weigh upon India's foreign and defence policies, and this pattern got established over time. For one, yet again, India had consented to the entry of a foreign power in Indian affairs; for another, yet again, what were essentially bilateral issues were permitted to be internationalized; and, thirdly, this marked the beginning of a period of unacceptably high Soviet presence in India's defence policies, particularly in the acquisition of military hardware – a dependence which eventually, by the end of the eighties had reached a crippling level of near 70 per cent quantitatively. The Indian political-military class during this period brought no new sense of leadership or guidance to the war effort. This was perhaps too much to ask for, since the experience of the military reverses of the 1962 war were too fresh. Besides international reverses following upon the Sino-Indian war, Pandit Nehru's death and the Kutch episode had not lent to the conduct of Indian foreign policy either any greater status or a surer touch. What characterized the Indian national effort was that the highly emotional '*Jai Jawan Jai Kisan*' became a kind of rallying cry hailing both the farmer and the soldier. Those were also the years when India was beginning to feel the food shortage. There were, however, significant intelligence failures, for example, in not fully assessing the real intentions of Pakistan in, say, the Kutch deflection. This short Kutch conflict had been accompanied by a rapid Indian deployment all along the Punjab border in early 1965. With cease-fire Indian troops withdrew to rear locations. In the process very useful intelligence was provided about India's mobilization plans and timings.

A Punjab deployment also amounted to an announcement of the possibilities and the potential of Indian reactions. Yet the Indian Army was soothingly withdrawn soon after the Kutch cease-fire and the Commonwealth initiatives. When, however, Pakistan launched its offensive against Kashmir in early August of 1965, a rapid deployment of troops was hindered by the monsoon. At Tashkent, gains made at great cost in Jammu & Kashmir were yet again bartered away on the negotiating table. The important pass of Hajipir was bargained for a Pakistani withdrawal from Chhamb sector. Withdrawals from Rajasthan followed as a matter of course. This, too, set a pattern for the future. In international relations this conflict was not accompanied by any great efforts of the country's foreign policy. In sum the second war between India and Pakistan ended as inconclusively as it had begun tentatively.

THE THIRD INDO-PAK WAR, 1971 – LIBERATION OF BANGLADESH

The seeds of the emergence of Bangladesh lay in a reassertion of some of the more ancient verities; for example, the constituents of nationhood, and an assertion of the cultural identity of a people against the demands of subscribing to a common faith and on that basis alone nationhood. It was also a telling comment upon the division of the Indian subcontinent on grounds of religion alone. Bangladesh owes its independent existence as much to the reality of the Bengali culture as to the identifying vehicle of its expressions: the Bengali language. An earlier division of Bengal by the very same imperial power in 1904 under the Viceroyalty of Lord Curzon had resulted in vociferous protests, reminiscent almost of 1857. Yet in 1947 a partition of the very same Bengal into East Pakistan and West Bengal was actually sought. Inter-religious passions fuelled this separation. Later, however, at just about the midway point of the half century of an independent India and Pakistan, yet again the Bengali sentiment in East Pakistan asserted itself over the insensitivity of a dominant western wing. On this occasion unity of faith was challenged by the particularity of culture and language. This too was clearly a consequence of political mismanagement by the Punjab-dominated martial law government of General Yahya Khan, and a cynical exploitation of the difficulties of his country by the late Z. A. Bhutto. Was there, in the emergence of independent Bangladesh a lesson which had not been learnt from a history of this subcontinent? And, of course, it has a lesson for the future. There is a significance too in the post-partition names adopted. Both the Indian and Pakistani parts of Punjab retain the original Punjab, not East Punjab for India and the Western part, now in Pakistan being called West Punjab. Conversationally, they are sometimes even referred to by an older, more sub-cultural, delineation, Majha and Malwa, but much less often as East or West Punjab. In Bengal, however, the case is entirely

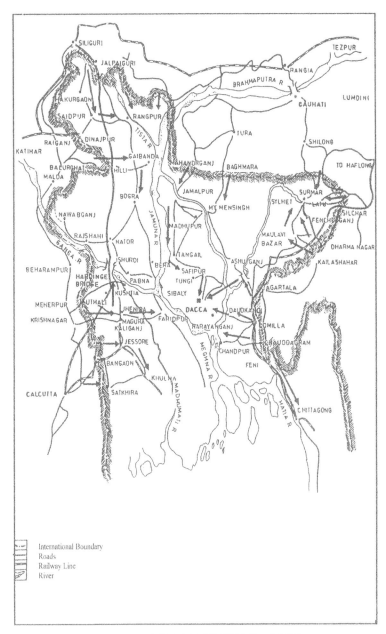

THE EASTERN SECTOR, 1971

different – the Indian part always from the beginning has been West Bengal, whereas, East Pakistan, that eastern wing, was frequently referred to as East Bengal. And now as Bangladesh, it assumes, in only a slightly altered form, the name of the original whole thus asserting, even if by implication, a continuity of a larger cultural oneness.

But this is almost a digression. There is no doubt that the emergence of Bangladesh owes its genesis to a gross mishandling of the situation by the then political-military class of an undivided Pakistan; however India also did certainly contribute. Our purpose, however, is not to trace the political history of the creation of Bangladesh here; it is to study the Indian decision-making and the higher direction of war by the Indian leadership. That is why we will not dwell for too long on a sequence of the purely military aspect. As to when the war actually started – in September 1971, when the Indian paramilitary, the Border Security Force, began early actions in the border areas of the then East Pakistan, or two months later when Pakistan proclaimed a state of emergency on 23 November and imposed curfew in Dacca city on 24 November 1971 – is largely an academic question now. On the same day, Prime Minister Indira Gandhi informed the Indian Parliament that some thirteen Pakistani Chafee tanks had been destroyed near Bogra when Indian troops repulsed a Pakistani attack. During this phase there was almost constant shelling by Pakistani troops, with civilians being killed often. Later, on 2 December 1971, three Pakistan Sabre jets strafed Indian positions. On 3 December 1971, unwisely the Pakistan Air Force provided a cause to India for full-scale operations by repeating almost exactly what they had done six years earlier. A dusk raid by the PAF simultaneously on a number of Indian airfields and other strategic targets was mounted. The Third Indo-Pak war had begun. Operations commenced in the West and the East almost simultaneously, also, of course, in Jammu and Kashmir. As in 1965, so also on this occasion. However, the Indian Army, Navy and the Air Force were employed in this conflict much more purposefully and tellingly. And as per past pattern, the UN became an early participant in attempting to resolve the conflict.

The war in the East went badly for Pakistan. The Indian armed forces exploited their all-round superiority tellingly. Within a week of the commencement of hostilities, by 11 December 1971, the Pakistani troops had begun to surrender in certain sectors, also in Dacca. Major General Farman Ali flashed an appeal to the United Nations pleading with the Security Council to arrange for an evacuation of Pakistani troops and official civilians to Pakistan. The Pakistani hierarchy was by then clearly divided. Making use of this discord (in the Pakistani Army), the Indian Army Chief, General Manekshaw, broadcast his first message to Dacca advising surrender. On 14 December 1971, in the afternoon, the US Embassy in New Delhi passed on the Pakistani Commander General Niazi's offer of surrender. A formal surrender took place on 16 December at Dacca. Cease-fire followed in the West too, after India had unilaterally offered it. Many years after the event, the Indian Defence Ministry, almost as an afterthought, has lately begun to observe 16 December as 'Vijay Divas' (Victory Day).

This was a significant military victory of Indian arms. All possible cards had by then been stacked in India's favour: international, internal and military; some by Pakistan's gross mishandling of the situation; others by an adept and dexterous management of the opportunity by the Indian political-military leadership. But was it really as surefooted as the ultimate outcome of the event demonstrates? What were India's strategic aims? Were these achieved? Are they still subserved – a quarter century after the event?

Militarily, in the East certainly, Pakistan had virtually lost the war even before it had commenced: the long lines of communication with the Western wing; a hostile local population in East Pakistan, where Pakistani troops from the Western wing had begun to behave and operate as forces of occupation; early and total control of the skies over the East by the Indian Air Force, thus facilitating helicopter-borne troop deployments over the otherwise formidable river obstacles of East Bengal are only some of the reasons. The morale of the Indian Army was high, while that of the Pakistanis was very low. The Indian military leadership displayed farsightedness in both planning and in the timing of operations; in resisting political pressure for a hastening of the events, and most tellingly in planning the logistics of this war with accuracy and forethought. The Indian Navy virtually sealed off the Bay of Bengal. The war in the West was wisely kept to a kind of a re-run of the 1965 operations – as a limited purpose holding operation only. And thus, in the process, the Indian military demonstrated another ability: to conduct a two-front war.

As in 1965, the apprehended Chinese hand did not materialize though it could almost verbalize, about stray sheep and goats, also yaks and similar other occurrences on high and distant Himalayan grazing grounds. But China's conduct was telling in different ways, about their approach to relations with India and Pakistan, then more tellingly about Indian intelligence assessments, and equally about the Pakistani leaders misleading their own citizens about a 'helping hand' coming to their rescue. The US did something not too dissimilar by ordering their Seventh Fleet into the Bay of Bengal, though for no ostensible purpose other than of providing the Indian leadership with a useful propaganda stick, which was naturally fully used.

What 1962 had done for the People's Republic China – demonstrated their power without earning unacceptably high international odium – so 1971 achieved for India too. India had taken a large number of Pakistani troops as prisoners, 93,000 of them. They were all transferred to India soon after Bangladesh came into existence. The Indian Army too withdrew rapidly, almost immediately after Sheikh Mujibur Rehman had taken over as the new President of Bangladesh. Indo-Bangladesh treaties of significance followed. Most of the refugees, victims of the military repression of the Pakistan Army and of attendant uncertainties also returned in 1972.

In the Shimla talks that took place between India and Pakistan – Mrs Indira Gandhi and Z. A. Bhutto being the two premiers respectively – a great mistake of earlier years was avoided: there were no foreign umpires or overseers; the matter was negotiated entirely bilaterally. An unassessed, perhaps even unintended, consequence of thus re-recognizing an older subcontinental reality of keeping external influences out has been the imparting of a longer stability to this first, entirely Indo-Pak Agreement of 1972. Since the Shimla Agreement India and Pakistan have not engaged in overt hostilities. But if this mistake was not repeated, others were. Yet again an opportunity for finding a more lasting solution to the Kashmir tangle was lost, particularly by India. The Shimla Agreement recognizes the respective position of the two countries 'as without prejudice' to the stated position of either. The cease-fire line went through an adjustment as also a nomenclature change: it became the Line of Control. However, the task was left incomplete for it describes the LC as running up to map grid reference NJ 9842 and then vaguely as 'thence North to the glaciers'. This obvious lack of precision became the root cause, in turn, of a subsequent conflict about the Saltoro ridge and the Siachen glacier – the battleground at a frozen height of 18,000 feet for Indian and Pakistani troops. And all on account of that lack of a sense about geography, territory, even of map-making and reading.

But some larger questions remain. That India sought to exploit Pakistan's discomfiture is self evident; even a resort to arms was acceptable as the means. But had Indian planning assessed the long-term strategic consequences of the birth of Bangladesh? What would that do to India's East and North-East? What would it do to Pakistan, which had to shed the responsibility of an unwieldy, distant and culturally separate Eastern wing? Would such a smaller Pakistan be more or less powerful, or even antagonistic? And again, how would the new state be disposed towards ourselves?

As we examine India's higher direction of war, the first of our concerns becomes an assessment of the factors that influenced Indian decision-making on East Pakistan.

The refugee issue was certainly important, but probably not decisive; indeed, it is doubtful whether New Delhi would have resorted to direct armed intervention if the refugees had been the only issue. Of greater importance to New Delhi was the potentially destabilizing influence of the conflict in East Pakistan on strife-ridden West Bengal, as well as on the tribal hill states and Assam in northeastern India, in which the basic political alignments pitted the "indigenous" communities against the "outsiders" – mainly Bengalis. The problem for India was not just the "existence" of refugees, but where they existed.[16]

Therefore,

In New Delhi's view it was not sufficient that East Pakistan gain independence or autonomy if, in the process, a radical government were established in Dhaka that (1) had ties with leftist "extremist" factions in West Bengal and the northeast and (2) carried out internal policies (for example, land nationalization) that would result in another outpouring of refugees to India. What New Delhi wanted in Dhaka was a government that was both democratic and politically moderate – but with emphasis on the moderate. . . . Thus, for crucial Indian political purposes, Bangladesh had to be neutralized to the extent possible as a factor in northeastern Indian politics.[17]

There was also the calculus of domestic polity.

A successful war would also reap domestic political rewards for Mrs Gandhi and her party. At the national level, the opposition was so weak and divided as to be easily ignored, but state assembly elections in several key states were scheduled for early 1972, and something was needed to counter the charges that Mrs Gandhi's government had done nothing to implement the "Garibi hatao" (Abolish poverty) slogan that the Congress party had campaigned on in the March 1971 parliamentary elections. A victorious war with Pakistan was the answer. . . .[18]

The international factor, unlike earlier occasions, was handled with professional competence and clarity of purpose.

The conduct of attendant diplomacy was purposeful. 'The Indian government wanted to give the international community and the United Nations sufficient time to attempt to mediate a viable political solution in East Pakistan or, in the process, expose beyond all doubt their inability to do so. [Thus] Mrs Gandhi's visits to Moscow in September [1971] and to Western Europe and the United States in October and November [1971] were intended to serve this purpose. Mrs Gandhi returned to New Delhi in mid November, [1971] and the order went out to initiate another "military solution according to plan" immediately.[19]

This timing was right, diplomatically, militarily and against the criteria of local factors, too. Even though the UN General Assembly would be then in session. . . . Soviet Union would forestall, or at least delay through the use of its veto power, any action by UN Security Council, but it also understood that this would embarrass Soviet relations with the Islamic . . . other South Asian states, as well as affecting its emerging detente with the United States and even relations with a large proportion of countries in the nonaligned movement, which tended to be critical of India on this issue. These factors made it even more important that the Indian army accomplish its tasks as quickly as possible.[20]

Strategic deception was not intended but it followed India's decision to provide only the necessary help to the Bangladeshi resistance groups. India was not raising another army, it could not, it was encouraging the resistance movement. This

> limited support of the Mukti Bahini raised a difficult question, . . . for the Pakistani government and military, . . . one that complicated Pakistani decision making throughout the fall and winter of 1971. Did New Delhi have a limited objective in mind – the establishment of a section of East Pakistan under Mukti Bahini control, with Indian military support, in which a government of Bangladesh could be founded and internationally recognized? Or was all this carefully disguised military intervention by India in fact the prelude to an all-out invasion of East Pakistan?[21]

In this conflict, much more than in 1965, China and the United States

> had a substantial impact upon decision making in the South Asian states. The 1965 Indo-Pakistani war and the Tashkent conference in February 1966 had led to some interesting innovations in Soviet, Chinese, and American policies in South Asia, based primarily on their perceptions of the political and strategic environment in the subcontinent in the post-Tashkent period. The most apparent changes in regional policies during 1966 to 1971 were made by Moscow and Washington, but Beijing also began subtly and indirectly redefining its role and policies south of the Himalayas. . . . [For] the Soviet Union [which] had initially become involved in South Asia in the mid 1950s

in order to forestall and counteract US 'intervention' in that region through Pakistan's membership in US-sponsored military alliance systems and through massive American economic aid programmes to India. India was the critical state in the subcontinent . . . it had [thus] become a basic objective of Soviet policy to prevent any serious disjunctures in its relationship with India.[22]

It is in this period that Brezhnev had propounded an 'Asian Mutual Security' concept. The Indian response was cautious at first. But of

importance to the Soviet Union was the receptivity of Mrs Gandhi's government to Moscow's proposal for a treaty between the two states if, in response, the Soviets terminated, or at least reduced, their military aid to Pakistan. Moscow considered such a treaty an important step in the direction of an Indian endorsement of Brezhnev's June 1969 'Asian mutual security' proposal, which was an integral part of the Soviet Union's 'containment of China' policy. A broad agreement on the proposed Indo-Soviet treaty was reached during negotiations conducted by the Indian ambassador to Moscow, D. P. Dhar, in mid 1969, and it is probable that the treaty would have been signed in the first half of 1970 if the political situation in India had permitted. For its part Moscow informed New Delhi in April 1970 that Soviet military aid to Pakistan was being 'suspended', though in fact some arm shipments to Pakistan continued through 1970 and into 1971.[23]

But these supplies were already in the pipeline; they were not any new initiatives.

Of the three major external powers China was probably placed in the most difficult position by the events of 25 March 1971 in East Pakistan. Beijing concluded that it had nothing to gain, but much to lose, from these developments, no matter what the outcome might be. China was clearly unenthusiastic about the military crackdown in East Pakistan, which after all was directed against pro-Chinese political factions there as well as against the Awami League. On balance, however, Beijing was far more concerned with avoiding any actions that would weaken or alienate its 'ally', Pakistan. . . . . At the same time that China was taking a public position seemingly supportive of the Pakistani government, however, it was also informing the Pakistani embassy in China and the foreign ministry in Islamabad privately that it would not intervene directly in hostilities, either internal or international, on the subcontinent. Thus, by mid April the core group in the Yahya Khan government – but not the Pakistani public – had learned that they could not expect Chinese military support in the event of another war with India. . . . The Pakistani government therefore decided to approach Beijing once again with a request for assistance – to reverse its April policy position – and a deputation consisting of Bhutto, Air Marshal Rahim Khan, and Gen. Gul Hasan was sent to Beijing on 7 November. In a meeting with Zhou Enlai, Rahim asked the Chinese to provide thirty fighter planes, as well as sundry other military supplies on an emergency basis, while Bhutto sounded out the PRC premier on whether China would consider coming to the assistance of Pakistan in the event of war with India. Zhou replied that war was unlikely, but that if it occurred Chinese military forces would not intervene directly in support of Pakistan, although China would support Pakistan politically and provide material assistance.[24]

New Delhi, therefore, had made a reasonably accurate assessment of possible Chinese response.

Indeed, India doubted that China had the capacity to intervene effectively even it wanted to. The Chinese military forces in Tibet had not been reinforced and resupplied . . . even more important in New Delhi's calculations was the September 1971 'coup' attempt by Mao's designated successor, Lin Biao, supported by some elements in the Chinese air force and army.[25]

Even though China behaved exactly as Pakistan and India expected during the 1971 war, there is some doubt about the reactions to such an assessment. Cautious India could simply not repeat the intelligence errors of 1962. Thus Indian troop deployments all through this short war did not result in any significant milking of the divisions on either the Eastern frontier or in Ladakh. 'US policy in South Asia [was much] less consistent, and hence less predictable, than either Soviet or Chinese policy.' Obviously the US establishment was divided on the whole war

not over the objectives of US policy but over the public position [to be] taken by the government. More specifically, the dispute focused on the question of whether the United States should publicly criticise the Yahya government for its repressive actions in East Pakistan.[26]

The logic behind this approach was outlined in a Kissinger report to the Washington Special Action Group (WSAG) on South Asia in early September. What were the listed options?

First, it could have condemned the government in Pakistan and cut off all assistance. The purpose of such a stance would have been to rely on the political 'shock effect' to change Pakistani policy. A secondary purpose would also have been to take distance from a government that, in much of the world's eyes, was responsible for a great deal of human suffering.

Or, second, it could have expressed concern and restricted the actual flow of assistance but stopped short of an act of open condemnation. The purpose of such a stance as have been to try to maintain effective communication with Islamabad while making clear that a normal US-Pakistani assistance relationship could not be resumed as long as the present disruption in Pakistan continued.[27]

Leo Rose explains that the US Government had chosen the second course 'not with any illusions about being able to shift sharply the course of events', but because it 'would offer the best chance of conserving our limited ability to influence' Pakistani policies, as well as offering 'the best chance that the United States could take effective action to help meet the human needs of the people of East Pakistan.'[28] For the US Government India's intentions towards West Pakistan were critical. In Kissinger's words again:

There was no question of 'saving' East Pakistan. Both Nixon and I had recognized for months that its independence was inevitable; war was not necessary to accomplish it. We strove to preserve West Pakistan as an independent state, since we judged India's real aim was to encompass its disintegration.[29]

'Gun boat diplomacy', it was called, the dispatch of the Enterprise – Task Force 74, or "Oh Calcutta" as some cynics [termed it].

On 10 December the Enterprise and four escorts were ordered to sail from their station in the Gulf of Tonkin toward Singapore. On 12 December they met another naval detachment off the Singapore coast and on 14 December, after two days' unexplained delay, sailed down the Strait of Malacca during the daylight hours into the northern most section of the Bay of Bengal. Task Force 74 then turned south and was operating in the Indian Ocean to the Southeast of Sri Lanka when Dhaka surrendered on 16 December and the war ended the next day with the ceasefire on the western front.[30]

What was it doing?

Kissinger and Nixon have generally tended to explain and justify the Enterprise episode in broader geopolitical terms, primarily the supposed impact of this symbolic gesture of support for our Pakistani "ally" on China, just at the time when the United States was beginning the process of normalizing relations with the People's Republic. Some others in the State Department placed greater importance on the impact of American support of a Muslim state on the international Islamic community. Both were factors that were considered, but in and of themselves would not have been decisive.[31]

There were no Soviet naval forces in the region then and the first did not arrive until 18 December 1971. By then the war was over. Besides, the orders to the US Task Force were vague and intended not towards any specific task, they seemed almost advisory: to conduct 'naval, air and surface operations . . . to support US interests in the Indian Ocean area'.[33] Predictably the Indian response was bitter.

What then is the score card 26 years later? The social (and economic) aspects of Indian concerns about unrest in the region have altered only in form, not in substance. Unchecked immigration continues as does the option of inciting anti-Indian feelings for the sake of the domestic politics of Bangladesh. But the country now has a large and increasing trade with India. Besides there is no strain on the Indian military from this quarter.

This, in sum, is one security issue about whose

management the Indian political class can express satisfaction.

THE INDIAN PEACEKEEPING FORCE IN SRI LANKA, 1987-1990

Though the categorization of this particular example of India's management of conflicts is a study of bilateral peacekeeping/peace- enforcing in Sri Lanka during the period 1987-1990, two central and ancient coefficients of the origins of policy merit reiteration. The first, which we established earlier is that – notwithstanding the fact that this was military cooperation between two sovereign states, India and Sri Lanka – both approached it as an issue of restoring internal order only. There were not, in the essence of it, any aggressive or territorial designs. India had neither any intention nor did it actually mount an expedition of conquest. A launching of the Indian Peacekeeping Force (IPKF) (wrongly and unhappily so titled) was, at least in part, to ensure that the ethnic ·and linguistic strife of Sri Lanka did not spill over into the adjoining Indian state of Tamil Nadu. For this a solution was sought through the agency of surplus Indian military power – that which could be employed outside the territory of India.

We examine, therefore, the genesis of the problem in Sri Lanka; the Indian assessment of it; the employment of the Indian Army, its role, tasks and performance; and finally whether the Indian venture succeeded, and why not?

The decade of the eighties was marked by a surfacing of many insurgencies in India: in Assam, Punjab, Jammu & Kashmir, and deep in the south with the LTTE in Sri Lanka. Mrs Indira Gandhi mishandled all of these.

The student movement in Assam (1980-83) for the preservation of Assamese identity against unchecked and illegal immigration from adjoining Bangladesh was brutally put down. This gave birth to a more virulent form of separatism in that state in the form of ULFA (United Liberation Front of Assam) and various other smaller groupings like that of the Bodos. To combat these the Army had to be employed.

In Punjab the insurgency boiled over in 1983 just as Assam was being restored to relative normalcy. The armed assault on the Golden Temple, Operation Blue Star, was in the June of the following year. In 1984 Mrs Gandhi became the victim of a foul assassination – the first Indian prime minister to be so killed. About then the Kashmir Valley too began to go into a phase of renewed insurgency, a phase which concluded in good part only with elections to the State Assembly of Jammu & Kashmir in 1996.

That is why it is difficult to appreciate how or rationally even why Mrs Gandhi opted in 1983 following the language riots in Jaffna (Sri Lanka) to begin overtly to, not simply espouse the Tamil cause, but covertly to actually launch India on a policy of aiding and abetting the LTTE. It was here, through an arming of the LTTE, of providing them with financial assistance, of training them on Indian soil, in special camps that the genesis of the IPKF experiment lay.

What was it that India apprehended? J. N. Dixit, then India's High Commissioner in Sri Lanka and later the Foreign Secretary of the country, offers some answers. (There is a reason for relying on his version, for no other official account exists.)

> India's involvement in Sri Lanka . . . was unavoidable not only due to the ramifications of Colombo's oppressive and discriminating policies against its Tamil citizens, but also in terms of India's [own] national security concerns. . . .[33]

And yet again repeating the internal order arguments.

> There was a perception that if India did not support the Tamil cause [the] rise of Tamil militancy in Sri Lanka and the Jayewardene Government's serious apprehensions about this

SRI LANKA

development [would be] utilised by the US and Pakistan to create a pressure point against India in the island on the strategically sensitive coast of peninsular India.[34]

There are more internal order arguments.

There was a perception that if India did not support the Tamil cause in Sri Lanka and if the Government of India tried to question the political and emotional feelings of Tamil Nadu there would be a resurgence of Tamil separatism in India.[35]

This was a double-edged weapon for

if India were to endorse the demand for the establishment of a separate state on the basis of ethnicity and religion which would disintegrate a neighbouring multi-ethnic, multireligious and multi-lingual state, then India would find it difficult to maintain its own unity and territorial integrity facing the challenges of separatism in Punjab and Kashmir. Her intention was only to provide support to the Sri Lankan Tamils to generate sufficient pressure on the Jayewardene Government to make it responsive to Tamil aspirations so that Sri Lanka does not disintegrate. The political exchanges between India and Sri Lanka between 1980 and 1983 confirm this assessment.[36]

The argument is a bit tortured but not much is gained by engaging with it. The consequence of this assessment resulted in:

Tamil militancy [receiving] support both from Tamil Nadu and the Central Government not only as a response to the Sri Lankan Government's military assertiveness against its Tamils, but also [as] a response to Jayewardene orchestrating military intelligence presence of the US, Israel and Pakistan in Sri Lanka. The assessment was that these presences would pose a strategic threat to India, as they might encourage fissiparous movements in the southern states of India.[37]

The stated objectives of Indian policy, discernible so far, can be identified thus: protect the Tamil minority in Sri Lanka with arms, money, training, etc. but short of secession; and discourage US, Israeli and Pakistani presence and influence in Sri Lanka as this was inimical to Indian national interests. To achieve these objectives the entire structure of encouraging the LTTE was established.
    Was this approach correct or even appropriate? We are provided an answer.

In normative terms and in terms of international law and principles of morality . . . the answer, obviously, has to be in the negative, Sri Lanka should have been allowed to sort out its own problems. India should not have interfered in any way, even if developments in Sri Lanka and its Government's policies endangered India's interests. India should have tackled them domestically.[38]

But this is not a doctrine being stated, only a kind of morality being suggested. Our yardstick can, however, only be judgement against stated objectives.
    Towards the end of 1984, and following Mrs Gandhi's assassination, her son (and that really is only why he was chosen as the Prime Minister) succeeded to office.

He maintained continuity in Indian policies but with certain significant shifts in emphasis and nuances. . . . The then Foreign Secretary, Romesh Bhandari, described the shift as "India intends to have an Indian rather than a Tamil Nadu policy towards Sri Lanka".[39]

This 'Indianizing' of the policy presumably meant a 'militarization' of the response. For that is the 'significant shift in emphasis' that did take place. Rajiv Gandhi's changes are listed:

(a) India should firmly oppose the Sri Lanka Government's military operations against Tamils; (b) more direct political pressures as to be generated against Jayewardene to implement the devolution package which had been finalised in negotiations between 1985 and 1986; (c) if India succeeded in the above two objects, India should persuade Tamils to come back to the negotiating table; (d) if these negotiations succeeded and a set of solutions resulted from the discussions India should directly guarantee the implementation of the solution in one form or the other through appropriate agreements; and (e) India apart from being a mediator, should become the guarantor of compromises to give a tangible sense of security to Sri Lankan Tamils and to ensure that Colombo implements the solutions agreed upon.[40]

These were not simply 'significant shifts'; they amounted to a radical departure from the earlier policy of covert assistance only to the LTTE. What was now prepared amounted, in reality, to being an agenda for intervention, with India guaranteeing, enforcing and ensuring – in reality imposing its will upon both Sri Lanka and the insurgent LTTE. How did Rajiv Gandhi arrive at such a major decision – of employing the power of the Indian State in such a manner, to this cause? 'These elements in the evolving policies of India were the result of a series of internal discussions which Rajiv Gandhi held with his political and civil service advisers.'[41]

This is very disturbing, for the suggestion here is that as momentous a decision as the one outlined above, of such total Indian involvement, was taken on the basis only of 'internal discussions', and that too with a set of 'personal advisers'. Having arrived at a set of policy objectives these were tested on the specific question of the merits and demerits of executing an agreement with Sri Lanka. The response was supportive. But was it so because everyone already knew the decision and simply concurred?

Intelligence agencies, armed forces and the Ministry of External Affairs, including myself [the High Commissioner] told him that the initiatives being taken for signing the agreement were valid and practical. My advice to him was that it was time to bypass the LTTE if they remain obstinate, garner support from other Tamil groups and sign the agreement directly with the Jayewardene Government. Representatives of the Research and Analysis Wing told him that since the agreement has been explained to all Tamil groups, including the LTTE and since they had given their overall consent, the agreement could be signed. In response to specific doubts raised by my colleagues in the IB and myself about the likelihood of LTTE pulling back from the agreement, the representative of RAW told Rajiv Gandhi that they had sufficient influence with the LTTE to prevent them from resiling from the agreement once Prabhakaran gave his commitment. The phrase used was, 'These are the youth whom we have dealt with, we can manage this eventuality.' In the same vein when a query was raised about the likelihood of the Indian armed forces having to militarily confront the LTTE and the possibility of these forces getting involved in guerilla or anti-insurgency operations in Sri Lanka, the then Chief of the Army Staff, General K. Sundarji told Rajiv: 'This should not be a matter of concern. The Indian armed forces can neutralise the LTTE in a fortnight or three to four weeks.' It was on these confident assertions that Rajiv Gandhi went ahead with the agreement. He did not overrule the professional advice given to him. That the advice was wrong and the political judgement on which this advice was based was erroneous has to be acknowledged with the benefit of hindsight.[42]

The complicated, often complex, occasionally even coercive efforts that went into finalizing the Indo-Sri Lanka Agreement of 27 July 1987 are a matter for historians to unravel. In India the response was, in part, falsely eulogatory as when the Congress Party predictably termed it as (the usual) 'pathbreaking, historic, visionary', etc. It was seen by some as extending India's 'glory' and power. For the majority, however, the whole Agreement was perplexing, with attendant tones of disbelief and incomprehension. Strenuous efforts were then made by the establishment to put it across as an act of great statesmanship; as a step by which India (read Rajiv) had masterfully thwarted all international designs in the region, asserted India's position subcontinentally, and simultaneously resolved the internal dilemma of injured Tamil sensibilities, and thus potential separatism.

In Sri Lanka, however, the portends were disturbing. The Indian premier's inauguration of the Agreement in Colombo was accompanied by an unprecedented act of protest. At the Ceremonial Guard of Honour, while inspecting the parade, the Indian Prime Minister was attacked by one of the Sri Lankan Servicement lined up as a 'Guard'. This was unprecedented, humiliating both individually and nationally, and an early message to the Indian political-military class. Thus the beginnings of what was being projected in India as a major international achievement were not auspicious.

The first of the Indian troops began landing in Sri Lanka hours later. The Indian Peacekeeping Force was born. It was put together by various milked Indian formations and from a small initial force of just about a Brigade, eventually it grew to Corps-plus strength with a separate headquarters and all the attendant military paraphernalia and bureaucracy.

The advance elements of the IPKF reached Palali Air Base near Jaffna on 27 July 1987 itself. It might seem like carping or making a petty point, but they actually were not in possession even of appropriate or even adequate maps. They had to initially make do with Sri Lankan road maps. The advance elements were in the form of 54 Division advance units, largely sappers and signaleers, with infantry elements, too. This build-up continued until the commencement of Operation Pawan which was on 10 October 1987.

Other formations were to follow: four full infantry divisions plus an independent brigade group and all attendant supporting arms and elements. The total strength of IPKF's deployment was, however, a little over five divisions, with naval and air force detachments not included. This misadventure cost India a total of roughly 1230 dead and about 8000 injured. The last elements of IPKF, including the General Officer Commanding, left Trincomalee harbour on 30 March 1990. Upon return to Madras the IPKF was not even received properly.

Why did the IPKF fail?

According to the impressions which I gathered from IPKF officers at the highest levels of command was [sic] that the IPKF was itself handicapped in terms of the brief given to them about the objectives of their mission. They carried out operations in a disciplined manner according to instructions received, but I was constantly queried as to why they found themselves in a situation where they are fighting the Tamils whom they were supposed to protect and whose cause they were supposed to uphold by helping in the implementation of the Sri Lankan Agreement. Somehow there was a failure in giving them a detailed and multi-dimensional briefing about the complexity of the task which they had undertaken. Their actions therefore were not backed up by a shared and informed conviction about the purpose of their operations.[43]

The High Commissioner further explains:

I am not knowledgeable in detail of many problems
which the IPKF faced as has [sic] been articulated
by some of the divisional commanders. Some
of these commanders themselves were not convinced
about the logic of IPKF's presence and operations
in Sri Lanka. Their second complaint was that
sufficient operational authority had not been
delegated to them. There was unnecessary
interference in field operations. According to these
officers command and control was highly centralised.
And yet, the IPKF restored order and stability
in the northern and eastern parts of the island.
They were the main factor enabling elections
in the Tamil areas of Sri Lanka and the creation
and establishment of a Tamil provincial
government. They were an equally important factor
assisting the Sri Lankan government to hold the
presidential and parliamentary elections in 1988
and 1989. By the end of 1988 and beginning
of 1989 they were in the final phase of containing
and neutralising the LTTE. It is my [the High
Commissioner's] assessment that had the IPKF
been allowed to stay on in Sri Lanka for another
six months or so, the LTTE would have been
under sufficient pressure to give up violence and
join the mainstream of politics.[44]

Whereas the IPKF was certainly an attempt by India
to generate and export surplus military power, neither
was the nature of this power fully grasped, nor were
its limitations. There was thus early confusion about
the role of the IPKF. What was it? A force to play
umpire between two combating groups and thus maintain
peace? Or was the IPKF itself a combatant, a party
to the conflict? And if the IPKF did indeed, as an
extension of the policy of the Indian state, play a combatants'
role, was it against the Sri Lankan forces, with
which Government there was after all an Agreement;
or against Tamil militancy in the form of the LTTE,
for the protection of which Tamil interests (in both

Sri Lanka and India) this whole effort had in the first instance been mounted? This early confusion bedeviled the unfortunate IPKF constantly: at the beginning; through the entire duration of the operations; and in the final withdrawal in 1990 too. Confusion about the whole enterprise persists till date. The only explanation that we have is that the

> criticism that Rajiv Gandhi should not have militarily intervened in Sri Lanka following the signing of the agreement begs the definitional question whether it was a military intervention or whether it was military assistance given in response to a specific and formal request from the Sri Lankan Government to meet the situation emerging in the country after the agreement was signed.[45]

Some fundamentals of peacekeeping operations and forces need to be outlined. Obviously there must be a clear definition of the role: keeping peace or warring parties apart, or enforcing it by employing military force? About this there must not be any ambiguity, as so self-evidently there was in the case of IPKF. Whereafter, such a 'force' must be despatched only if there exists a broad enough acceptance of it from the local population, even the warring elements of it. It must then be for a specific period announced in advance so that a withdrawal route and date is always available as an option in case of change of circumstances. Such a force must retain its military character and not attempt too many additional responsibilities, for example, policing, or civil administration or even relief, as the IPKF was so confusingly required to shoulder. A force such as the IPKF must act conjunctly with local forces; as a force that assists, in contrast to one that occupies or pioneers.

Did India succeed; did IPKF achieve its tasks? No formal assessment is needed for the outcome has itself passed judgement on the event. The High Commissioner says that the criticism that the agreement did not fulfill its objectives, and the IPKF's withdrawal without completion of its tasks was a foreign policy failure is valid.[46]

And again,

that the Agreement failed because there was no cohesion in operational aspect of Indian policies and harmonious coordination between different agencies of the Government of India dealing with the Sri Lankan crisis. In fact, there were periods when the Indian defence establishment, the intelligence agencies and the Ministry of External Affairs were working at cross-purposes. The Sri Lankan operation is in glaringly negative contrast to the harmony, cohesiveness and coordination which characterised Indian policies related to the Bangladesh crisis in 1970-71.[47]

He apportions blame:

Rajiv Gandhi could be partially blamed for the contradiction which characterised Indian policies. Though he had to instruct the armed forces to confront the LTTE, once they reverted to terrorism, there was perhaps an emotional and psychological inhibition on his part to take drastic action against the LTTE. He had an innate sympathy for the legitimate rights and aspirations of Tamils. It is perhaps because of this mind-set that he permitted representatives of our intelligence agencies to continue negotiations with the LTTE even as the Indian forces were engaged in military operations against them. The consequence was that the LTTE and the Sri Lankan Government took advantage of this two-track policy and its contradictions, and thereby reduced the efficacy of the IPKF operations.[48]

As for the principal combatant

the LTTE itself had a perception different from India's about Indian intentions behind the signing of the agreement. Prabhakaran from the initial period of his emergence into leadership had an emotive perception that India's real intention was to support his ambition of creating "Eelam", a separate Tamil state in Sri Lanka. His understanding was that by signing the agreement and becoming a direct guarantor of it, India will acquire a legitimate direct politico-military presence in Sri Lanka. Once this presence is consolidated India will give full support to his struggle against the Sri Lankan Government leading to the creation of "Eelam". He discovered that Rajiv Gandhi's motivations as manifested in the Indo-Sri Lanka Agreement were genuine and sincere and that India had no plans of clandestinely helping him create a separate Tamil state. He was not just disappointed but bitter. He waited for the first opportunity available to go back from the agreement and revert to violence.[49]

We need to dwell a bit longer in this attempt at understanding the LTTE phenomenon. The Indian peninsular point is after all just 22 miles from the Sri Lankan port of Jaffna. In reality this India-Sri Lanka Tamil insurgency relationship has its origins in the 1970s. 'The initial contact between the Tamil Nadu government and Sri Lankan Tamil activists was established in 1972.' And proceeding from that it has continued. Will it in the future? It is a relationship that will have its ups and downs but it is a relationship that will nevertheless continue. Despite the fact that the LTTE eliminated Rajiv Gandhi, the last of the Gandhi-Nehru dynasty, there will always be a segment of the Tamil Nadu leaders and people that will support the LTTE.

The contradiction stems from India's own structure

- the diversity within India, particularly the
disparity in antagonizing India at the southernmost
point of peninsular India meant the permanent
closure of the door for creating Tamil Eelam
and Prabhakaran becoming its ruler.[50]

It is time to take stock. The IPKF decided to withdraw
in 1990 when the Indo-Sri Lankan Agreement of 27
July 1987 expired. But it has left in its wake the
inevitable debris of such failed endeavours. Of course,
the more frequently pronounced objectives were not achieved;
the conflict continues; Sri Lankan Tamil interests have
not been subserved in the process, thus the possibilities
of a spillover into peninsular India have not receded.
That first objective of better internal order has not
been met.

The second objective of countering or discouraging
an extension of foreign influences inimical to India's
security interests has not been achieved either. These
have, on the contrary grown, for India failed to obtain
the geopolitical security that it sought through the
Agreement and the IPKF. It weakened Indian as well
as Sri Lankan domestic security.

In many ways, the presence of a foreign military
strengthened the fighting spirit of LTTE and weakened
the anti-terrorist capability of the Sri Lankan
forces. The organization gained mastery of guerrilla
warfare by fighting the fourth largest military
in the world. The LTTE suffered heavy causalities
but replenished their ranks and gained a confidence
paralleled by the Viet Cong and the Afghan mujahidin.
LTTE also innovated new weapons, mostly projectiles
and mines. Johnny mine, the anti-personnel
mine invented by Prabhakaran, has at least
claimed 5,000 Indian and Sri Lankan war
casualties. . . .[51]

India's credibility as a mediator and as a regional
power capable of controlling critical developments
and stabilising the situation suffered seriously

in the region and in the world at large. The Central Government's credibility with the people of Tamil Nadu has also been affected over the years because of the failure of the agreement.[52]

What were the flaws? What were the operational errors? Where did India go wrong? The flaws in our Sri Lankan policy in holistic or moral terms were as follows.

1. While Mrs. Gandhi's support for Sri Lankan Tamil aspirations was correct and justified, her policy of materially supporting Tamil militant separatists was wrong. India's interests and the Tamil cause which oriented her towards generating pressure on Jayewardene could have been pursued by political and diplomatic means instead of extending material support to Tamil militants.

2. Rajiv Gandhi's approach was more impartial between the Sinhalese and the Tamils. He pulled back from giving material support to Tamil militants. He and all of us who advised him were, however, not perceptive enough to fathom the deep psychological and emotional chasm between the Sinhalese and Sri Lankan Tamils which went beyond socio-economic and political factors.

3. We were over-optimistic about the change of mind in the Jayewardene Government and about the capacity for reasonableness amongst Tamil militant groups and Sri Lankan Tamils generally, which led India to sign the Indo-Sri Lanka Agreement. Both Jayewardene and Sri Lankan Tamils acquiesced in the agreement only for tactical purposes. Though being aware of this undercurrent, we expected our political will be backed by military force would overcome this lack of sincerity and reasonableness on the part of the Sinhalese and Sri Lankan Tamils. Our predications and expectations in these regards were wrong.

4. The Indian mediatory effort leading to the signing of the Indo-Sri Lanka agreement and the despatch of the IPKF to Sri Lanka in a manner were the inevitable consequences of the activists posture that we took

on the internal affairs of Sri Lank due to our strategic concerns and domestic ethno-political compulsions.

The power structure in India was initially unable to totally pull back from involvement in Sri Lankan affairs. Over and above all, all of us in the government of India involved in the Sri Lankan developments between 1983 and 1990 did not comprehend the collective mind-set and political psyche of the Indian people which has generally been averse to assertive or intrusive postures in inter-state relations, even if it affected our national interests. The Indian state despite desiring a regional power status and despite being keen on safeguarding national interests does not have the stamina to stick to controversial policies in an adversary ambience.[53]

Nor perhaps the desire or ambition.

In the concept of the IPKF and its employment there were repeated errors. For one, as observed, the power of a state is not its military alone, there are other elements: persuasive, economic, coercive, diplomatic. In the present instance, India perhaps emphasized only one, that is, the military, and not so much the others; for of the others it simply did not have any surplus, leave alone the exportable. Obviously there was no coordination between the agencies but was the assessment of intelligence itself adequate? Not if we examine the RAW-LTTE relationship. There was a failure even in assessing the LTTE supremo's personality attributes which High Commissioner Dixit, who dealt with him – indeed had to as a part of his duty – describes as being 'passionate, even obsessive' in his commitment to the cause of Tamil Eelam, his authoritarian and single-minded nature, his tactical cleverness and his resilience in adversity. But what do we attribute the other, greater failure to – of the lack of cohesion in operational aspect of Indian policies and harmonious coordination between different agencies of the Indian state in dealing with the crisis? To the incapacity of the political leadership of the time alone.

NOTES

1. Sir George Cunningham, the Governor of NWFP, has this entry in his Diary on 26 October 1947: 'Apparently Jinnah himself first heard of what was going on about 15 days ago, but said. "Don't tell me anything about it. My conscience must be clear." ' [Lt Gen (retd) ML Chibber, Lt Gen (retd) Sir James Wilson, 'The Truth', *USI Journal,* April-June 1997, p. 253.]
2. Jinnah also asked Mudle, the Governor of Punjab, to pass this order to Douglas Gracey from Lahore. There was some heated exchange on the telephone when Gracey did not agree. Ibid, p. 253.
3. Ibid., p. 254.
4. K. Subhramanyam, 'Terror Tactics: Pakistan's Hypocrisy on Kashmir', *The Times of India,* 21 October 1997.
5. *Peking Review,* May 1959.
6. Parliamentary proceeding Part 1 (1 12 of 1962).
7. Lorne J. Kavic, *India's Quest for Security: Defence Policies, 1947-65,* (Berkeley and Los Angeles: University of California Press, 1967) p. 21.
8. Ibid., p. 21.
9. Ibid., p. 21.
10. Ibid., p. 21.
11. R. MacFarqualer, 'War in the Himalayas, Crisis in the Caribbean' (notes from a forthcoming book).
12. Ibid.
13. Ibid.
14. Ibid.
15. K. Subhramanyam, *Evolution of Indian Defence Policy (1947-64).*
16. Richard Sisson and Leo E. Rose, *War and Secession: Pakistan, India, and the Creation of Bangladesh* (New Delhi: Vistaar Publications, 1990) p. 206.
17. Ibid., p. 207.
18. Ibid., p. 208.
19. Ibid., p. 209.
20. Ibid., p. 210.
21. Ibid., p. 211.
22. Ibid., p. 238.
23. Ibid., p. 239.
24. Ibid., p. 251.
25. Ibid., p. 252.
26. Ibid., p. 252.
27. Kissinger, statement to the Washington Special Action Group Dated 2 September 1971 (FOI document; the date of the meeting is not indicated in the records made available).

28. Richard Sisson and Leo E. Rose, op. cit., p. 260.
29. Ibid., p. 262.
30. Ibid., p. 263.
31. Ibid., p. 263.
32. Ibid., p. 263.
33. J. N. Dixit, *Assignment Colombo* (Delhi: Konark Publishers Ltd, 1997), p. 327.
34. Ibid., p. 328.
35. Ibid., p. 328.
36. Ibid., p. 329.
37. Ibid., p. 329.
38. Ibid., p. 330.
39. Ibid., p. 331.
40. Ibid., p. 332.
41. Ibid., p. 332.
42. Ibid., p. 338.
43. Ibid., p. 341.
44. Ibid., p. 342.
45. Ibid., p. 338.
46. Ibid., p. 338.
47. Ibid., p. 339.
48. Ibid., p. 339.
49. Ibid., p. 340.
50. Rohan Gunaratne, *International and Regional Security Implication of the Sri Lankan Tamil Insurgency* (International Foundation of Sri Lankan, 1997) p. 22.
51. Ibid., p. 22.
52. J. N. Dixit, op. cit., p. 343.
53. Ibid., p. 350.

4

Defence Spending and Force Structure[1]

PART 1

INTRODUCTION

Independent India inherited a post Second World War military. It had thus to simultaneously cope with partition, division of forces and military assets, reintegration, reorganization along with demobilization, even as the first and socialistically inclined Indian Government endeavoured to build a new India. Inevitably, therefore, the defence budget was as sharply reduced in quantum as were the Armed Forces devalued in the national hierarchy. The very first military challenge, the first war with Pakistan, following their invasion of the Indian state of Jammu & Kashmir, and the UN-sponsored cease-fire of 1948 sharply posed the question: was it to be defence or development?

This classic dilemma of guns or butter provided grist for a debate that effectively lasted until 1962, when it was brought to a sudden and a rude stop. As neither defence nor development ever have enough public funds, a search for the correct balance between security and development was not even seriously attempted. The accent was invariably on development; it was in any case both politically easier to make, as well as the right choice in terms of the challenges facing the country. But these decisions were not easy, because the two competing sets of demands were concerned with problems which had a definite impact on the polity. India on attaining independence was one of the least developed countries in the world, besides being one of the most endangered from the point of view of both external and internal threats – though the latter aspect was not at that time sufficiently appreciated. In the event, development received its due but at the expense of defence. In those early years, there could be no recognition of the fact that the armed forces were the weapon of last resort, the ultimate guarantor of law and order in the country.

There were other early inputs. Firstly, the entire process of defence budget allocations in an independent India was inherited from the British with no conceptual or procedural changes. Next, the aspects of winding down the special efforts of the just concluded world war. Thirdly, and specifically, the sheer difficulty of deciding "How much was enough?" for defence led the Indian Government and the people at large to adopt certain relatively simple criteria. This confusion was added to by the widespread ignorance of military matters (both within and without the Government) combined with an inherited sensitivity about the subject (being an imperial preserve till then) and an uncritical attitude towards both foreign and defence policies.

The ensuing analysis, delving into the actual budget figures, will show, among other things, that development was never actually sacrificed on the altar of defence. In this sense the debate was false as indicated by the fact that the country's defence has grown at an annual rate which consistently lagged behind the spending growth rate on social welfare and developmental programmes, as indeed even on debt servicing. That the debate is false is further proved by the fact that the heavy demands of capital for military equipment acquisition, upkeep and modernization notwithstanding, the defence capital allocation as portion of the Government's 'Non-

Plan' capital expenditure and of its total capital expenditure is on a sliding curve. But this was a traditionalist, non-innovative, rather bureaucratic, some might even say 1937, approach. The familiar, the known, the precedent always took precedence over change, and the undeniably vital need for it. In consequence, as this analysis will suggest, India's relative impecuniousness, far from motivating the armed forces into pursuing economical and innovative force-structuring policies, did not even keep them from getting locked into a capital-intensive mode of expenditure. What has been obtained is an in-date force featuring major weapons hardware but one that is short-legged and unable to fight wars of long duration. The analysis will further show that this was, and is, a relatively wasteful and skewed response to threats, present and potential.

The deconstruction of the Indian defence budget undertaken in this chapter does not go all the way back to the first of the defence budgets and for obvious reasons. The point that we attempt to make is that whatever the exigent circumstances, the apportionment of the defence funds between the Services and between the various arms/capabilities within the individual service, was invariably according to dated rationales, to ratios established long ago. This rigid pattern of military spending resulted in lopsided expenditures and in the building up of certain specific capabilities at the expense of other equally, if not more important missions. Also, this inflexible budget together with the fixation of each service to acquire evermore sophisticated weapons platforms meant that cost-effective solutions based on a more rational, combined arms approach, and a policy of incremental augmentation of capability (rather than of wholesale modernization by replacement) of the current inventory using force-multiplier technologies and by retrofitting advanced technology systems and subsystems on existing hardware, were eschewed.

The exercise that we undertake, though confined to the last twelve years only out of the five decades of independence, fully illustrates the fundamental shortcomings highlighted here. Threats multiplied and situations altered, but the system remained fixed, constant and unvarying.

ANALYSIS OF THE
INDIAN UNION BUDGET, 1985-97

National security is acknowledged as the first charge on the Treasury. For reasons not entirely clear, defence expenditure was early relegated to the 'Non-Plan' category within the ambit of a Soviet Union-inspired centrally planned economy established in India under the first prime minister, Jawaharlal Nehru. This socialist economic philosophy coupled with the secrecy phobia – a hangover from the British colonial rule – resulted in a permanently opaque military budget system. Thus, information about the impact of defence spending on the fiscal deficit, the inflation rate, the national debt, and on any other part or whole of the national economy is not easily available. Also, there is no information pertaining to the defence component of the country's manufacturing sector and of the Gross National Product, or the Gross Domestic Product, the fiscal multiplier effect of defence spending, and the returns on investment in defence research and development and in defence industrial plants in the public sector.

The following analysis is, therefore, based on the assumption that defence spending is 'exogenous' expenditure (unrelated to the state of the economy). This is taken to mean that in absolute numbers, the defence allocation in any given year may be more, but never less, than the floor established in the previous year.

METHODOLOGY IN GROUPING BUDGETARY
HEADS AND SUBHEADS

In order to get an analytic handle on the budgetary data, the heads and subheads or sub-aggregates are grouped as follows. For the macro-level expenditure analysis,
1. all plan and non-plan expenditures on revenue and

capital accounts for 'Economic Services', 'Social Services' and on 'Subsidies' (fertilizer, food, etc.) are consolidated separately and drawn together under the heading of 'Social welfare' expenditure;

2. all transfers in whatever form and through whatever channel in the revenue and capital budgets and in-plan and non-plan categories are aggregated as devolution to the constituent states and the Central Government-controlled Union Territories (UTs); and

3. an umbrella category called 'Total Developmental Expenditure' is conceived as the sum of the above two categories plus the spending on 'General Services' (meaning, roughly on the Government itself) and is a broad-based concept to indicate the end-benefit of government spending. (The 'benefit' is very loosely defined: it assumes that there is positive 'social benefit' even from a 'services' delivery system which delivers 'zero' benefits to the people.[2])

In this analysis, the 'actual', 'revised' and 'estimated' expenditure figures are held to be on par.

In the period 1985-97 when India's population grew by some 210 million, from about 750 million to 960 million, the total Government expenditure of Rs 43,632 crore increased over threefold to Rs 2,32,176 crore. In the same time-frame, the defence spending grew from Rs 7,061 crore to Rs 35,620 crore – a decline from 16.2 per cent to 15.3 per cent in the defence share of the Central Government budget, though obviously a fivefold increase in absolute terms. There was a corresponding tapering off of the double digit annual growth rate of the mid-to-late 1980s to an average 7.4 per cent in the 1990s. (The 21 per cent increase in the 1997-98 defence expenditure is mostly on account of the expected hike in the wage bill owing to the higher salaries and allowances recommended by the Fifth Pay Commission.)

Resources allotted to 'social welfare' (as defined above) ballooned from Rs 17,490 crore to Rs 1,16,501 crore, thereby retaining its top sectoral ranking. Indeed, as a proportion of the Union budget, it actually grew

FIGURE 1

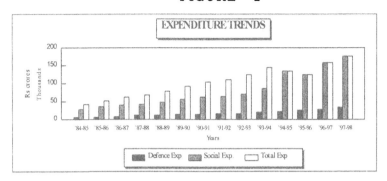

FIGURE 2

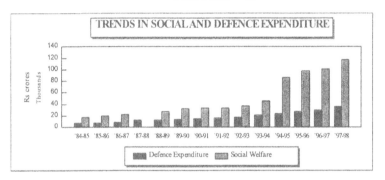

from 40 per cent in 1993-94 to 53.3 per cent the following year before sliding a little to 50.2 per cent in 1997-98. This expenditure, moreover, enjoyed a healthy 17 per cent annual growth rate for the last 13 years. This point is asserted by Sanjaya Baru:

Before assuring the Fund [International Monetary Fund] that there would be no cuts in expenditure on "social sectors and other core sectors of the economy", including rural development, welfare programmes and population control, the "Memorandum of Economic Policies for 1992-93" submitted by the Union Finance Minister Dr Manmohan Singh to the Managing Director of the IMF in June 1992 states: "Total defence spending is budgeted to rise by 7 per cent in nominal terms, resulting in a further real decline to 2.5 per cent of GDP." Clearly defence spending was not viewed as "core sector" expenditure (Sanjaya Baru, paper presented at an IDSA seminar, "Defence Expenditure: Management Budgeting", New Delhi, 1 February 1998).

The volume of transfers as loans and grants by the Centre to the provinces and Union Territories too jumped from Rs 9,709 crore in 1984-85 to Rs 43,983 crore in 1997-98. States are 'closer' to the people than the Central Government is the organizing principle of any federal polity. In the event, all manner of financial transfers to the constituent units should, in theory, be expected to percolate more quickly as benefits to the people. The direct Central grants-in-aid and other assistance to 'social welfare' programmes are likewise supposed to have downward beneficial reach and lateral spread (in terms of directly serving or affecting the people). Together they represent the two main avenues of delivering social welfare and development benefits. But, apart from subsidies (which herein are a component of the expenditure on social welfare), these two broad expenditure categories, along with defence, are sliding in terms of their growth rates.

The only consistently growing segment (at a healthy 14.9 per cent rate from 1984 to 1997) of the Indian budget, other than debt servicing is the 'General Services' head, which refers to the cost of Government and of the law and order apparatus. This suggests that economic liberalization and the pruning of Government-run programmes are all very good, but in the still overly bureaucratized Indian state the Government is the only proven growth industry.

Per capita expenditure is another universally recognized criterion to judge the slant of Government spending. Assuming the country's population for the base year 1984-85 as 75 crore and an annual rate of growth of 2 per cent, the per capita defence expenditure over the last 13 years has risen fourfold from Rs 94.5 in 1984-85 to Rs 371 in 1997-98. Meanwhile, per capita expenditure in every other major category has grown more impressively. For example, the per capita debt servicing has grown by over 18 times, the 'Social Welfare' spending by five times, and the per capita 'Total Development Expenditure' in excess of four and a half times.

This analysis has been generous in its acceptance of the broad expenditure rationales in that the value of a rupee spent on defence (in terms of output/outcome, in other words, performance) is assumed to be the same as that of a rupee expended on social welfare. In reality, of course, no such equivalence can be postulated simply because defence spending is more focussed and more result-oriented. Due to comparatively greater discipline and accountability and less leakage and wastage, the defence rupee secures more value-for-money and more 'public good' in terms of strengthened national security than an equivalent sum does for social welfare. However, the fact that the defence rupee is better utilized and higher defence outlays may be merited because of an increasingly unstable and unpredictable threat environment does not necessarily buttress the argument for increased levels of funding for the defence effort.

It is self evident that resource inelasticity affects all Government spending, including expenditure on defence. But it stands equally established that the armed forces cannot be permitted to degrade by denying them the monies to modernize and to keep them in fighting shape. That would be to court grave national danger.

This, however, is precisely what is perhaps inadvertently being achieved in terms of the mostly negative rates of growth (in seven of the last 13 years) of defence expenditure – in a period when the Government of India is supposed to have been particularly sensitive to defence requirements. In absolute terms, the defence capital budget as a proportion of the Government's Non-Plan capital budget and its total capital budget is sizeable, averaging 17.44 per cent in the former (since 1986-87) and 43.6 per cent (experiencing a sustained high in 1995-97 of some 61 per cent and a shocking low of 6.7 per cent in 1993-94) in the latter. However, when measured against the unpredictable increases from year to year of between 50 per cent and 350 per cent in the price of modern military equipment, spares and replacement systems, such levels of investment nevertheless have proved inadequate. For these reasons modernization of the armed forces and the beefing up of its holdings of equipments and spares have been slow, insufficient, fitful and very ad hoc.

Over the years it has resulted not only in sustained, appreciable and an all-round improvement in the warfighting abilities and stamina of the Indian military, but also in a fall-off in these respects, as later analysis will make clear.

DEFENCE EXPENDITURE TRENDS AND IMPLICATIONS, 1986/87 – 1997/98

India's defence budget is ordered on the basis of some archaic principles, which makes reliable analysis difficult. For example, purchase of capital military stock (major weapons systems) by the individual service is permitted under 'Aircraft and Aeroengine', while 'Heavy and Medium Vehicles' and 'Other Equipment' heads in the defence capital budget. The generic category 'Stores' in the defence revenue budget subsumes all spending on war stock (the totality of equipment spares, POL – Petroleum, Oil

FIGURE 3

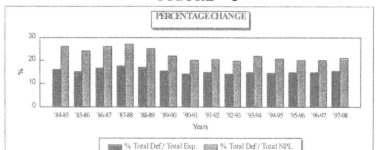

and Lubricants – food, apparel, tentage, and such other items necessary to sustain the existing forces in the peacetime training mode and during war). Stores also include maintenance spares (required for routine upkeep and servicing of all equipments and to replace material wasted in training and in war exercises), and on the War Wastage Reserve (WWR) – the total stock of ammunition, artillery shells, missiles and chemical explosives of all kinds. This hoary budgetary scheme has apparently been found to be not unsatisfactory.

In its desire to provide the Services with a consolidated sum of capital with which to meet all their material needs, whether new and replacement weapons, command and communications systems, technology add-ons and retrofits, spares of all kinds, ammunition, POL and other consumables, the Ministry of Defence (MoD), starting several years back, erased the distinction between the capital and revenue streams of the defence budget, even as the budget's traditional form was retained.[3] This has freed the armed forces from worrying about accounting problems but, and more importantly, it

1. confounds the problem of distinguishing the end-use of sanctioned funds,
2. conceals the extent of their allocations set aside for hardware and other buys, and
3. precludes criticism that funds that should have otherwise been used for replenishing the holdings of maintenance spares, WWR and the war stock, have been diverted mostly towards acquiring expensive armaments.

All defence expenditure, in theory at least, strengthens the country's military prowess. But this approach does not help to analyse the end-use of the defence rupee. Therefore, for the analysis of the defence budget which follows, an analytical schemata has been devised to focus on the quantum of budgetary resources spent on, or directly related to, warfighting or combat capability. Hence, all servicewise expenditure on 'Stores' in the revenue budget and on the acquisition of militarily useful material under various heads on the capital account is bunched together under the heading 'Combat Capability/

Warfighting'. It excludes capital expenditure on 'Land' and 'Construction'. (This is so because a good part of these expenditures pertain to social welfare infrastructure like housing, hospitals and clinics, for the use of servicemen and their families, which bear only indirectly on the country's warfighting capability. Such spending may, of course, include the construction of obvious warfighting assets, like 'hardened' hangars, blast walls in forward air bases, etc.)

To clarify some more, the expenditure on the 'warfighting or combat capability' for each of the three Services will comprise only the sums allotted to them for 'Stores' on the revenue account and for 'Aircraft and Aeroengines', 'Medium and Heavy Vehicles', and 'Other Equipment' on the capital account. The budgetary head 'Naval Fleet' in the capital budget will be the additional component in the Navy's expenditure on 'warfighting capability'. All spending to do with defence science and industry are clubbed under the category 'Defence Industry'. This includes the generic accounting heads 'Research and Development' and 'Special Projects' in both the revenue and capital budgets, and 'Defence Ordnance Factories' exclusively in the revenue budget and 'Naval Dockyards' in the capital budget.

ANALYSIS

Unlike elsewhere in the Government, the wage bill is not amongst the fastest rising elements in the defence budget. Nevertheless, it is ratcheting upwards at an average rate over the last ten years of 19.43 per cent, with extraordinary increases of 37.2 per cent in 1988-89, 18.6 per cent in 1992-93 and 52.3 per cent in the 1997-98 budget owing to the periodic revision in pay and allowances of all Government employees. The sum for pay and allowances has grown from Rs 2,943.6 crore and 28 per cent of the total defence budget of Rs 10,477 crore in 1986-87 to Rs 12,870.6 crore and 30.6 per cent of the defence allocation of Rs

35,620 crore in 1997-98.

While the pensions bill has nothing formally to do with the defence budget as such – being a separate charge on the Exchequer – its growth rate averaging three times as much as the expenditure on pay and allowances, suggests the kind of problems that may have to be faced in the future through overlarge pension liabilities to ex-servicemen. The former was Rs 694.58 crore in 1986-87 and Rs 3,715 crore in 1997-98, with an annual rate of increase in excess of 20 per cent. This figure will climb precipitously in the future when the retirees will draw much higher pensions pegged to markedly higher salaries as recommended by the Fifth Pay Commission. This further represents the snowballing effect of the pensionable 17-year-colour service norm, notwithstanding a near freeze in the numbers of those employed in the armed services.

Consider first the expenditure on the warfighting capability (as defined above) of the armed forces as a whole. It was Rs 5,202.62 crore and 49.7 per cent of the total defence budget in 1986-87. Some 11 years later, it is Rs 16,635 crore and 46.7 per cent of the 1997-98 budget of Rs 35,620, a slide that is especially worrisome considering the skyrocketing costs of military goods, both imported and indigenously produced.

If importation of defence wherewithal is not the answer considering the high foreign exchange outlays involved, there is no compensating policy to rely growingly on locally developed products either, since they will require enhanced and sustained investment in the domestic R&D projects and defence manufacturing sector. The spending on 'defence industry' (a category that was earlier described) has remained at the 4-6 per cent level of the defence budget, a niggardly sum considering that China's expenditure was over $5 billion in the defence R&D sector, i.e., some 8-12 per cent of its defence budget of $45 billion in 1994-95.

It is a different question altogether, whether higher spending without a radical overhaul of the defence public sector's way of doing things will produce substantially different results than in the past. Owing to the unrealistic requirements of planning by the Services, equally unrealistic R&D project planning by the Defence Research and Development Organization (DRDO), and the absence of long-term production planning by the 40-odd ordnance factories and research units and, worse, the continuing reluctance to sell indigenous arms abroad, the returns on the huge investments in the defence industry have been nowhere near commensurate. The capacity utilization moreover is abysmal, resulting in 'sunk costs' not being amortized and very high unit cost of Indian manufactured items whose quality the Services do not always trust.

The expenditure increases on warfighting capability grew at an average of 12 per cent every year from about the mid-eighties to 1993 before plunging to 4.9 per cent in 1997-98. On examining this expenditure, we find that the spending on 'Stores' as a proportion of the defence revenue budget, which had stabilized around the 40-45 per cent level in 1986-96, has slipped to the 35.5 per cent mark. Even as a proportion of the total defence budget, this spending has subsided from 46.3 per cent in 1986-87 to 26.6 per cent in 1997-98. But the expenditure on capital military stock for the three Services as proportion of the defence capital budget has risen quite spectacularly, from 46.3 per cent in 1986-87 to 82 per cent in 1994-95 before dropping marginally to 80.4 per cent in 1997-98.

Examining the defence expenditures more closely, the established pattern of slicing up the budgetary pie, servicewise, is discernible. The total outlays on defence are found to be cut up roughly in the ratio 1:2:4, with the Air Force and the Army getting some twice and four times as much as the Navy. This principle of division of financial resources is based on the presumption that the main threats to the country are land-based and the main instrument to deal with these threats, therefore, is the Army and, in a progressively high technology warfare milieu, the Air Force as a powerful adjunct to the land forces (but in the expenditure on the all-important consolidated warfighting capability category, the ratio falls to 1:2.6:2.7, with the Navy for the years 1986-87 to 1997-98 accounting for approximately 17 per cent of the funds expended on combat capabilities compared to 40 per cent for the Air Force and 43 per cent for the Army). However, the reasons for these expenditure ratios are hard to explain except in terms of accepted convention. Indeed, there is a built-in budgetary mechanism of dividing up the monies with the least recriminations and to cater to the Service ambitions of the Navy and the Air Force, as we shall see later.

The percentage breakdown of expenditure on 'Stores' in the revenue budget is 8 per cent for the Navy, 30 per cent for the Air Force and 62 per cent for the Army, in the ratio 1:3.75:7.75. However, it is in the investment in major weapon systems that the resource distribution evens out dramatically with the spending ratios of 1:1.2:1.7, with the Army and Air Force having only 1.2 times and 1.7 times the quantum available to them for purchases in the capital budget as the smallest (manpower-wise) Service, the Navy. This is the budgetary device which permits the 'junior' but more capital-intensive Services, Navy and Air Force, to garner, relatively speaking, an equal or larger chunk of the funds meant for procuring technologically advanced and prestigious armaments. This helps to mitigate inter-Service rivalry somewhat, realize individual Service ambitions and address status considerations (in terms of weapons profile).

It is significant that whatever the size of the total defence budget in any particular year, the ratios in which the budgetary allocations are divided do not depart greatly from these seemingly sacrosanct spending ratios.

On scrutiny, however, certain anomalies evident in the formal budgetary expenditure heads and figures are scrutinized. The expenditure on 'Stores' ought ideally to be correlated to the spending on new weapons and battlefield systems. Depending on the weapon system, holdings of maintenance spares and WWR worth anything between three and ten times the initial cost of the particular weapons system are recommended. By this reckoning, the Indian Army is slightly more prudent

FIGURE 4

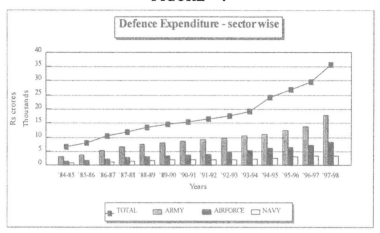

FIGURE 5

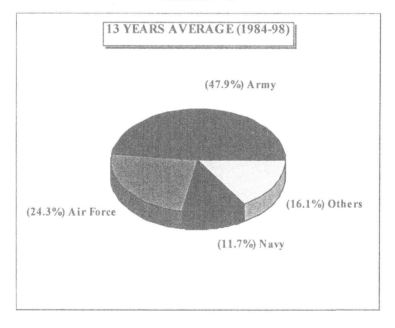

than the Navy or Air Force.
Expenditure on 'Stores' in recent years reveals that

the Army spent between two and three times as much on building up its WWR, and in replenishing its holdings of maintenance spares and of war stock for its inventory, as it did in buying new or replacement equipment. The record of the Navy and Air Force is more tilted. The Navy's capital expenditure has not only far exceeded its expenditure on 'Stores', but has grown disproportionately. Thus, while it bought Rs 332.80 crore worth of maintenance spares and Rs 753 crore worth of hardware in 1987-88, in 1996-97 and 1997-98, it paid out Rs 899.9 crore and Rs 990 crore on spares and for replenishing its WWR and Rs 1,954.75 crore and Rs 1,636.68 crore

FIGURE 6

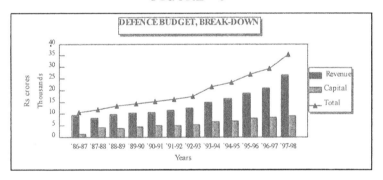

for capital acquisitions, respectively. It manifests the tendency to acquire major new weapons platforms first and worry about maintaining them in an effective state of war readiness later. This tendency is the starkest in the case of the Navy, with the Army having a record of two to three-to-one ratio of expenditures on spares and new equipment while the Air Force has achieved near parity between the expenditures on stores and major hardware acquisitions.

But such spending (reflected in the doing away of the line separating expenditure on the revenue and capital accounts) would appear to aggravate the problem of force readiness and staying power in war for all the three Services, especially so in the case of the

Air Force. Its need for spares support is much greater and far more critical than, say, the Navy's. A frigate or a submarine requires expensive servicing and refit periodically, but does not need the frequent maintenance attention a fighter aircraft does, for instance, with the consequent call-up and rapid use of spares. So even a one-to-one expenditure on spares support, new aircraft and other major systems is guaranteed very quickly to thin out the 'presence in the sky' by drastically cutting the ready availability of the fighting complement in the case of war. It is this paucity of spares which has, in fact, cut aircraft serviceability rates down to unacceptable levels.

DEFENCE DEMANDS:
PROBLEMS IN THE FUTURE

Financial planning for defence and force planning is an activity that centrally planned systems like India's are supposed to handle better than polities that do not believe in planning. Whether or not this was ever the case, the fact is that disjunctions between financial planning for defence and force planning have grown sharply in recent years and especially since the extension of the Eighth Five-Year Plan from its original end year in 1995 to 1997, necessitating the revision of the Eighth Defence Plan enabling it to converge once with the National Plan.

The Government of India refers to three main causative factors for this dislocation:
1. The cessation of defence credits from the erstwhile Soviet Union forcing the Indian military procurements to be done on a 'cash and carry' basis;
2. the economic restructuring in Russia and CIS leading to persistent demands for steep price hikes for defence exports to India; and,
3. the steep fall in the exchange value of the rupee resulting in an equally steep increase in the debt repayment obligations for past purchases from both

Western and Russian supply sources.

The consequences are the erosion and depletion of the already lean defence resources which is likely to continue into the foreseeable future. Hence, India's defence financial planning will continue to be out of sync with the Services' force planning and also because Russian/CIS pressures will persist owing to the 70-85 per cent dependency on ex-Soviet military equipment. This situation cannot be reversed quickly because the effects of, at best, a slower devaluation of the Indian currency relative to hard currency will mean restrictions on what and how much a shrinking defence rupee can buy from alternative Western sources.

India's defence demands are caught in a pincer of rising ruble and dollar value conjoined to, pricewise, dearer internationally available military hardware, spares and services. Therefore, almost any reasonable level of funding of defence programmes will be found to be inadequate to sustain the existing and planned force structure.

The three Indian armed services have 'Financial Planning' cells that are known to compute the costs of prospective modernization/acquisition programmes and of raising and maintaining various fighting units and formations; in this Part a very rough costing is, therefore, attempted.[4]

Perhaps the most difficult factor in calculating the cost involved in the upkeep of fighting formations and military hardware in good repair, are the figures assumed for 'military inflation'. From year to year, there is no relation in the increases in the cost of spares and whole replacement systems. The trends in cost growth cannot be anticipated and what financial planning and force planning is done is, therefore, routinely off-target, upset by factors and circumstances beyond the MoD's control.

ARMY

The Indian Army is today composed of three armoured divisions, nine independent armoured brigades and 29 infantry divisions. (In this analysis, no distinction is made between plains infantry divisions and mountain divisions because cost-wise there is little to distinguish them.)

An official study estimates that the initial and recurring costs of these three field formations for the years 1987-88 and 1989-90 (for which authoritative figures are available) show that in the two intervening years, the initial cost of forming an armoured division, independent armoured brigade and infantry division had gone up by 36 per cent, 54 per cent and 32 per cent, respectively. Similarly, the recurring costs (which includes the manpower cost, the cost of spares, POL, replacement equipment, and depreciation) for each of these three field formations rose by 140 per cent, 122 per cent and 55 per cent, respectively. Assuming the annual rates of growth in the initial cost and recurring cost of these field formations to be half of those prevailing in the above two-year set, the recurring cost in 1997-98 works out approximately to Rs 1,710.72 crore for an armoured division, Rs 587.52 crore for an independent armoured brigade and to Rs 397.44 crore for an infantry division. By this reckoning the total cost to upkeep the Indian Army's full strength could be in the neighbourhood of Rs 21,945.72 crore. Thus the total of the recurring costs (there being no new raisings and hence no initial costs) of three armoured divisions, of nine independent armoured brigades, and of 29 infantry could be Rs 5,132.16 crore, Rs 5,287.80 crore and Rs 11,525.76 crore, respectively.

The budget documents, however, show that the estimated total expenditure on the Army in 1997-98 is Rs 17,818.75 crore. The difference is due to a number of reasons. Firstly, as analysed earlier, the bulk of the Army formations, especially the armoured and mechanized forces and the artillery division-equivalent are, by and large, staying put in their bases or built-up areas, taking extreme care to minimize the wear and tear on equipment and to conserve holdings of spares, POL and war material generally, in order to free capital for acquisition purposes. In this regime of austerity, therefore, the full cost of running fighting formations will not be reflected. Secondly, there seems to be no accounting in the Services' budget of the cost of fielding the 36-odd Rashtriya Rifles battalions in the Internal Security (IS) role in Kashmir and elsewhere. The Rashtriya Rifles is a specialist counter-insurgency force, manned, officered and controlled by the Army, and paid for by the Ministry of Home Affairs (MHA). But the MHA, is not as quick in paying the Army for their use as it is in calling up the Rashtriya Rifles.[5] Consequently, the Army has to make an allowance within its current budget to absorb the cost of their deployment until such time as it is reimbursed by the MHA.

NAVY

Factoring capitation rate for personnel, fuel, spares support, etc., the actual cost of putting major naval combatants out to sea is enormous.

Due to reasons mentioned earlier, Indian Navy ships are out at sea only about seven days a month, i.e., only a third of the time they would normally spend on operational tasks which could be between 168 and 252 days. Even so, the actual running costs for 84 days of sailing in 1997, for instance, for all classes of ships are huge. For the 26 Corvettes (or smaller sized ships) it will cost Rs 76.4 crore, for the 19 frigates Rs 100.6 crore, for the 13 submarines around Rs 61.2 crore, for the 38 OPV/minesweeper-countermeasures ship/survey vessels Rs 71.5 crore, for the five destroyers Rs 29.4 crore, the lone aircraft carrier Rs 20.14 crore, and for the two tankers Rs 7.3 crore. The total running costs for all ships is in the order of Rs 360.4 crore.

The Navy's allocation in the 1997-98 budget meant for fighting assets and capabilities is Rs 2,626.68 crore.

Deducting the running costs (of Rs 360.4 crore) will leave Rs 2,266.28 crore. (There's an element of double debiting here because the stated running costs have factored into them personnel costs. But, because the complement of naval manpower ashore is larger than that afloat and because the numbers of personnel out to sea are relatively small due to operational restrictions in force since the early nineties, the double debiting problem is considered negligible.)

In the absence of financial and other constraints, the running costs for a normal time of 168 to 252 days at sea would have totalled between Rs 677.2 crore and Rs 1,081.4 crore. The Navy apparently caters for this level of expenditure for 'days at sea' but uses the savings generated from only 84 days on operational duty to make up for the shortfall in funding of, among other things, sanctioned shipbuilding programmes, which have escalated several-fold in cost. This much is obvious from the higher price tags for designated warship-building projects underway. For example, the Cabinet Committee of Political Affairs (CCPA) approved Rs 120 crore for Project 16A, the Brahmaputra-class frigate, the follow-on to the Godavari class. However, it is likely to end up costing well over Rs 400 crore, i.e., a cost escalation of 333 per cent. (The comparable cost for the Godavari class rose from Rs 93.4 crore in 1984 to Rs 161.33 crore for the INS Gomti in 1989, a hike of 172.73 per cent.)

The cost escalations of other programmes are expected to be just as large for other projects approved by the CCPA. For instance, the sanctioned cost of the Delhi-class missile destroyer (a Kashin derivative) under Project 15 will increase by 238 per cent (i.e., from Rs 294 crore to Rs 700 crore per ship) and the Kora-class corvette (four on order) under Project 25A by 390 per cent (i.e., from Rs 57.7 crore to Rs 225 crore). Compare such cost escalations – a penalty for the essentially indigenous nature of designing and manufacturing these ships – with the capital funding for the Navy in the 1997-98 budget, of Rs 1,636.68 crore.

Indeed, if the escalating costs of continuing shipbuilding programmes are added up and matched with new inductions into the Navy over the last several years and the level of naval expenditure considered in these years, it is clear that the Indian Navy could not have afforded to at once maintain a high state of readiness and to continue with the warship construction and, albeit, a slower rate of induction of finished vessels. The pattern of diminishing ship strength is reflected in the 1976-96 period when the major seagoing surface combatants – the frigates and destroyers – declined in number from 31 to 24, a decline in ship strength of 22 per cent. The second aircraft carrier, Virat, added to the fleet in the second half of the eighties, was a replacement boat and along with the HDW and Kilo-class submarines, did nothing to compensate for a diminished force profile. Most of the Soviet Foxtrot-class submarines and the carrier Vikrant had to be formally retired in 1997, as they dropped rapidly in operational effectiveness.

In the event, with the Service being reduced essentially to a one-carrier Navy since at least 1991-92, the surprise is that it has continued to add to the carrier-borne aircraft fleet. There are 39 Sea Harriers in the Indian naval inventory. With only 12 such planes embarked on Viraat, the surplus holdings of 27 aircraft would appear to be excessive and is indicative of an uneconomical expenditure choice, even if there is an 'air defence' ship available to replace Vikrant.

In brief, because the phasing-out rate of old ships outstrips the induction rate of new ones (as we shall see in another Part of this chapter) and the funding in the defence budget has not kept pace with the increases in the costs of new vessels, the Indian Navy is resorting to desperate measures, diverting funds even from operational tasks to shipbuilding and replacement in order to retain the present ship strength into the future.

AIR FORCE

To state the conclusion first: The Indian Air Force has focussed, like its sister services, to a significant extent on acquiring a larger and technologically more advanced arsenal. Limitations of the defence rupee has resulted in less than necessary outlays on expensive spares support and aviation fuel. In turn, this has imposed severe restrictions on operational training resulting in lower pilot combat skills and a reduced all-round state of readiness.

Taking the 1997-98 budget as a representative one of the last few years, we see that of the total Air Force budget of some Rs 8,763 crore, about 81 per cent is ostensibly meant for acquisitions (with the Stores category in the revenue budget showing Rs 3,253 crore and the 'Aircraft and Aeroengine' and 'Other Equipment' heads in the capital budget another Rs 3,817 crore), 14.4 per cent is to meet the payroll liability and 4 per cent of the remaining outlays spent on the bases and support structures. The Air Force budget in 1997-98 available for combat capabilities (including acquisitions) is about Rs 7,070.58 crore. With each new aircraft costing Rs 155 crore (calculated on the basis that the contract signed in 1996 for 40 Su-30MKs was worth Rs 6,200 crore), this sum will procure no more than 45 advanced fighter aircraft along with some spares support. The numbers of aircraft that need to be replaced (because of obsolescence) and owing to a high 'Category 1' or 'Category E' accident rate averaging a loss of 22 frontline aircraft or a squadron every year,[6] exceed the number of replacement aircraft that the IAF can theoretically buy for the allotted sum.

If there is seemingly little money left over for operational flying and to maintain a high state of readiness, it is because combat aircraft are very costly to fly and to upkeep.

Given the financial stringency and the service's own priority, IAF pilots on an average log only around half the hours in the air per month as compared to US

Air Force pilots. Moreover, because of problems with the Russian suppliers and the need to conserve spares, the serviceability of aircraft is down to an average of 50 per cent for all types of aircraft. Assuming the squadron strength (which differs) to be a uniform 16 aircraft and the average flying time to be 10 hours/month per aircraft the cost of operating the various types are approximately as follows: for four squadrons of MiG-29 Rs 883.2 crore, three squadrons of Mirage 2000 Rs 662.4 crore, five squadrons of Jaguar Rs 1,104 crore, the squadron of eight Jaguars converted to maritime strike role Rs 110.4 crore, and for the four Su-30 MKs Rs 110.4 crore.

Additionally, the bill for flying 22 squadrons of MiG-21 is Rs 728.64 crore, six squadrons of MiG-27 and two squadrons of MiG-23BN Rs 358.28 crore, six squadrons of AN-32 is Rs 66.24 crore and 45 Ilyushin-76s Rs 207 crore for a grand total of Rs 3,177 crore for all operational flying by the IAF. This leaves Rs 3,893.58 crore out of the service budget nominally provided for all combat-related activity, other than limited operational flying.

The cost of imported combat aircraft, as indicated by the Sukhoi deal notwithstanding, we shall assume that only the accident losses of 22 or so planes every year are to be made up but exclusively from the indigenous MiG-27 production line costing Rs 35 crore. The replacement bill will then amount to Rs 770 crore, leaving Rs 3,123.6 crore for building up reserves of spares, purchase of new aircraft, hardware like aerial refuellers, funding programmes for aircraft/systems updatement and retrofitment for force augmentation. This cost estimate is because of the best possible spin being put on the IAF's requirements and liabilities and by leaving out whole categories of aircraft out of the reckoning, like transport planes and helicopters. All the same, this breakdown of expenditure does not make sense for one main reason, i.e., it leaves too little money to invest in the many ongoing high priority infrastructure programmes like improving the surveillance radar along the western border.

This suggests that the present policy of favouring a fairly high level of new aircraft induction has been bought dearly at the expense of force readiness. This appears to have been the norm for the IAF over the last 15 years as it has boasted of a 40 per cent increase in the costliest element of any air force, namely, in the strength of the sophisticated strike and air superiority/counter air aircraft with the entry into squadron service of MiG-29s, Mirage 2000s and lately the Su-30MKs. The result is two-pronged: the pilot's flying and aerial combat skills degrade and the force experiences a lower state of readiness/preparedness because of diminished aircraft serviceability rates.

Unbalanced Force Development
The professed aim of the military in major countries is to have a 'balanced' force size-wise comparable and comprising capable land, air and naval forces. This is true of the Indian defence services, but with a telling difference. What balance has been achieved over the years is between the various mission capabilities within the service, not across service lines and in the national force structure as a whole.

The Navy, for example, spends a nearly equal amount on the 'sea control' mission, i.e., on capital ships (aircraft carriers, frigates and destroyers) and on coastal defence (corvettes, minesweepers/mine countermeasures, fast missile attack craft, inshore boats), in which the expenditure is 1.8 times more than on the 'sea denial' assets (submarines). There is likewise a semblance of parity between the spending on armour and plains infantry within the Army's budget and between the Air Force expenditures on, say, the air superiority/counter air forces and the air strike capabilities.

However, there is simply no balance between the expenditures on mission capabilities (as percentages of the total defence budget) across the services. While the monies for all naval mission capabilities amount to only 1.22 per cent of the defence budget and the combined expenditure on all mission capabilities for the

Air Force – the most technology- and capital-intensive service – in terms of buying and maintaining the wherewithal, amounts to just 12.87 per cent of the total defence budget, the spending levels on the Army's armoured forces, the plains infantry and mountain divisions (which constitute the principal mission heads) are 29.25 per cent, 21.20 per cent and 11.16 per cent, respectively.

When the individual service expenditure pattern is deconstructed and then juxtaposed against each other and the total defence budget, the extent of the sheer imbalance between the prevailing military capabilities becomes obvious. For instance, the spending on the potentially decisive strike capability (in any future war) – the Air Force's Jaguars, MiG-23s and MiG-27s – account for only 4.71 per cent of the total defence budget. The Mirage 2000s and MiG-29s in the air superiority/counter air role enjoy funding which is just 4.34 per cent of the defence expenditure, with the bulk air defence aircraft, the MiG-21s, accounting for 2.05 per cent, the strategic airlift important for resupplying troops in mountainous areas, for facilitating the switching of forces between different theatres of war and for out-of-area operations, 1.77 per cent of the entire defence expenditure.

This is an egregiously skewed expenditure pattern and reflects priorities which are, correlation-of-forces-wise, growingly irrelevant and which may begin to exact a heavy cost in terms of neglected capabilities in the

FIGURE 7

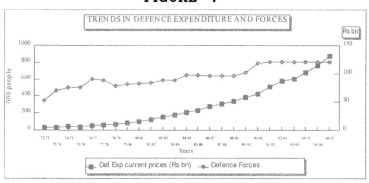

future. Such an expenditure mosaic also disproves the by now classic belief that South Asia is inclined towards an arms race, initiated by India or Pakistan, implying a certain action-like reaction sequence at work. What is established however is that India's defence expenditure priorities have largely become autonomous. Not being geared to any realistic assessment of threats, they serve only to strengthen certain, already formidable, select warfighting capabilities, while de-emphasizing others which, considering the military developments, weaponization and technology trends in the region and the world at large, legitimately require more attention.

PART 2

DEFENCE SPENDING AND FORCE PROFILES (INDIA, CHINA AND PAKISTAN)

India's defence policy since independence has had a limited compass, both in terms of geography and operational latitude. Pakistan and China apparently define the limits of India's national security interests, and the ability militarily to counter them has determined India's forked force structure – the fighting capabilities for mainly plains warfare against Pakistan and the quite separate and distinct mountain warfare assets to tackle the Chinese threat.

Moreover, there are similarities in the closed, essentially dyadic, India-Pakistan, India-China loops in the regional security system. For instance, each of the constituents have in the recent past undergone a cathartic military defeat – India's military humiliation in the 1962 Himalayan War, Bangladesh's secession from Pakistan with Indian military help and China's costly intrusion into Vietnam in 1979. These led to higher defence expenditures which has come under pressure in recent years due to economic constraints. Consequently, defence expenditures are plateauing out in the case of India and Pakistan, and slowing down in China. However, the still significant part of

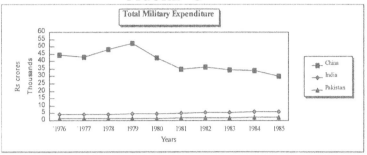

FIGURE 8

the Chinese GNP dedicated to defence, combined with an economy growing at an average of 12-15 per cent in real terms annually, means that the Chinese defence establishment continues to have increasing growing larger financial resources at its command, even as the defence share of central government expenditure and GNP declines.

The impact of this disparity in funding levels between India and Pakistan on the one hand and China on the other, is seen in the inadequate numbers and inferior quality of force augmentation and modernization. Besides, the military doctrine and thinking undergirding these programmes of force upgradation and reorientation (in the wake of their respective military crisis) in China and Pakistan took different routes with a differential impact on Indian security. India, consequently, is losing ground, as we shall see, in terms of deployable weapons platforms, combat capability and of an operational edge vis-à-vis the larger, more long-term threat, China, and in some crucial respects against Pakistan too.

In the ensuing sub-sections, the defence spending and force structures are analysed in five-year sets, starting with 1976-77. Appreciable changes since the mid-1970s in the inventories and hence in the weaponization trends and in war doctrines (as reflected in the extent and quality of the arms holdings) are clear and can be studied as the effect of defence spending over the preceding 4-5-year periods.

DEFENCE SPENDING

There is a methodological difficulty in estimating the true national security expenditures of China and Pakistan. Official Chinese data is supposed purposely to leave out vast defence expenditure streams out of the public view by accounting for most military capital expenditures on weapon systems acquisitions and on defence R&D under such obscure heads as 'Building National Strength' and 'the Central Military Commission' or in some other guise.[7] Budget documents in Pakistan traditionally carry only a one-line mention about the size of defence funding and little else.

Many organizations are involved in the annual exercise of deducing the defence budget figures for such countries. The computational difficulty is best reflected, for instance, in the case of the Chinese defence expenditure, say, for 1990. The International Institute of Strategic Studies (IISS), London, playing it safe, gives the figure as ranging between $11 billion and $23 billion – an implied range of error amounting to $12 billion or exactly twice the size of the Indian defence expenditure in 1994-95! The IISS figure of $11 billion is at the low end with the highest estimate being $36.5 billion as calculated by the Stockholm International Peace Research Institute (SIPRI), with the Indian Institute of Defence Studies and Analyses (IDSA)'s assessment of $20.02 billion and the US State Department Arms Control and Disarmament Agency (ACDA)'s $22.33 billion falling in between.

INDIA-CHINA

Defence spending is a function of the size of a country's economy. Considering that China and India were amongst the most impoverished in the 1950s, the pronounced gap in the military expenditures of the two countries can only be explained by the different strategies and plans and the matching priorities accorded to defence by their Governments. The data shows that the Indian defence outlay for 1956 (used as the startline and appropriate as 1956 saw the first definite indications of the coming border clash with Communist China) of $760 million (compared to $174 million for Pakistan) was one-twelfth that of the Chinese level of $9.1 billion (at 1973 dollar value).

This degree of disparity was maintained right up to 1959, with the gap actually growing in 1961 when the Indian defence outlays were one-thirteenth the size of its Chinese counterpart. In 1962, India's level of military spending was one-eleventh of the Chinese, closing to a little less than one-eighth in 1963. The margin widened to one-twelfth in 1966, dipping down to one-thirteenth of the Chinese quantum for several years running (1967-74) before beginning to close very gradually.

The Indian defence spending level became one-seventh in 1981, one-fifth in 1985, and rose to half of the Chinese level during the years of the sudden 'bulge' in Indian defence spending (1987-90). In more recent times, however, the disparity in expenditures is beginning to grow yet again from one-third of the Chinese level in 1991 to approximately a quarter in the mid-1990s. What is most striking is that while in the case of China, wars and crises are invariably anticipated and planned for and financial provisions appear to be made well in advance to ensure that the military has both sufficient time and resources to prepare itself for any eventuality, there seems to be no such corresponding relationship between threat and military preparation with regard to India.

Indeed, the Indian Government's reading of threat and the possibility of conflict has been consistently wrong at least *vis-à-vis* China and forward contingency planning has all but absent. This much is obvious from the lack of increased military funding in the years prior to the 1962 crisis, which could have signalled Indian readiness to respond forcefully if provoked and conceivably deterred the potential adversary. In India, increases in defence spending have occurred usually as a panicky reaction to impending hostilities or, as in

1962, a disastrous war. Consider the evidence. From 1956 to 1962, China simultaneously prepared for two major conflicts – over the offshore Quemoy and Matsu Islands and the Sino-Indian border. The defence budget registered a steep rise over the seven years, from $9.1 billion to $13.7 billion, indicating sustained military build-up prior to hostilities.

In the early 1970s, there were border clashes with the Soviet Union on the Ussuri River and by the middle of that decade the possibility of a full-scale war loomed large. Chinese defence outlays doubled (at 1973 prices) from $15.5 billion in 1963 to $32.3 billion in 1974, jumping in 1976 by over a third (at 1980 prices) to $44.7 billion. This experience compelled China in 1978 to include military upgradation as one of the 'Four Modernizations' that the country was programmatically embarked upon. The aim was to realize a modern, technologically advanced military which could, by the year 2000, hold its own both tactically and strategically against a first world rival. In 1979, the defence spending level touched $52.6 billion, some 10.4 per cent of the GNP and accounted for 32.8 per cent of the total central government expenditure.

The years of consistently high allocations to the military had apparently provided the People's Liberation Army (PLA) with the confidence and the wherewithal to teach a 'lesson' to Vietnam, with whom Chinese relations were quickly souring. The ensuing defeat further confirmed the weaknesses of a primitive foot-soldier-dominated PLA and spurred the military modernization thrust.

In the period 1956-61, Indian spending levels stayed low, rising from $760 million (at 1973 prices) to $914 million in 1957 before, incredibly, subsiding to $905 million a year later and to $844 million in 1959. It rose notionally to $848 million in 1960 and reached only $911 million in 1961, registering a negative rate of growth in two of these five years and a near zero level growth in the third at a time when the situation was 'hotting up'. The spending level did rise by 7 per cent to $1,256 million in 1961 but with, predictably, little impact on the war in the following winter. Compare these figures with the Chinese expenditure levels in 1960 and 1961 of $10,000 million and $11,800 million, respectively. The difference in the outlays hints at the differing levels of combat capability the two sides were able to muster for the fight.

The defence spending pattern subsequent to the war points out another disturbing characteristic of Indian policy, namely, the slide quickly into complacency once the immediate crisis was over. The 1962 war proved the need, heretofore neglected, for vigilance and the emplacement of a strong force on the disputed border in order to deter China and, in the worst case, successfully to fight the PLA. To have a meaningful conventional deterrent, however, required the mobilization of massive resources on a sustained basis. This did not happen. The defence expenditure galloped upwards all right, by 37.8 per cent to $2,055 million in 1963 – still only 1.9 per cent of the country's GDP and 19.61 per cent of the total central government expenditure, but apparently only as a reaction to the military defeat the previous year. Almost immediately thereafter it began slipping again, until 1971 and the prospect of another war, when the defence budget broke the $2 billion barrier last breached eight years earlier!

INDIA-PAKISTAN

The higher defence spending of the post-1962 period no doubt enabled the Indian armed forces in the 1965 war with Pakistan, but the fact remains that that war eventuated in an impasse revealed the inadequacy of this kind of funding when faced with the situation of dealing with two disparate, and nominally collaborating enemies active on geographically diverse fronts.

To get a better perspective on what level of defence spending can reasonably be afforded by a country and what priority is accorded by the government, let us look at the Indian and Pakistani defence expenditures as proportions of their respective Gross Domestic Products and of their central government expenditures. In 1963, the Indian defence expenditure was 4.4 per cent of its GDP of Rs 185.5 billion; its share of central government expenditure was 25.5 per cent. Two years later, these figures were 4.02 per cent (even as GDP increased to Rs 220 billion) and 22.5 per cent. Pakistan's GDP was only Rs 23 billion in 1963 (roughly one-eighth of India's) and its defence share was some 5 per cent. The Pakistani defence outlay accounted for fully 55.8 per cent of the central expenditure.

In the year (1965) of two discrete wars (over the Rann of Kutch in February and along the entire border in September), the Pakistani defence expenditure as a proportion of the GDP had grown to 9.9 per cent and of the central expenditure to 63.5 per cent. This last was the highest level reached except for the 74.2 per cent share of all government expenditure a year later in Pakistan. These relatively high levels in that particular timeframe can be attributed to the Army (Field Marshal Ayub Khan) run government in power. Interestingly, civilian rule in 1972-79 and since 1985 has, if anything, improved upon some of these proportions. In 1972 Pakistan spent 7.5 per cent of the country's GDP and nearly 54 per cent of its central government expenditure on defence.

It was during the first Benazir Bhutto regime that

FIGURE 9

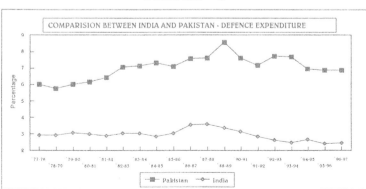

Pakistani defence allocation in 1988-89 reached 8.56 per cent of GDP, the highest ever after the 9.9 per cent level achieved in 1966-67. In any case, the Pakistani defence spending has hovered in the plus/minus 7.5 per cent of GDP range throughout the 1980s and so far into this decade, indicating the very high priority accorded to defence.

Contrarily, the Indian defence expenditure level got pegged to the GDP and floated between a low of 3.19 per cent to a high of 3.78 per cent (except for the unusual 4.04 per cent in 1986-87) in the last decade. It further plummeted to 2.5 per cent and 2.44 per cent of GDP in 1992-93 and 1993-94, respectively. The defence portion of the central government expenditure has, likewise, been dropping steadily, from a high of 25.63 per cent in 1969-70 to 19.19 per cent ten years later to 14.45 per cent in 1991-92. There has, however, been an upturn to 15.3 per cent in 1997-98. In the context of both the Chinese and the Pakistani defence expenditure trends, the prospects for India are not bright.

FIGURE 10

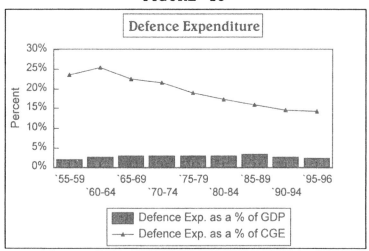

Looking at the whole picture, it is clear that India has got caught in a spiral of relative decline in military expenditure. The Indian defence expenditure as a percentage of the central government expenditure has come down, from 17.55 paise of every rupee in 1986-87, to 13 paise in 1997-98. 'Even Jane's Sentinel Regional Security Assessment, India 1997 concedes that India's defence spending "remains modest compared to other countries with major security concerns" ' (Sanjaya Baru, op. cit., quoting from Jane's Information Group, Surrey, UK). The outcome is that China is placing a greater distance between itself and India in terms of ever larger resources allotted to the military with Pakistan catching up.

Besides, the difference in spending levels between India and Pakistan is not quite as telling on the latter because the funds that India sets aside for defence have to be expended on a force structure with its attention split between two very different kinds of threats posed by Pakistan and China, requiring in the main two entirely different types of military wherewithal. Pakistan's military focus, on the other hand, is exclusively on India.

FORCE STRUCTURING

Post-1962 War

The 1962 winter war with China was a watershed. Far more political attention began to be paid to the armed forces and commensurately greater financial resources were channelled for their modernization. It may be surmised that beginning formally with the 1963 defence budget, programmes to strengthen the military were initiated on the basis of a long-term perspective plan. The programmes that were realized make sense only if it is assumed that in the 15-year defence plan framework ending around, say, 1978, the chief concerns were to develop capabilities to deal with primarily landward threats from China and Pakistan. The war with Pakistan in 1965 and again, over Bangladesh, in 1971, combined with threatening moves made by China on both occasions, tended to validate the Indian military's threat appreciation embedded in the planned augmentation of its capabilities in that period.

Thus, the 'baseline' force obtaining in 1964-65 after the initial beefing up comprised 16 infantry divisions, nine of them for mountain warfare, with four more infantry divisions forming; an armoured division with the heavy British Centurion Tank, an armoured brigade with the Second World War vintage Sherman Tanks and two light tank regiments each with the French AMX-13s and the British Stuarts; a naval fleet of one aircraft carrier, two cruisers, three destroyers, five anti-submarine frigates, three anti-aircraft frigates and five other escort ships for a total surface combatant force of 19 ships; and the Air Force of ten fighter-bomber squadrons (six with the British Hunter aircraft, four with the indigenous HF-24 Maruts), eight squadrons of interceptors (four Gnat, four Mystere IV) and four squadrons of light bombers, Canberras – altogether 22 squadrons (not including several transonic squadrons of French Ouragon and British Vampire fighter bombers phasing out) out of a sanctioned force of 45 squadrons.

What is particularly remarkable is that the accelerated pace set for mountain warfare capability meant that within a year and a half of the 1962 war, the bulk (nine divisions) of the authorized 11 mountain divisions – mainly against the Chinese threat – had been formed and forward positioned. Most of the accretions in the Army's mountain infantry strength, the Air Force's Gnat, HF-24 and Canberra squadrons, and of the aircraft carrier Vikrant to the Navy, were financed by defence expenditures totalling Rs 1,579.57 crore (current prices) for the years 1961-62 to 1963-64. By 1967-68, the defence expenditures in the intervening three years totalling Rs 2,599.15 crore, the 1964-65 baseline force in the main had grown too: to the seven plains infantry divisions (marked for action against Pakistan), five more divisions were added (even as the mountain warfare capability remained static at nine divisions); into the Navy were inducted four Soviet F-class submarines. Air Force strength grew to 500 (from 430 combat aircraft, with 60 MiG-21 interceptors joining 20 more Gnats to replace the aging Mysteres and the under-performing HF-24s.

At the time of the last of India's wars in December 1971, the Indian orbat featured a further increase in the 1964-65 baseline force with, in the main, the armoured division of 200 Centurions buttressing two independent armoured brigades with 450 T-54/55 and 300 newly inducted Vijayanta tanks. The 13 infantry and ten mountain divisions had, as backups, six independent infantry brigades and two parachute brigades. Other than the coastal defence variety of ships, one general-purpose frigate joined nine new destroyer escorts (ex-Soviet Petya class) in the seagoing naval holdings. All this new weaponry was acquired with the total defence spending (from 1967-68 to 1971-72) of Rs 5,827.12 crore.

In this period, only one mountain division was added for the China front. Taking 1978 as the last year of the hypothesized 15-year Defence Plan set in motion in the fiscal year 1963, where was the change and growth in the Indian force profile from 1971-72 to 1979-80? The mountain divisions reached their sanctioned strength (11), one new armoured division was formed and three new independent armoured brigades raised (with 1,900 tanks in all, divided equally between the Soviet T-54/55s and the Indian-built Vijayantas of British Vickers-Armstrong design), and the plains infantry strength went up by three divisions (achieved by reconstituting the six independent infantry brigades and one of the two parachute brigades). The artillery arm which, as late as 1967-68, had 2,500 pieces, mostly ex-British 25-pounders, had ten years later a predominantly Soviet look (100 mm, 130 mm, 203 mm guns and 120 mm and 160 mm mortars). The destroyer/frigate flotilla was consolidated at 22 ships (including the four Leander class but otherwise a growingly Soviet-origin fleet) and to the seaward defence capability were added 16 Osa-class fast missile boats and three Ninochka corvettes. The IAF had by now 620 combat aircraft (16 FGA squadrons – four Su-7, four Hunter F56, three HF-24, five Gnat), 14 interceptor/FGA squadrons (with 252

MiG-21 PF/FL/PFMA/MF/bis/U), and three squadrons of Canberra bombers.

From the time the deal was struck for the off-the-shelf purchase followed by licensed manufacture of the MiG-21 in the mid-1960s to the time when the force structure was dominated by ex-Soviet equipment, a little over a decade had elapsed. This Sovietization of its arsenal has had deep ramifications for India's financial and force planning and, more importantly, for the operational readiness of Indian forces, as we shall presently see.

The post-1962 military growth in India may have been primed essentially by the twin China-Pakistan threat, and the subsequent force was planned on the basis of the capability to fight two wars at the same time. But the substantive growth in operational strength was keyed to the demands of the western front. This may be seen in the growth over the next 15 years and thereafter of the armoured forces and plains infantry in the Army and of the relatively short-range strike, interception and interdiction aircraft in the Air Force capabilities which could be used mostly against Pakistan.

As we have seen, by 1964-65 nearly 82 per cent of the authorized mountain warfare capability was already in place with no further major expenditure undertaken in this field. No major weapons meant specifically for the over-the-Himalayas kind of operations, were acquired as an obvious follow-up. For instance, the only sure way to deter Chinese actions across the Tibet, Sikkim and Arunachal Pradesh borders is to be able to hit valuable strategic targets, like those in Xinjiang (where most of the Chinese nuclear weapons installations are located) or deeper into China proper. The India-China war had actually exacerbated the late 1950s' Sino-Soviet rift and the Soviets further tried to strategically discomfit China by offering India long-range bombers including the Tu-22 with the necessary reach.

Only in 1996 was this requirement discovered in order to justify the procuring of 40 Su-30 MK aircraft with the long-range and nuclear-ordnance carrying capacity to deal with the Chinese threat. Prior to the Sukhoi deal, there were no Indian aircraft with the radius of action to reach targets even midway inside Tibet, let alone mainland China, and no aerial refuellers in the inventory – there still are none – to permit the existing strike aircraft (like the Jaguars and the Mirage 2000s) to extend their range.

On its part, the Indian Government is in a hurry to obtain the genuine strategic strike capabilities afforded by the Agni intermediate range ballistic missile, even as some 20-30 nuclear warhead-carrying medium-range ballistic missiles emplaced in Tibet are targeted at India. The Indian Navy too does not have the comparable reach and clout of the Chinese Navy which has conventional and nuclear-armed, nuclear-powered submarines that can operate at will in the Bay of Bengal or anywhere else in the Indian Ocean. In its Xia-class boats embarking a dozen submarine-launched ballistic missiles, moreover, China has the means to hit any Indian target when fired from positions as far away as in the Yellow Sea.

THE TREND TOWARDS 'HEAVY' WEAPONS SYSTEMS

It is a corollary of military growth that the forces over time gravitate towards the heavier equipment. This growth in the size and the sophistication of weapons systems, ends up being expensive as the cost penalties imposed by this growth trend in weapons means that no country can afford a continual across-the-board transition to growingly bigger, better, more lethal, weaponry. In the event, the choice of which combat capability to 'modernize' and 'upgrade' gets restricted. The consequence of selecting certain types of warfighting wherewithal for modernization means that other mission areas suffer relative neglect.

Worse, the initial measures taken, perhaps prudently, for a massive enhancement of capabilities in these select spheres, creates a momentum, an internal dynamic, which thereafter ensures that increasingly larger investments are channelled into these very same capabilities. Sometimes, even supporting capabilities get funded (whatever the doctrinal justifications offered for it) to, in essence, protect the manifestly growing physical and institutional stake in the favoured warfighting spheres.

ARMOUR

The Indian Army fought the 1965 war with Pakistan with mostly light tank forces. All of the Indian tanks, including Centurions, were basic fighting machines with rifled guns (of 105 mm calibre or less) having simple target-sighting and line-of-sight gun-ranging devices on board. The Pakistani forces, none of them dedicated armoured formations, were equipped with the American M47, a technologically better tank (because of laser-ranging and the incorporation of other advances) than those in the Indian orbat. But, notwithstanding this ostensible Pakistani 'edge', Indian armour registered successes on the battlefield of a kind not repeated in 1971 when the Indian armour had heavier, more in-date items. At the time of the Bangladesh war, the Centurion and the Sherman Tank forces were augmented by ex-Soviet T-54/55s and Vijayanta Tanks, built under license.

The mix was 950 medium tanks to 500 light tanks, in the ratio of 1.9:1. The most useful tank of the war was the light, amphibious PT-76, able to manoeuvre without problems in the deltaic terrain of East Pakistan. The heavier tank forces fought to an impasse on the western front, where Pakistani armour too had gained in weight – the 100 M47 medium tanks being joined by 100 of the newer M48s, the then Main Battle Tank (MBT) of the US Army and the 375-odd Chinese built T-54/55s and the T-59s. In all, Pakistan fielded round about 575 medium tanks, to India's 1,450 tanks. India's quantitative superiority overall was two and a half times as many tanks as Pakistan had. In the bulk category of tanks,

Indian armour still had the 'gap' on its side, 950 medium tanks to Pakistan's 500 like tanks.

Less than five years later, by 1976-77, the Indian and Pakistani armoured strength had grown but in tandem, maintaining the two to one edge as before (2,030 Indian tanks to 1,050 Pakistani tanks). As of 1980-81, the tank strengths seemed to have stabilized at 2,170 Indian tanks to 1,065 Pakistani tanks, a percentage growth of 6.9 per cent and 1.43, per cent respectively. This was the lull before a windfall (for Indian armour). A new chief, assisted by a supportive government, set the Army on a course of 'mechanization' in the mid-1980s that added substantively to the 'manoeuvre mass' that could be mustered. The new programmes – RAMIDS (Reorganized Army Mountain Infantry Divisions) and RAPIDS (Reorganized Army Plains Infantry Divisions) – sought to speed the Indian Army into a mechanized fighting mode.

The plans, in the main, involved providing mobility to the foot soldier, more lorries and transport for the mountain infantry to take them as near to forward positions as possible and huge numbers of wheeled armoured personnel carriers (APCs), progressively replaced by an equally impressive fleet of tracked armoured Infantry Combat Vehicles (ICVs), enabling a RAPIDS jawan to keep pace with the tank-led penetration of enemy territory. The concept was for an autonomous mechanized division of tracked ICVs carrying infantry speeding alongside the tanks and, now and again as the situation demanded, peeling off in discrete groups in order to firm up Indian control of the invasion corridor and to capture nodal points along the way. This, it was thought, would enable the tanks to charge ahead without having to worry about flank attacks, enveloping enemy movements or other obvious dangers.

Further, an Army Aviation Corps of attack helicopters was conceived to provide an airmobile anti-tank punch to clear the path for the onrushing tanks. The mechanization policy by 1985-86 resulted in the Indian strength jumping by 22 per cent to 2,650 tanks (up from 2,170 tanks in 1980-81) and the ICV fleet growing by as much as

21.43 per cent to 850 vehicles (from 700 five years earlier). At the same time, the Pakistani armour, following a simpler route just increased its strength to 1,506 tanks (a gain of 41.4 per cent), even as its numbers of APC/ICVs declined (even if infinitesimally). But India's two-to-one lead in tanks was not disturbed. The Indian drive was now getting into its stride. By 1989-90, the tank strength increased again, by nearly 23 per cent, but the ICVs in service grew by over 35 per cent (in five years) to reach a fleet strength of 1,150 vehicles.

A Pakistan trying to catch up in this period added some 16 per cent more tanks (now numbering 1,750) and 47 per cent more ICVs (800), but was engaged in a losing contest. India was pulling away from Pakistan both in quantity and now in quality as over 650 T-72M1 (with a laser-ranging gun, autoshell loader for rapid fire, thermal imaging sights, etc.) formed the cutting edge of the Indian forces. Pakistan meanwhile had nothing more modern than the 1960s' vintage US-made M48. In 1993-94, the Indian and Pakistani tank numbers grew by roughly 8 per cent over their 1989-90 strength. The Indian ICVs increased in the same time frame by some 17.39 per cent (to reach 1,350 units). Meanwhile, the Pakistani ICV growth has apparently stalled at 800 fighting vehicles, the same number as in 1989-90, perhaps indicating a Pakistani decision to consolidate its armoured strength rather than keep adding to its mechanized-support capabilities.

However, the inevitable has happened. The trend path of the foot infantry being carried into battle zones aboard APCs and ICVs led naturally to the growth of a whole new arm in support of mainline armoured forces – the mechanized division with the ex-Soviet BMP1s and BMP2s mounting a 30 mm cannon and an anti-tank missile. In the time, it led, as is now the case, to upweighting this division into a full-fledged MBT-equipped third armoured division. (The Army brass, impressed by the mobility of the mechanized division in war exercises but ruing its lack of fire power, decided on its conversion.) In the event, the specially raised, lightly armoured, mobile force as a tactical adjunct to heavy tanks to afford operational flexibility as per the original RAPIDS concept, is no more. In its place is another very heavy T-72 tank division.

The policy of gradually heavier armourization of the forces – whatever the realistic tactical needs of the subcontinental battlefield – has begat three strike Corps (I, II and XXI) built around three armoured divisions and four and a half armoured divisions equivalent in the form of nine independent armoured brigades, and 20 divisions of growingly BMP2 mounted plains infantry. It is exacting a heavy toll of the defence budget.

The logic of the fairly rapid transformation of the Army with a significant mobile and armoured component now requires that the other major support arm, the artillery too becomes equally mobile and acquires armour for self-protection. Thus the demand is created for priority expenditure on a fleet of self-propelled long-range heavy guns fixed on tank chassis and needed, it is argued, to advance with the thrusting tank columns to neutralize enemy positions. This tilt towards the armoured warfare capabilities is slated to continue into the future. The list of so-called 'inescapable' requirements in the Ninth Defence Plan, for example, reportedly features at the very top of the list of programmes dealing with the modernization of the T-72 tank fleet, the conversion of the Vijayanta regiments to T-72, and the acquisition of long-range, armour-supporting, self-propelled and towed 130 mm and 155 mm artillery.

Actually, with the plains infantry growingly mounted on ICVs ostensibly to take them, among other places, to the Forward Edge of the Battle Area (FEBA), the infantry too is turning into another adjunct of the armoured forces. So a good part of the expenditure on plains infantry can also legitimately be clubbed with that of armour. Whereupon, the disproportion in the budgetary support of mission capabilities becomes even more marked. The spending on armour and plains infantry, together accounting for just over half (50.45 per cent) of the entire defence allocation in 1997, is 4.5 times that on mountain divisions,

256 / DEFENDING INDIA

in excess of 49 times the total expenditure on the Navy, specifically, 120 times that on the sea control and coastal defence assets and nearly 297 times the expenditure on sea denial capabilities afforded by submarines – the only effective means of deterring hostile activity off peninsular India which, defence-wise is the country's weakest, most vulnerable, frontier.

There has to be some correlation between defence expenditures and the threats supposedly faced by the country. Such resolute and sustained weighting of defence expenditure on the side of certain select warfighting capabilities at the expense of other capabilities to deal with equal, if not more serious, threats naturally raises doubts about the efficacy of MoD/Defence Services' so-called 'threat based' requirements planning. Assuming that there is a correspondence between the threats and the defence expenditure, then, to justify the investment/ ongoing expenditures in armoured and plains warfare capabilities, the threat from Pakistan would have to be some four times as great as the one posed by China across the mountains? But is that the case? And this Pakistani threat, moreover, would have to be nearly 50 times as onerous as the threat from any source on the sea. Again, is it so?

This is the central weakness at the heart of the Ministry of Defence's threat assessment. It appears to be driven more by the capital acquisitions plans and programmes of the Services – Army, Air Force and Navy, in that order. Considering the 'continental mindset' of the Indian political and defence establishment, the Indian Army and its threat orientation have a leading role in filling out the defence effort.

The trouble is the threat requirements paradigm has been inverted. The Army's primary interest in having a heavy, sophisticated and prestigious mobile armoured warfare capability has defined the threat and the country's expenditure priorities. In this context, the 'Pakistan threat', at once validates the capital-intensive armoured warfighting wherewithal acquired over a long time and the ongoing and future programmes to beef up the same.

This is so despite the fact that after 1971, Pakistan has lost even the will to wage an all-out war with India (opting instead for the low-cost, low-risk, low-intensity operations in Punjab and Jammu & Kashmir). The incontrovertible proof of this, as our study of weaponization trends has shown, is that it is reconciled to an armoured plains warfare edge – the decisive element in any war – resting with India.

The China threat, meanwhile, remains unaddressed in its larger context. But it is narrowly conceived as an inaccessible border problem able to be adequately dealt with by the mountain forces in place, which at a maximum are designed to prevent a repeat of the debacle in the 1962 war, and by political moves towards compromise and accommodation. An asymmetric military relationship with China is compensated by a military build-up against the manifestly lesser adversary, Pakistan. This then is the basic policy map apparently used by MoD for force planning purposes and reflects an inflexible threat assessment, which has remained unchanged virtually since independence in a period encompassing major geopolitical upheavals.

Threat estimation, untouched by international and regional developments, not only does not inspire confidence but raises questions about the thinking of the military. Worse, defence and weaponization policies based on such reading of threats tend, in the long term, more to waste resources than to boost national security. The pattern of Indian defence expenditures shows a skewed and generally unsatisfactory threat analysis at work.

COMBAT CAPABILITY: DYNAMIC INDICATORS

A weapon system is only as good as the least competent member of its operating crew. This is an old military adage and hence the Indian armed forces' emphasis is on training. But rigorous training regimes in relatively modern armed forces require expenditure of vast quantities of ammunition and POL and entail intensive consumption of spares and other war material. Care, therefore, has to be taken to see that reserves of these items meant for use in case of war are not run down.

Thus, the separate stocks of spares meant to sustain and upkeep the existing orbat, and which are used for training purposes, like in field and higher level war exercises considered routine activities are called maintenance spares. Those held in reserve for war are called War Wastage Reserves. And then there is the War Stock concerned with the stores of ammunition, chemical explosives, shells and missiles of all kinds for all varieties of weapons in the arsenal, which are drawn down for live firings and in other training regimes, but which are continually replenished.

The size of holdings in these three categories for each item is according to a 'practical' scale which, in turn, is dictated by the authorized firing rates (for ammunition), spares wastage rates of every individual system, the expected rates of attrition/usage based on the past record and experience in peacetime and in war, and the priority accorded the replenishment of these different categories of holdings. But the spending to make up attrited spares and consumables of all kinds, because it comes out of the same budgetary capital pool, competes with the expenditure on modernization and acquisitions.

The 'practical' scale of holdings are usually lower than the 'authorized' scale, because even in storage many of these high value items, like missiles, for instance, begin to degrade. The 'wastage' of ammunition is estimated at a high 10 per cent of the holdings worth some Rs 100 crore annually and may occur because of the storage practices. Ammunition and artillery shells are kept in large open air stacks covered only by tarpaulin in huge ammunition depots, in the rear and in forward area dumps. Regarding spares, 17 per cent to 20 per cent of the original unit cost of aircraft is supposed to be the value of spares expended every year if the aircraft is in full (peacetime) use.

Normal training at the rate of one major level field exercise per year supplemented by lower level unit manoeuvres and exercises throughout the year, result in firing of ammunition by the Army estimated to be worth Rs 700-900 crore annually and the consumption of POL yearly amount to 25 per cent of the operating costs of any unit (regiment upwards).

Spares, ammunition and POL are heavily consumed. Factor into this high consumption context the uncertainties introduced by the disruption of spares supply from the Russian source. Now complicate this situation by the natural drive and desire of the defence services to acquire more and more advanced weapons platforms and related hardware requiring huge expenditures of capital, continually to keep their force profile technologically advanced. Place all this is in the context of the shrinking (in real terms) of the defence allocations, and what you have is the risky policy of internally generating 'savings' to be used as capital for new acquisitions.

These savings are secured, as our analysis shows, by conserving spares and cutting down the expenditure on POL by restrictive training regimes and by dipping into and diminishing the WWR in order to sustain a minimal level of activity without, however, restocking maintenance spares and the WWR. The unreplenished WWR, holdings of maintenance spares and warstock are the main reasons, moreover, for the very large 'voids', i.e., unmet demands, claimed by the three Services. The Army and Air Force each claim a void in excess of Rs 30,000 crore and Navy Rs 10,000 crore.

But such overlarge claims are keyed to the authorized scale of spares, POL and ammunition for every type of operating system in the inventory. These large figures suggest precisely the size of the problem facing the Indian military, which seems unwilling to use the defence allocations for the purposes of filling these 'voids' created in the first place by not channelling enough funds over the years for the buying of critical war material.

The result is the dropping of the mission operational rate for all capital military stock to 33 per cent and in the diminution of war reserve to levels permitting fighting for only 15 days. The Government-sanctioned size of stockpile, however, is supposed to ensure that there is enough ammunition and spares to wage the first 30 days of war at 'intense' rates and a further 30 days at attrition rates.

Though there has been some improvement in this situation since the early 1990s, the situation is still grim in the field where the impact is felt most. For instance, some two-thirds of all tanks in the Army (including those in the frontline armoured formations) are either mothballed or under-used, all capital ships and submarines not in dry dock or undergoing repairs are out at sea only seven days in a month, rather than the 21 days that they are supposed to spend. And, in the Air Force, of the 16 or so combat aircraft in the average combat squadron, eight aircraft and a trainer are in the hangar for extended time, owing to paucity of spares (40 per cent-50 per cent serviceability). Each of the 20-odd pilots in a frontline squadron, therefore, get to sortie no more than two times a week in the eight aircraft in flying condition.

The spares shortage is one side of the coin. The other side is the weakness in the service infrastructure, seeded by the Soviet 'short leash' arms supply policies that did not sufficiently stress support services or stocking of spares in the total arms package. Fortuitously for the defence services, such Soviet policies meshed with the latters' overarching drive to acquire capital hardware, even if this meant acquiring hardware without an adequate and assured level of spares support. (In contradistinction to the Russian aircraft, like the MiGs which average 8-10 hours, the serviceability of Western origin aircraft, like Jaguars and Mirage 2000s, is around 15 hours per aircraft per month. The normal rate is 20 hours/ aircraft/month for any type of aircraft.)

At the grassroots level, the spares and POL-saving austerity regime hurts the training of the average Indian trooper, who has to be imparted a certain level of battlefield skills without which he will be endangering himself, the weapon system, and cumulatively, will affect the performance of his immediate unit and still larger formations. For the still semi-literate soldiery only the hard grind of physical training that drills them repeatedly in certain weapon and battlefield functions can pull them up to the desired level of performance. But it is this training that suffers from severe truncation with obviously unsatisfactory results.

Take the case of a frontline mechanized battalion mounted on a BMP2 ICV. The designated missile firer gets to loose off one live missile per year. The reserve/ alternate firer gets to trigger a live missile once every two years, the tactical commander of the unit once every five years and the average crewman who in an emergency is supposed to be able to guide (earlier the Faggot anti-tank missile, and now the Malutka and progressively the Konkurs missile) to target once every five years. The Modified Logistic System (MLS) which was introduced to rationalize consumables usage, seems to be an attempt to garb the deficiencies in spares support with managerial jargon. Thus, in order apparently to save on imported spares, which comprise 40-50 per cent of the T-72 tank, the maintenance support has been scaled down in the MLS. Another example: serious depletion in spares has resulted in the Aircraft-On-the-Ground (AOG) rate in Army commands of as high as 65 per cent.

If spares are to be conserved, so are POL. In a regiment of about 45 tanks, only 15 are allowed to participate in routine training exercises, with each tank being restricted to 200 km of running. It leads to very perfunctory training. Further, the policy to conserve ammunition means that tank crews practise firing in their unit ranges with the help of a 0.22 mm rifle aligned with the tank gun shooting pellets at targets. Curtailed training snowballs in air-land exercises, involving combat aircraft squadrons honing their skills for close support missions, complaining that the under-strength armoured units in the exercise area do not provide 'realistic warfighting experiences'. Likewise, restricted spares and POL eventuate in a short time at sea, a situation aggravated by the fact that the ships in order to limit spares/POL usage, practise only suboptimal naval manoeuvres. The training of officers and ratings in this situation is consequently also 'suboptimal'.

INTERNAL SECURITY

If the spares and POL conservation has dented military efficiency, the growing use of the Army for Internal Security (IS) duties, senior Army officers fear, has affected the morale and fighting qualities of the soldier by
1. realigning his mission and adversary orientation from external to internal enemies, which can be potentially very dangerous,
2. blunting his battlefield skills – the time he would otherwise spend in training for conventional war is spent on IS duties,
3. providing him no rest and respite, and
4. exposing him to, and infecting him with, the lax and corrupt values of the police and paramilitary forces. It is not the occasional but fulltime 'aid to civil power' which is the problem.

Take the case of the Northern Army. A major proportion of the forces in the Srinagar Valley of the Command's central sector were until lately engaged in internal security functions. These are part of the two Corps supposedly tasked for war on a front stretching from Siachen to north of Gurdaspur in Punjab. The IS role impinges adversely on the fighting units in this sector. Nearly a quarter of the present strength of frontline units under the Army's Northern Command are composed of soldiers who have pulled three years or less in service, mostly in operations. Other than basic training, these soldiers have seen little else and have had no advanced training/ retraining in actual warfighting nor, more importantly, rest.

Tasking the Army for IS duties has other penalties. There is degradation of the force posture, equipment-wise, necessitating greater utilization of spares – the very thing the Army strives most to avoid. There being no railways, the upkeep of a military presence in Kashmir, let alone sustenance of full-scale operations, depends upon the military transport system. Deployment of the Army in 'aid to the civil power' ends up whittling away at this lifeline. How? Say, one Army column is ordered from Jammu to Doda. At a minimum this will require 200 vehicles to move with troops in full gear. The wear and tear on the trucks and other equipment, with repeated deployments of this kind, will in quick order render the mass of vehicles in the concerned division inoperative. Given that replacement of equipment in 'peacetime' is uncertain at best, in case of sudden war, there will only be a hugely depleted and weakened road lift capability to take the troops to the front or to staging areas, and to move war material.

NOTES

1. Saadet Deger and Somnath Sen of the Stockholm International Peace Research Institute are of the view that 'Nowhere in the world is the inherent conflict between economic development and strategic security as acute as in the Indian subcontinent.' See their 'Military Security and the Economy: Defence Expenditure in India and Pakistan' in Keith Hartley and Todd Sandler (eds.), *The Economics of Defence Spending: An International Survey* (London and New York: Routledge, 1990) p. 189.

2. Prime Minister Rajiv Gandhi in a speech during the ruling Congress Party's centenary celebrations in Bombay in 1985 famously revealed that not more than 15 paise in every rupee tasked for social welfare reached the people at the grassroots level as benefits and that the rest was lost in 'leakage' and 'wastage'.

3. See Amiya Kumar Ghosh, *India's Defence Budget and Expenditure Management in a Wider Context* (New Delhi: Lancer Publishers, 1996) p. 371. Mr Ghosh was formerly Financial Adviser, Defence Services.

4. Serving and retired Indian military officers informally volunteered the data but in bits and pieces and on a non-attributable basis. These have been patched together, projected and extrapolated as the purpose of this part is indicative.

5. The MHA is reported to owe the Army almost Rs 1000 crore

on this account. See Manvendra Singh, 'Home Ministry Owes Army Rs 950 Crore', *Indian Express*, 12 August 1997.

6. See Dinesh Kumar, 'IAF Lost 82 Aircraft Since April '93', *The Times of India*, 11 November 1996. This level of losses is beginning to stir public criticism; see the editorial 'A Crashing Force', *The Hindustan Times*, 14 February 1997.

7. *Asian Strategic Review 1992-93*, Institute of Defence Studies and Analyses, New Delhi, p. 35.

In the research for and the writing of both the sections of this chapter Bharat Karnad has provided very valuable analysis and inputs.

5

The Future

We near the end of our enquiry, and here as we attempt to peer through the uncertainties of the future the only signposts that are discernible are the examples of the past. That is why the way India handled the challenges of the past half century perhaps gives a fair idea for assessing how it will respond in the future too.

An oft-repeated truism, still worthy of repetition, is that errors in the realm of strategic planning, management of foreign or defence policies have consequences that trouble many succeeding generations. This applies in particular to India's management of its security issues. We need to reflect only upon, for example, a major failure in the seventeenth and eighteenth centuries to make a proper assessment of the importance of the Indian Ocean and of the sea routes to India. This failure resulted in the arrival of foreign powers on Indian shores, at first to trade, and thereafter to conquer.

It was not the eventual conflict on land, not so much the oft-cited Battle of Plassey or even the earlier Third Battle of Panipat that were the true turning points of Indian history. Of course, these battles were of great consequence that is irrefutable. But a simple citing of these examples is inadequate for they do not account for a vital reality. In this instance victories on land only followed a conquest of the sea. That was the great divide, this domination of the sea routes by foreign powers. Here it was that the seeds of an ultimate colonialization of India were sown. Had Shivaji's naval fleet not been destroyed by the machinations of the Peshwas the European trading powers could never have established themselves in peninsular India.

The need then was to recognize that a strategic shift of great significance had occurred; that land routes had been replaced by the sea passage. During the earlier centuries ingress into India had always been a land invasion; now, whereas that could still occur, a new element had been introduced. And thus a conquest of India took place but in the wake of trade, which in turn was entirely dependent on free movement over the oceans. In the path of that and resisting it could stand only a naval force, for that alone would have denied access to India. But perhaps it is unfair to so judge; for the times were different, and we view through the magnifying lens of hindsight. But yet another limitation is illustrated here: not to pre-empt; just as in the earlier centuries no attempt was ever made to pre-empt an invasion by the land routes, by confronting well beyond even local (as against national) territorial boundaries, so too in this case of seaborne aggression. The response was late and in Indian waters. The destruction of the Maratha Navy was, therefore, a fateful strategic error for which India paid the price in the next two and a half centuries.

Studying the five major conflicts of independent India and their management, similar characteristics are found repeating themselves. In 1948, against that first invasion a lack of a comprehensive strategic sense about what was involved was perhaps inevitable. There was a saving feature, however: an institutional mechanism that supported decision-making did exist. It functioned as a Cabinet Committee on Defence which asked for assessments, analysed them and then sent recommendatory analysis to the Prime Minister. That all this was transitional, and therefore, errors of profound importance to India were committed is now explained away on various grounds; yet there was at least an instrumentality and an institution. Even then mistakes that currently trouble India, half a century down the passage of time, were made. These happened on account of an inadequate sense of territory; of an absence of sufficiently developed historical perspective; of a sense of our own geography, and it is then that we made the first error of trading space with illusory peace; we gave up territory for a UN-sponsored – albeit temporary – absence of conflict. Unfortunately, true peace was even then not found though territory had been conceded, almost permanently. That is why the consequences still trouble us. India remains possibly the only country of its size and importance that has for so long had an undefined land frontier; it is amongst those few countries of importance that continues to have major border disputes with two of its principal neighbours. To what do we attribute this? To that very same legacy: of an absence of proper strategic thinking, planning and execution on the part of the early political military leadership of the country. This continues to bedevil India to the present day.

In like fashion the humiliating episode of 1962 brought into existence yet another line of control, which after all was again a compromise of the country's fixed land boundaries, but not a solution. But by this time, only 15 years after independence, even that inherited and somewhat rudimentary institutional support system had been lost. A characteristic of the Sino-Indian War of 1962, of which the very first forewarning came in the short earlier episode of Goa, was the near total erosion by then of institutional decision-making, particularly of the country's foreign and defence policies. Institutions by then had been replaced by entirely personalized cliques; decisions were taken by small coteries, all centred around the Prime Minister. And there existed no system either of review, or of questioning assumptions, or professionally examining options. That is why it is pathetic to read outpourings like those of Pandit Nehru that no one asked that earlier cited question, 'What if the Chinese behaved differently from what they had till then been doing?' It is telling that 25 years after the Sino-Indian border war, in 1987, when the occasion arose to send Indian forces into Sri Lanka – yet again on an issue that posed important questions to the country's foreign and defence policies – no proper assessment of the LTTE and its responses was carried out. Questions were asked: 'What if the LTTE does not behave according to expectations?' but the instant response 'We will deal with any unpredictability' demonstrates an absence of the institutional. There was a greater degree of professionalism in 1965 and in the conflict of 1971 though more as an outcome of the lessons of 1962. Decisions, however, even in these two examples of conflict management continued to be made by a small group with access to the Prime Minister. What sets these two conflicts apart is the loss of militarily acquired gains on the negotiating table. The gains of 1965 were bartered at Tashkent; and real possibilities of a durable peace, accompanied by a definitive and concluding settlement of bilateral contentions between India and Pakistan, were lost on the negotiating tables of Shimla. But these we have already examined.

It is not a very encouraging conclusion, though it is unavoidable. In the last half century the Indian political-military leadership has not displayed the required strategic sense. Indian national interests were not adequately served. The leadership failed if even just one criterion of evaluation is taken into account – that of maintaining the frontiers of India as inviolable. What therefore, is the legacy of the past 50 years? An absence of certainties in security-related issues; no established land boundaries; an absence of a secure geopolitical environment; a devaluation of India's voice in global affairs and worrisomely, not even a beginning of any institutional framework for conceptualizing and managing the country's defence.

The twentieth century, the bloodiest of the centuries, closes. With it closes the first half century of Indian independence as well. This century saw the end of the British Empire in India, as of several other empires globally; and the collapse of many monarchies. It witnessed freedom from colonialism, emergence of democracy and mass movements. It is the century in which more revolutions took place than in any earlier century but it also witnessed the collapse of the principal one. Uniquely, in the span of just one lifetime the twentieth century witnessed a flowering and then domination of the thought of Marx, and then most remarkably a collapse of communism. As for India, the first half of the century saw it as a subject nation struggling for independence; the second half saw it endeavouring to address itself to the challenges of statehood and building anew in a post-colonial, post Second World War global polity.

Early management of the country's foreign relations was inspired; it was marked by the sustaining strength of a philosophical and conceptual base; it was identifiable too by finesse and a certain adeptness. That world has now altered beyond recognition. Its bipolarity has dissolved. With the great meltdown of 1989 and a defreezing of the cold war the supporting contours of the non-alignment movement have lost their sharpness. In this situation of asymmetry as India addresses itself to the challenges of the twenty-first century what is it that it seeks? And it is not simply the certainties of foreign relations that have changed. Concepts and nature of warfare too have altered, almost beyond recognition. As new international accords about weapons of mass destruction are arranged, there is a poignant irony in recognizing that it was in the twentieth century that the world experienced the use of all of them: atomic, biological and chemical. Whilst social and environmental inequalities arising from a free play of market forces place serious question marks on today's suggested panaceas order is sought through experiments like the World Trade Organization. New issues arise, for example, the loss of a monopoly of the state over both knowledge and weapons; and the preponderant importance of factors like environment, drinking water and movement of people; these issues now enter our concerns as areas of new security challenges.

Warfare of the future, with the 'greater democratization of knowledge and resources', including weapons, and their 'concentration in uncontrolled private hands' has been altered beyond recognition. It is no longer possible for nations (and this despite the apparent example of the Gulf war of 1991) to conquer another country, to subjugate an entire people or to take into captivity as a booty of war the adversary state as a colony. There is an inescapable conclusion to be drawn about the nuclear reality: of recognizing both the deterrent factor of such weapons and, paradoxically, their actual non-usability in conflict. This dilemma confronts India more directly and much more pointedly than perhaps any other country in the world. Even as environmental aggression becomes a factor in today's security considerations, so too does the question of energy dependence. Without doubt the economic is the determining criterion, but no economic progress is possible without energy sufficiency.

In the transformed nature of war what India is experiencing and shall have to contend with is not so much open, direct conflict as covert war, clandestine war. This has, in any event, been waged against India for almost the entire half century of independence. In turn this altered and transformed nature of war will require a total transformation of our concepts and response mechanisms too. On the other hand, in the absence of any social, cultural, political or economic commonality or interdependence, a bland policy of 'improving relations' with China could, over time, convert into an opiate, consequentially persuading us to mortgage the future yet again for illusions about the present. The Chinese strategic culture remains what it has always been: wedded to domination; not so much through occupation of the (real or potential) adversary's territory as through a psychological subjugation of mind, an emasculation of the adversary's response options. India, therefore, needs to pose to itself some unsettling questions. It is in this broad backdrop that we address ourselves to drawing a contour map of India's tasks in the coming decades.

INSTITUTIONAL

The problem is not so much of form, it is of the substance. The debate in India has got fixed upon the need for a national security council. Arguments against it are best summarized by a statement of the Indian Prime Minister made in the Indian Parliament on 16 May 1995.

A question was raised about the National Security Council. It is true that we had a National Security Council, first established in 1990, and it had only one meeting. After that nothing happened. . . . In the Government, a lot of thinking has gone into it. . . . I had occasion to promise a National Security Council, or somebody which takes into account the questions of national security and we have examined the entire gamut of possibilities and options available to us. . . . It is not because a new government has come that we wanted to change everything, it was because of the experience of the National Security Council as it existed from 1990 was found a little unworkable. A Strategic Policy Group headed by the Cabinet Secretary and including the Service Chiefs, Secretaries of Ministries concerned like Defence, Home, External Affairs and Finance and Heads of Agencies was also set up to consider the strategic policy papers. Now, according to the decision at that time the National Security Council had Ministers In-Charge of Defence, Home, Finance and External Affairs as members as well as some others. . . . Essentially, it was, what is known as, the Cabinet Committee on Political Affairs, plus one or two added. [This] was a kind of mechanical addition: it was not a functional addition. A fairly large advisory board comprising experts, academics, scientists, journalists, former Government officers, some Chief Ministers and MPs was also constituted to enable interaction with non-official resource persons . . . this big body was found to be a little unwieldy and its deliberations tended to become a little diffused in the sense that we could not, in matters of national security come to a particular decision or particular conclusion after deliberations. . . . My opinion is – after examining the working and whatever happened in that meeting – that this objective cannot be achieved by a body of the size and composition. We have undertaken a thorough review of the above mechanism and come to the conclusion that . . . for one thing, the National Security Council as set up in 1990, as I have just submitted, is not much different from the CCPA. Secondly, the advisory board as proposed in 1990 appears to be somewhat unwieldy . . . [making] the whole exercise blurred and confusing.

National security is a very wide subject. . . . We therefore feel that instead of having one large advisory board, it would be more appropriate to provide for meaningful interaction with selected experts in each specific field under study or discussion. Such experts can be associated at the stage of preparation of strategic policy papers as well as during discussion of such papers at a higher level. Our review of the system prevailing in other countries shows that different structures exist for dealing with national security issues depending upon the type of system of government prevailing in that country. Generally, the national security council set-up is found in countries where the Presidential form of Government has been adopted, the most notable example being that of the United States. We find that it is difficult to have such a system transplanted in India because here the business of the Central Government has to be ultimately transacted in the Cabinet or Cabinet committee with Ministers Incharge being responsible for their subjects to Parliament. In the United Kingdom, for instance, no single national security council has been set up and the work pertaining to national security matters is considered in different Cabinet Committees, for example, the Committee on Defence and Overseas Policy, the Committee on Nuclear Defence Policy, the committee on Northern Ireland, the Committee on Intelligence Services, etc. In our case, a system more akin to that prevailing in the U.K. might be more appropriate. We are, therefore, veering to the view that specific committees of Ministers or groups of Ministers could be set up for different aspects of national security whenever strategy or policy papers are brought up for consideration of the Ministers. The Joint Intelligence Committee in the Cabinet Secretariat constantly interacts with the concerned Ministries and agencies. There is regular consideration of the defence aspects of national security in the Chiefs of Staff committee who have their own Secretariat. The Chairman, Joint Intelligence Committee and Heads of other agencies interact with the Service Chiefs. We have all these working even now. The core group of Secretaries is also there. They look into these matters of internal security. These mechanisms and systems have been working well but this is where the difference comes that we are not satisfied with the present dispensation.

We would like to have an over-arching body which looks into the conclusions drawn, the reports sent by these different mechanisms. While these mechanisms and systems have been working well, we still feel that there is a need for strengthening the present arrangement in certain respects. . . . There is also need for having papers prepared from a central point of view instead of from one Department or Ministry. Therefore, the need for an over-arching body is felt here. . . . This is what I would like to say. It is more or less ready, in its final stages and before

losing any more time, I would come back to
Hon. Members for their views.

The rationale of and arguments for an institutional
framework remain; for that which has been asserted as
'more or less ready' has not been delivered, and time
has been lost, irretrievably.

ECONOMICS - THE PRINCIPAL DYNAMIC

"Nothing is more dependent on economic conditions than
precisely the Army and the Navy" (Engels).
    Currently the principal global dynamic for change
is the economic, along of course with technology; and
these two being supportive fuels are interdependent. An
intermix of these two (the economic and the technological)
impacts differently on different societies, variations being
determined by the political, economic and the strategic
cultures involved. The velocity too of this change, though
unprecedented in its totality, varies from one country
to another, dictated largely by different individual applications
of it. One constant alone remains: the vital importance
of the economic.
    Though evident that economic prosperity does not
'always and immediately translate into military effectiveness;
still, all the major power shifts in the world's military
power balances have [always] followed alterations in the
productive balances' of nations; but much more important,
that 'victory has always gone to the side with the
greatest material resources'.[1]
    That is where a dilemma confronts nations. If they
be economically weak, or poor, or if their economic
strength declines in direct relation to the challenges
they face, then obviously the authority of that nation
is enfeebled both internally and also internationally. This
then compels them

    to allocate more and more of their resources
    into the military sector, which in turn squeezes

out productive investment, and over time leads
to the downward spiral of slower growth, heavier
taxes, deepening domestic splits over spending priorities,
and [a] weakening [of the] capacity to bear burdens
of defence.[2]

This is a cruel spiral, relentless in its logic. It
is also precisely the dilemma that India faces. The choice
is not between security or economic growth, it is really
security through economic growth. The challenge to India
is direct: how to achieve greater national security through
a more dynamic and distributionally equating economic
growth. There has to be a recognition by the political
leadership of the country that the more India pushes
ahead with economic growth and expansion, the more
will such a development by itself generate a 'power-
political' dynamic. This alone can give the nation the
kind of security that is its just and due destiny.

Two other economic aspects merit reflection and some
comment. The first is about economic sovereignty, while
the other is about combining social justice with economic
growth.

In this era of diffused sovereignties, nations have
to be far more flexible in their attitude, and in their
approach to where exactly the line of pure sovereignty
(if there be such a line) lies. Yet again, the only
measuring mechanism is that of vital national interests;
short, however, of that falls an enormous area, largely
grey, in which the choice of nation states is influenced
directly by the factor of economic self-interest. As national
interests, in respect of trading rights, for example, assert
themselves, inevitably then some of the larger tend to
swallow the smaller. India is currently passing through
a phase of shifting from one to the other; as a nation
it has changed its economic gear, but only just. A
great deal more remains to be done.

On the question of harmony between economic growth
and social justice, there cannot be a standard formula.
It is yet again a challenge to the management of change
that India's national leadership faces. The question

that needs to be addressed centres around economic growth and social cohesiveness. In the process of growth should India lose social cohesion then will it not be diluting its national will? Enhancement in gross national product must result in an increase in gross national contentment too, not in any exacerbation of disparities; for the commitment of citizens to a state is altogether more material in this age.

FOREIGN POLICY

> In the Post-Cold War world, . . . idealism needs the leaven of geo-political analysis to find its way through the maze of new complexities. That will not be easy. . . . In the 21st century, [India] like other nations must learn to navigate between necessity and choice, between the immutable constants of international relations, and the elements subject to the discretion of statesmen. . . .
>
> Because we need to balance especially between values and necessity, therefore, foreign policy must begin with some definition of what constitutes a vital interest – a change in the international environment so likely to undermine the national security that it must be resisted no matter what form the threat takes or how ostensibly legitimate it appears. . . .[3]

Just when the rest of the world was moving into the period of the great meltdown – a collapse of the fixed order of things which had come into being since at least the end of the Second World War – just then India, perhaps typically and perversely, chose to move into a phase of internal political uncertainty and rearrangement. Precisely when, therefore, India needed clarity and vision from its governments, it was found wanting. Indeed, governance as such became almost a casualty. And as the principal preoccupation became political survival, the demands of internal politics superseded the management of the country's external affairs.

Thus as we now move towards the twenty-first century, India seeks a reliable order out of this apparent and existing disorder; of the domination of one power but polycentrically, without fixity. This power shift is not simply geographic, it is also conceptual. What then are these new or other integrals of power in today's international relations? Can any nation, for example, today impose its will on another? And if it can, then how? Have not, therefore, knowledge and economics overtaken the purely military components of power? India ought to reflect deeply upon where it went wrong in the IPKF; or where the United Nations and the USA went wrong in Somalia; or why Europe fumbled for so long against the disorder of former Yugoslavia; why again, nearer home, is it that Afghanistan has descended into a vortex of fundamentalism and of unbridled tribal anarchy? And why this despite superpower interventions? Yet again we come to the conclusion that this entire subcontinent has an inherent order and an equilibrium, perhaps even a dynamic disequilibrium – to permit any force to intrude here thereafter results in prolonged destabilization.

In a post-non-alignment world, what is it that India ought to search for? Essentially it is that philosophical base for its foreign policy, from which it can distill national objectives and, thereafter, a harmonious conduct of diplomacy in service to vital national interests. Are we globally moving away from a confrontationist defence policy to cooperative security, or is that too idealistic? Is it a balance of power, or dominance, the supremacy of one that is the emerging global scheme? Are we entering a new phase of ever-widening spheres of influence? Or is it to be circles of hegemonies that we shall have to contend with? And does India stand on the crossed lines of any of these potential contentions? Between the idealistic aspirations of mankind, the reality of human nature, and the imperatives of national interests, lie some yawning chasms. How to so bridge them so that India's national security interests are best subserved?

Here are two additional thoughts: first, that strategic

frontiers of a power do not always coincide with the geographic delineation of its boundaries, this is a sufficiently well-established aspect of international relations. Therefore, what holds for others does so for India as well. Which takes us to our second point.

India's strategic frontiers lie where our vital national interests do. In the realm of strategy, compartmentalization into the purely diplomatic, economic or military is both unwise and ineffective. Challenge to any of the vital interests calls for a response that is total and national. It is axiomatic then that unless India gives some definition to its vital national interests it will fail to even conceptualize its strategic frontiers. Thereafter, a violation of any of those interests will, unfortunately, go entirely unchecked. In consequence, India's difficulties will be enhanced, future correctives will be made more difficult, and the country's national security will be adversely effected. This has been at the root of India's past mistakes; this critical deficiency lies at the heart of its present immobility, both of thought and of action.

The strategic situation, both globally and in Asia, is in a state of flux. As traditional alliance systems – of which India too has been a beneficiary – and the US decline in importance and effectiveness, no regional order appears ready to replace them. This reality dictates the primacy of 'state-centric perceptions', with the predominance of concerns about 'sovereign national interests and state influence'. That is the inescapable reality: around this reality, India's foreign policy has to structure both its concepts and its conduct in service of our national security.

ENERGY

Energy is security; deficiencies in this critical strategic sector compromise national security. The major issues in the Indian energy sector are the absence of an integrated long-term energy policy; inefficiencies in energy supply and utilization; an unsustainable energy mix; acute scarcity of developmental capital; a lack of rational energy pricing; insufficient environmental considerations combined with demonstrable sectoral changes which are in line with reforms in the economic, industrial and investment policies of the Government. These issues are all critically interdependent.

In the energy sector the overriding need continues to be for the enunciation of a long-term strategy, leading to the adoption of an overall energy policy; a policy that is marked by an optimum economic utilization of the nation's resources; is 'user-friendly' and duly accounts for the nation's special needs; is conscious of the debilitating consequences of a shortage of capital; a policy which combines growth in the energy sector with conservation; is uniform in its application throughout the country; is environmentally conscious so as to sustain development; and which addresses itself simultaneously to correcting the existing imbalances and preparing for the first decade of the twenty-first century.

TABLE I

Proven Energy Reserves

	Unit	India	World of the world	India as per cent
Coal	(bmt)	64.9	1,078.1	6%
Oil	(bbb)	5.87	1,000.9	0.59%
Natural Gas	(tem)	0.735	124.0	0.59%
Hydropower	(mw)	94,000	n.a.	

Table 1 reveals that proven reserves of hydrocarbons are small, accounting for less than 0.6 per cent of the global reserves. India is relatively rich in terms of coal and hydropower, but their exploitation is constrained by factors such as poor quality of coal, environmental concerns, and interstate water disputes in case of hydropower and non-availability of financial resources. The primary sources of energy available are thus coal, oil, natural gas, hydro and nuclear power. Even though coal dominates, persistent shortages of coal and power supplies during the recent past have led to substantial increases in the consumption of petroleum products (largely as swing fuels). This can be attributed to the relative ease in importing oil and petroleum products, albeit at formidable economic costs. Natural gas is a relatively new entrant in India's energy sector and could make a significant contribution as a source of fuel and feedstock in a number of sectors.

The issues which must be examined by the political-military leadership of India are the potential for energy independence through development of India's coal reserves; a sound and sustainable development of its hydel potential, and thereafter, an energy strategy based on natural gas, the potential and the dimensions of which can be gauged by examining the map on the facing page. Increasingly, what was earlier treated as an obstacle to smooth extraction of oil is now being employed as an additional energy source.

There is another area, atomic energy as a source of power. India can simply not forsake or even neglect its development. What is needed is for the political-military leadership of the country to separate the two strands: the entirely military from the purely peaceful. The current posture of ambiguity no longer suffices. On the contrary it is precisely on account of such ambiguity that the country's energy security has also suffered. This is best explained by a report of the Indian Parliament's Standing Committee on Energy, for the period 1995-96, on 'Nuclear Power Programme', of which it conducted an evaluation. This short report merits attention. It establishes as a finding that 'most inexplicably the stated objective of attaining 10,000 MW of nuclear power by 2000 AD has been abandoned'. The current production is just about 10 per cent of this goal and unless more investment takes place, this is the level at which it is likely to stay. But much more important are the views expressed by an expert, N. Srinivasan, that 'in the absence of a committed continuous programme, the technology built under heavy odds over four decades will be irretrievably lost'. This would be a grievous national loss, for which the political leadership alone would be responsible.

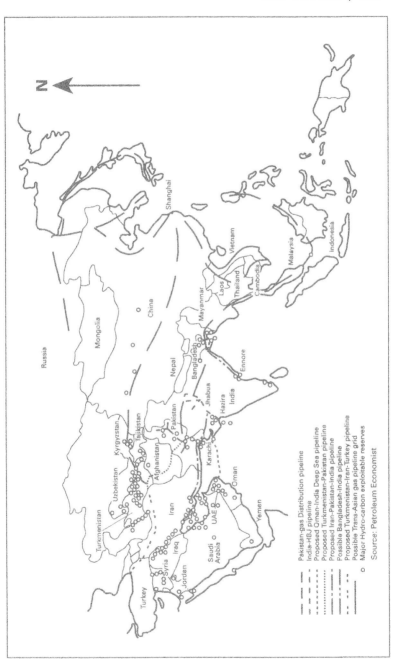

Natural gas supply options by pipeline: Asian region

Post Cold War Asia is in geopolitical transition.

The geo-politics of energy may be returning, once again, to the core of international relations in our region. Energy [is already] an important factor shaping the security dynamics in the Eurasian landmass, and could help redefine the relations among the Great Powers – the United States, Russia, China-and their alliances within our region. It could significantly reorder the balance of power in Eurasia and the world as a whole. Oil [is, arguably] at the heart of the ongoing turbulence in the Arabian peninsula and the [second] "Great Game" to exercise dominance in Central Asia and the Caucasus. The political developments in both the regions are likely to have a significant bearing on the foreign relations of most nations of the region, including India.[4]

A major component of this

emerging political milieu is competition for a secure energy supply and related tension regarding conflicting claims to potentially oil-rich [sources including the] seabed; and [of course] the protection of vital sea-lanes. In an increasingly energy-scarce world, such issues [will] become national-security concerns. If the major powers in the region fail to develop cooperative multilateral arrangements in the energy sector, competition over scarce resources could become the catalyst for regional conflict.[5]

ENVIRONMENT-FOOD-WATER

Global warming, and the consequences of that warming upon nations in India's neighbourhood, indeed even its own coastal areas, is the environmental aspect of security. Just as access to food and water or their denial can result in tension, so also the consequences of environmental degradation, deforestation, excessive siltation result in national problems. There exists in India, at present, neither any focused study in this regard nor any proper thought. Pollution of our rivers, and inefficient disposal of industrial wastes can choke our waterways and upset our agricultural lands affecting millions of people. Such a battered environment can cause violent upheavals and migration of population to already overcrowded cities.

As has wisely been observed and commented upon in an earlier section:

> Fusing ecology [or environment] and economics is an important advance on the road to sustainability. But fusing [environment] and economics gives us only two legs. For stability, we require the third leg of equity . . . because . . . sustainable society demands a wide consensus that we are all connected to our land and [to] each other.[6]

If water and food have an inseparable interrelationship, then monsoon-dependent India needs to reflect upon why its food production has apparently plateaued at around 185 million tonnes annually. Also we need to reflect upon why India, with almost twice China's arable land, is not yet able to produce the same quantities of food. That food is security; that no one can or will 'feed' India; that India must be entirely self-sustaining on the question of food security are axioms, not academic assertions.

The map on the following page best illustrates the problem in the case of water. There are two aspects here: the quality of water available for almost a billion human beings; in addition, India has possibly the largest domestic animal population in the world. They are equally dependent on potable water. All assessment of water needs must, therefore, take both humans and animals into account. Whereafter can be identified at least three major, potential conflict areas of the region, each related to water. They are the Indus, the Brahmaputra and the Ganga rivers.

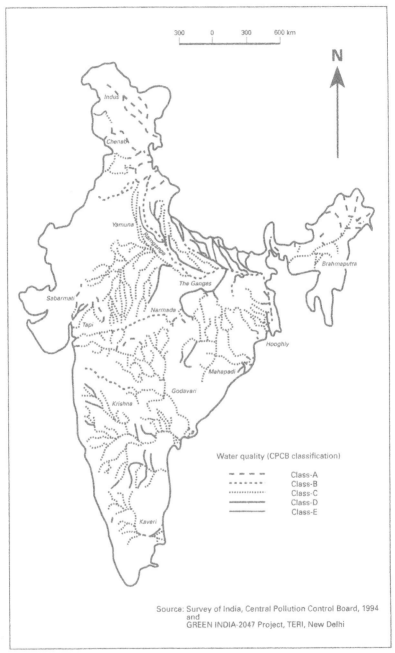

An overview of water quality in the major river systems of the country

For the first, India ought to reflect on the difficulties that it currently faces with Pakistan, which is dependent on the Indus. About the Indus there exists a water-sharing Treaty. However, various water storage projects in pursuance and in accordance with this Treaty are currently stalled. Potentially, they are all conflict points.

The Brahmaputra, on the other hand, poses problems that illustrate the aspect of international management of water, of environment, and of a more sensible utilization of a fast-diminishing natural resource, yet another potential conflict point.

In respect of the Ganga, the difficulties with Farakka and Bangladesh are only illustrative. A study by the Tata Energy Research Institute (TERI) suggests that by the turn of the century, the Ganga basin alone would be supporting a human population of around 550 million. If in this kind of dependence, problems were to arise, what then would be the consequences to national security?

DEMOGRAPHY AND ITS CONSEQUENCES

It is generally estimated that almost 20,000 km of the world's boundary framework is currently in dispute. This is but only the starting point of the demographic problem. The crux, of course, is the sheer dimension of numbers. But what we also have to examine critically is the aspect of demography's direct impact upon security.

This is a phenomenon of vast and stressful proportions: demographic migrations are now transforming not simply the geography but the sociology, the economy, indeed even the politics of various countries in the world. The United States struggles against unchecked immigrants from its south; Europe finds its problems as largely from across the Baltic and North African countries; and India faces it in the form of an explosive issue, on account of an unrestrained movement of people from the neighbourhood into the country.

India presents a diverse configuration of ethnic groups, castes and religious divides. As a nation it does not always stand together as a single ethno-political entity. This leads to clashes and confrontation between various ethnic, caste, religious and lingual identities. If demographic balances are disturbed by inept policies and political conflict, various demographic entities are bound to come in conflict, thus adversely affecting our security environment.

The political turmoil threatening peace in Arunachal Pradesh, tensions between India and Nepal regarding the changing demographic balance in the Terai region, suspicion in Bhutan about the influence India can wield through its Nepalese settlers are a part of the dangers of changes in the demographic balances. The ongoing conflict in Sri Lanka between the Sinhalese and the Tamils can pose a major demographic threat to southern India as large numbers of Tamil refugees pour into this region.

There is also then the larger aspect of refugees; the exodus and relocation of people creating new demographic equations within established national entities: a demographic invasion against which not just national geographic boundaries but political systems are also buckling.

To illustrate the problem, it is pertinent to share some official figures. These are from the Census Report of 1991, a sobering document and which contains some very alarming figures of population growth, particularly in the North-East. The growth rates in Mizoram and Nagaland during the last two decades are in the region of 50 per cent, in Manipur and Meghalaya it is about 32 per cent, and in Arunachal Pradesh and Assam the figures are 35 and 24 per cent respectively. An intelligence study of illegal Bangladeshi migrants in India shows that there are anywhere up to 12 million such settlers in the country. While West Bengal and Assam have borne the major brunt of the problem, almost three-fourths in these two states, Bihar and Tripura too have received their share of the migrants. The problem, however, spreads as far wide as Bombay and Rajasthan, and Delhi, which has an estimated 300,000 illegal Bangladeshis.

In this context, we will have to take note of suggestions now being made – that of redefining all the demographic factors, on a simple need basis in South Asia. This is an issue of very high volatility and importance, but also of very low attention, and in consequence, therefore, of gross neglect. As it impacts directly on India's national security there are reasons to undertake at least the very minimum first steps.

INTELLIGENCE

An intelligent appraisal of India's intelligence agencies is not possible for several reasons. The principal amongst them is lack of information. Intelligence requires secrecy and operates only on the basis of 'need to know'. The Indian public, therefore, need not know, and does indeed remain largely ignorant what their intelligence agencies are doing. That is an inherited attitude of the State, another legacy of the country's strategic culture and of long servitude. Intelligence agencies were earlier needed and employed as instruments of control, as extensions of the interests of the State from ancient to British to an independent India. They are, therefore, employed mostly against the citizens and other servants of the State; and it is in this respect alone that they have any degree of specialization. But accountability, and by derivation, loyalty, remains fixedly with the wielders of state power alone. This attitude cannot change because the essential nature of the Indian State has not altered, and that despite Independence.

Some other consequences have followed, though whether by design or completely unintendedly. India's intelligence agencies have deliberately been kept away from the scrutiny of the country's Parliament. They are thus, as in the past, answerable only to the political masters of the day. But in a democracy, as political masters change, loyalties too have to change. And if governments change with any rapidity, as they have been doing recently, then a spell of dizzy uncertainty must inevitably follow.

An unintended but debilitating consequence of all this has been a crippling of the professional competence of India's entire intelligence apparatus. Largely as a self-protective mechanism, these agencies tend to insulate themselves from any form of accountability whatsoever. They either stop reporting to the government of the day, and if that is not entirely or always possible, as it patently is not, they then become selective in what they share, or tailor it, or even invent intelligence. This, for intelligence, is unintelligently suicidal.

The Research and Analysis Wing (RAW) and the Intelligence Bureau (IB) are India's premier intelligence-gathering agencies for external and internal intelligence, respectively. The functioning of RAW and IB (predictably) overlaps, at least in some spheres. In consequence there is avoidable duplication, loss of purpose, and a diminution of efficiency in both. These organizations have also generally failed to give timely warning of impending national crises. There is no independent and effective agency to coordinate them. The Joint Intelligence Committee of the Cabinet Secretariat has proved not very effective, largely because it has become just another bureaucratic department. This lack of proper coordination and unavoidable rivalries have at times resulted in crucial information not being made available in time to the end users.

In 1962, this tendency cost the nation dear, though at that stage the IB alone was responsible both for external and internal intelligence. But another deficiency has prevailed over the years; scant attention is being given to the military. This has led to a downgrading of an effective source, that of Military Intelligence. Until 1959, for example, we had failed to even discover that the Chinese had built a highway across the Aksai Chin. Similarly, the concentration of Chinese forces at various points on our borders in 1962 also went undetected. The IB then failed then to analyse or report likely Chinese designs or military postures. In 1965, large-scale concentration and movement of armed infiltrators across the Cease-Fire Line remained undetected. Even commonly known information about the raising of tank destroyer battalions and an additional Pakistani Armoured Division was not sourced. In 1968, after RAW came into existence India's external intelligence did improve, but not in proportion to the resources employed. Therefore, in 1971 even operational intelligence of military value was inadequate. New roads and bridges were not known even in the border areas. An important piece of information like the conversion of Akhura-Ashugang railway line, or a tarmac road close to our border was also not identified.

The main problem here is a lack of an appropriate organization for acquiring, analysing and disseminating intelligence of value. A lack of perspective, also attention at the political level is in turn mainly responsible for this unsatisfactory state of affairs. The RAW, IB and MI can prove effective only if they are used effectively. The use of RAW sources to arm and train the LTTE militants who later fought against the Indian Army is a typical example.

India needs to reorganize, reorient and integrate its intelligence sources. It must also update its methodology. The technological revolution underway since the last decade now provides the tools to acquire real-time intelligence of value and give time to plan ahead. Electronic (ELINT) and Signal (SIGINT) intelligence has proved more reliable than simply the routine human intelligence (HUMINT). That, however, does not in any sense dilute the primacy still accorded to HUMINT. And for good reason, for besides being the oldest form, it is also of the most-high value kind. But then, mere acquisition is not enough; for intelligence is, after all, the distilling, analysis and processing of information so as to be made available, in time, and where required. It cannot remain a routine bureaucratic function. Areas of search and focus must be properly determined, and intelligence then obtained in a planned manner. A different culture of professionalism with accountability is needed. The need, above all, and once again, is unimpeachable selection, first-rate training, and most of all, an appropriate apparatus that oversees intelligence operations, with accountability as the benchmark.

NUCLEAR FIELD

The problem in this critical field, influencing India's nuclear policy directly is entirely of its own making. In 1974 with an underground explosion India demonstrated an ability, but disclaimed the intent. In retrospect, this step is to be faulted on both counts. India ought either not to have carried out such an experiment at all; a simple explosion as a capability-demonstrator would have sufficed if it intended to deny itself the capability thereafter. By demonstrating the ability India had effectively and explicitly entered the world of nuclear capability. Had it then conducted a series of other such tests and established its intent clearly, all the confusion of subsequent years, also these current international pressures, and all the other difficulties of today would have been easier to cope with. Instead, India went into a nuclear trance; pretence replaced policy. In consequence it has suffered the ill-effects of both, of being suspected of being a nuclear-weapons power, and not really being one. In the process India's options have also got severely curtailed. In the decade of the eighties, again from its own mishandling of the situation, India permitted yet another neighbour to confront it with a competitive posture. India then granted to Pakistan the status of strategic nuclear parity, which precisely had been the avowed purpose and intent of its policy to deny for decades. Now, in the nineties, India has repeated the performance: having successfully tested the IRBM capabilities of Agni, it has shelved the project.

It is a much more complex world now; our difficulties, therefore, are also far more intractable. The principle, however, is clear; the challenge to Indian statecraft remains unambiguous: how to find a stable and credible equilibrium between India's own perceptions of its national security, and just and valid international concerns about weapons of mass destruction. It is in seeking a proper balance here that India has to formulate for itself a policy on various aspects of this issue.

In meeting this obligation, however policy formulators

have to judge the matter through only one prism, that of the security of the nation. The currency for the conduct of international relations is 'power' and that remains, at least for the present, irrefutable. A failure to recognize this compounds the country's problems; an apparent intractability of issues thereafter, not reason enough to avoid even addressing them. For ambiguity and not deciding, over time, becomes a decision in itself but with many unintended and unforeseen consequences. The most illustrative example of such a strategic failure is curiously enough that of the US. In the period 1945-49, USA failed to appreciate the decisive political-military value of nuclear weapons. In the event, it did not utilize its nuclear monopoly to realize a primary political objective *vis-á-vis* the USSR: the domination over Stalin's Russia to Washington's political direction. And then not having so used its nuclear monopoly, the US Government did not even make appropriate changes in its nuclear weapons design and policy once the USSR acquired an atomic weapons' status from 1949 onwards. Subsequently, this great error was compounded by the US military establishment particularly by the US Strategic Air Command which inappropriately persisted with its doctrine of 'total war'; fuelled by the then current policy of 'massive retaliation'. But because 'total war' could be the answer only to an extreme provocation of a surprise and massive Soviet first strike, this policy could not address lesser contingencies or secure less important national interests, resulting in (and this was the great Kissingerian insight) 'power being growingly distanced from policy.'[7]

Global nuclear disarmament, a freeing of all humanity from the perils of weapons of mass destruction is a goal so worthy of achieving that India must strive unceasingly for it. But this noble goal cannot be attained if the route to it is through exclusivism, of new nuclear apartheid, in which some alone are 'haves', all others, permanently, 'have-nots'. National security is the responsibility of India's political-military leadership alone; this is neither transferable nor is it a function that can be appropriated by others.

292 / DEFENDING INDIA

THE SWORD ARM

The radically different nature of warfare that has been brought into relations in the subcontinental region, has placed demands upon the Indian state to respond with innovation and alacrity. That the policymaking structures have yet not instituted the changes required is amply borne out by the continuing conflicts in various regions of India. The fundamental point, however, resides on the premise that the future political-military leadership in India must address itself to institutionalizing decision-making. The practice of taking, and undoing, decisions simply on the basis of a personality-based regime has to come to an end. The preceding chapters amply underline the terrible price that India has had to pay on account of this, an inherently inefficient practice.

At the onset, therefore, this unworkable separation between the services headquarters from the Ministry of Defence has to be undone, and in place of this, the current inefficient structure, there shall have to be an integrated MoD. The three services have to be given the responsibility of handling the affairs of their organizations, rather than let that remain at the desk of a generalist bureaucracy. This responsibility carries with it accountability. The frequently fractured relationship between the military and the civilian bureaucracy will not then be the subject of comment, for then each will rely on the other to produce results.

The onus on efficiency, then, that confronts the MoD, in general, and the armed forces, in particular, demands the establishment a rational and a more current manpower and equipment policy. This by itself calls for the revamping of the entire force structure of the Indian Army, Navy and the Air force. The unilateral decision taken by Army Headquarters to suppress recruitments by another 50,000, admirable as it is, is not enough. For it is unilateral, and not in the framework of a national security policy, and neither is it in the context of a manpower policy which involves the entirety of the Indian state structure.

This rationalization of force structures will, by the sheer force of its momentum, also change the designs of India's war fighting capability. The concept of combined forces and capability based formations has to take root in the Indian defence and security planning mechanisms. No longer can the conventional formations undertake the tasks of tomorrows wars.

In the decades to come India shall have to continue to contend with covert operations or clandestine war. These are the changed face of combat, and they are the reality in the Indian subcontinent. The response mechanism and methodology, therefore, of the past 50 years will not work. For the last more than a decade, the changing nature of war has been apparent, as also the inefficiency inbuilt into India's decision making apparatus. Striking a balance between the ever burgeoning demand for resources and a scarcity of them, the country will have to review the structure of its forces and move towards not simply integrating them, but also build much higher levels of sustainability. And that is where, once again, concepts such as rapid action forces, task based forces for internal order, and three service's combined forces arrive. A national manpower policy, by its very nature, will be the genesis of a symbiotic relationship between the myriad of, most often competing, forces currently charged with the responsibility of India's security.

Rapid advances in technology beckon India to look at other dimensions in the methods of clandestine wars being fought all over the globe. Information technology is not merely an office tool, it is now a core element of combat, and in every spectrum of conflict. The military is not the only user to require this medium for efficacy in the field; there is just as much need for the political class and the civil services to understand this weapon, and master its usage. Only then will information technology or the cyber-space function in India as a major force multiplier. For, in the conflict environment that currently prevails, the leadership's ability to cope with India's already overstretched forces, (which in turn are shackled by decreasing resources) will have to be made good by rapid and continuous introduction of force multipliers. Given its high expertise in computer software, where the country excels, can India engage in information warfare or be a participant in the revolution in military affairs that has been set in motion by the United States? That is the real challenge to the future generations of military and political leaders of India. Till such time the debate about a National Security Council is not resolved what India must do is to appoint early a National Commission for Services, which will address all aspects of national security: from conducting a strategic defence review of the country's needs in the twenty-first century, to examining the altered nature of war, to making suggestions for force's integration and a new manpower policy that is premised on the technological revolution. The defects and deficiencies are apparent from the expanse that we have traversed. In order, therefore, to institutionalize efficiency, India will have to innovate, and adapt, so as to better ensure its security.

NOTES

1. Paul Kennedy, *The Rise and Fall of the Great Powers* (London: Unwin Hyman, 1988) in Jaswant Singh, *National Security* (New Delhi: Lancer Publications, 1996) p. 24.
2. Ibid., p. 25.
3. Henry Kissinger, *Diplomacy* (New York: Simon & Schuster, 1994) p. 812.
4. C. Rajamohan, 'Energy and Diplomacy', *The Hindu,* 25 December 1997.
5. Mark J. Valencia, 'Energy and Insecurity in Asia', *Survival,* Vol. 39, No. 3, London, Autumn 1997.
6. J. William Futrell, *Environmental Management System in a Global Market Place,* (New Delhi: The Rajiv Gandhi Foundation, 1997) p. 13.
7. Henry Kissinger, *Nuclear Weapons and Foreign Policy* (New York: Harper & Brothers, 1957) p. 365.

Index

Abdali, Ahmad Shah, 150
Afghanistan, iii, vii, 19, 38, 111, 145, 146, 148, 150
Africa, 33, 110
Age of Imperial Civilization, 24
Agreement in Colombo, 202
Air Force, Indian, ix, 61, 113, 128, 135, 136, 171, 175, 226, 227, 228, 235, 236, 248, 256, 259, 292
Air Power, xix
Air Staff Requirement (ASR), 137
Aiyer, Sir P. S. Sivaswamy, 95
AJT, 137
Akash, 139, 140
Akhnoor, 178
Akhura-Ashugang railway line, 289
Aksai Chin, 34, 112, 172, 288
Alexander, 64, 65, 67
Ali, Osman, 100
Americans, iii, xv, 57
American Ambassador, 36
American Eighth Army, x
Amritsar, 150, 176
Angrey, Kanhoji, 76, 77, 78, 79
Anti-insurgency operations in Assam, 142

Mizoram, 142
Nagaland, 142
Tripura, 142
Anti-Submarine Warfare, 115, 125
Anti-terrorist deployments in Jammu & Kashmir, 142
Punjab, 142
Antony, Frank, viii
Arab areas, vii
Arabian Sea, 3, 126
Armed Forces, 61-141
Armed Forces Reconstitution Committee (AFRC), 96
Army, ix, xiii, 45, 61, 113, 134, 225, 226, 256, 259, 274
Army Aviation Corps, 253
Army's Northern Command, 262
Arthasastra, 11, 12
Art of War, The, 12
Arunachal Pradesh, 53, 171, 286
Aryans, v
Ashok, 10, 44
Asia, 10
Asian Mutual Security, 190
Asian Relations Conference, 29, 30

Assam, 55, 152, 153, 154, 195, 286
Aswamedha sacrifice, vii, 16
Atlantic Charter, 20, 29
Attlee, C. R., 123
Auchinleck, Field Marshal Sir Claude, 96, 157, 158
Aung San, President of Burma, 24
Aurangzeb, vi, 14, 68, 72
Australia, vi, xi, 110
Austria, 99
Awamy League, 191
Azad, Maulana, 30
Aztecs, vi

Babar, v
Bajpai, Sir Girija Shankar, ix, 35
Baluchis, 75
Bangalore, 101
Bangladesh, x, 93, 153, 155, 180, 189, 285
Bangladesh war, 40
Barbarossa, 78
Bay of Bengal, 124, 126, 185, 194
Beijing, 162
Belgium, 99
Benedict, Ruth, 6
Bengal, 83, 84, 181, 132
Bhagat, General Prem, ix
Bhakti movement, vi
Bhandari, Romesh, 199
Bharat, 3
Bharatiya Janata Party, i, xvii, xviii
Bharatvarsha, 4
Bhawanji, Mohitay, 77
Bhindranwale, Sant Jarnail Singh, 154
Bhopal, 102
Bhutan, 50
Bhutto, Benazir, 245
Bhutto, Zulfikar Ali, 174, 176, 181, 186

Bihar, x
Bikaner, 100
Bolshevik 'operational code', 6
Bombay, 77, 78, 82, 83, 84, 101, 116, 125, 128, 286
Bombay Army, 90
Bombay European Regiment, 82
Bombay Grenadiers, 90
Border Roads Organization, 53, 113
Boxer Rebellion, 100
Brahmaputra, 154
Brahmin, 62
Brazil, 3
Brecher, Michel, 50
Britain, iv, vii, 5, 21, 97, 121
British, the, ii, iv, v, vii, xv, 14, 18, 20, 62, 64, 78, 87, 89, 93, 110, 130, 136
Admirality, 118, 119, 120
-American sources, 131
Centurion Tank, 248
Commonwealth, 116
dominance, 3
empire, 18
First Sea Lord, 119
Government, 123
Imperial, iv
India, 61
Indian Army, 100
Indian empire, vii
Indian Raj, iv
Navy, 79
Parliament, 18
period, 10, 19, 61, 81
Raj, 44
Stuarts, 248
troops, 97
Vice Chief of Naval Staff, 120
Brooks, Lieutenant General Henderson, 165
Budapest, xi
Buddhism, 4
Bulganin, 36
Bulgarian Party Congress, 171

Burma, 19
Burma Campaign, 131
Burr, Colonel, 90

Cabinet Committee, xv
Cabinet Committee on Defence,
  266, 267
Cabinet Committee of Political
  Affairs (CCPA), 233, 271
Calcutta, 85, 132, 193
Callaghan, L. J., 116
Cambodia, 24
Canada, xi, 3, 5
Cariappa, General, 41, 96
Caribbean, 170
Carlill, Vice Admiral S. H., 118,
  121
Carne, William, 118
Cavalry Commander, 66
Central Asia, v, 50, 67, 111,
  145, 282
Central Government, 152, 154,
  198, 219
Central Military Commission,
  241
Ceremonial Guard of Honour,
  202
Chatterji, Vice Admiral A. K.,
  126
Chaudhary, Sir Nirad, 57
Chetwode, Field Marshal, 95
Chibber, Lieutenant General,
  157
Chief of the Army Staff, 201
Chillianwala, 81
China, ii, iii, iv, ix, xi, xii, xiv,
  xix, 6, 10, 17, 20, 21, 24,
  32, 37, 39, 49, 50, 54,
  91, 104, 133, 151, 162,
  163, 164, 167, 168, 169,
  172, 190, 192, 194, 239,
  240, 241, 242, 243, 244,
  247, 249, 250, 251, 257
Chinese, the, 10, 49, 116,
  162, 163, 168, 169, 171
Chinese aggression, 52

Chinese Air Force, 50
Chinese cease-fire, 171
Chinese GNP, 240
Chinese invasion, 1962, 161
Chinese Navy, 250, 251
Choudhury, Rahul Roy, xix
Christian queen, iv
Christianity, vi, 4
Chrysanthemum and the Sword,
  6
Chushul, 162
Civil bureaucracy, viii
Clausewitz, Carl von, 12
Clive, Robert, 82
Coast Guard, 124
Coastal Defence Flights, 130
Cochin, 116
Coimbatore, 128
Commander-in-Chief, ix, 65, 95,
  96, 101, 108
Commonwealth Prime Ministers'
  Conference, 123, 175
Congress Party, i, viii, 30, 40,
  202
Constituent Assembly, 42, 47,
  54
Copland, Ian, 99
Copyright Office, xix
Cornwallis, Lord, 85
Council on Foreign Relations,
  xvi
Counter-Insurgency Operations,
  142, 151
Courtney, Sir Christopher, 102
Cuban Missile Crisis, 169
Czechoslovakia, 33

Dacca, 184, 187, 194
Da Gama, Vasco, 81
Defence Committee, 156, 158
Defence Minister, xviii
Defence Ministry, 105, 108,
  109, 157
Defence Ordnance Factories,
  223
Defence Research and

Development Organization (DRDO), 138, 139, 225
Defence Science Organization, 138
Defence Secretary, xiv, xv
Defending India, xix
Delhi, i, v, 51, 83, 286
Delhi Sultanates, 10, 14
Dhar, D. P., 190
Dharma, vii, 8
Dholpur, 14
Discovery of India, The, 46
Dixit, J. N., 196
Doda, 263
Dogras, 14
Dogra Regiment, 97
Dutch, 77
Dwarka, 125

East Asia, xiii
East Bengal, 183, 184
Eastern Sector, 1971, 182
East India Company, iv, 79, 82, 83, 85, 93, 129, 130
East Pakistan, 183, 184, 187
Economic Services, 217
Eighth Defence Plan, 229
Eighth Five-Year Plan, 229
Elphinstone, Monstuart, 71
England, 63, 68
English, 77
Englishman, 57, 63
Europe, v, 20, 130, 132, 146
Europeans, v, vi, 24, 79, 83
European nations, v
European political ideas, 9
European Union, v

Farakka, 285
54 Division, 203
Fifth Pay Commission, 224
First Chinese Attack, 170
First Indo-Pak conflict, 142
First Indo-Pak War, 155
First Sea Lord, 117
First World War, 94, 128

Forward Edge of the Battle Area (FEBA), 255
4 Infantry Division, 162
France, xii, 100
Fraser, Lord, Admiral of the Fleet, 119
French, iv, 85, 87

Galbraith, J. K., 36
Galtung, Professor Johann, v
Gandhiji, ii, 24, 41, 42, 43, 44, 105
Gandhi, Mrs Indira, 55, 153, 154, 186, 187, 188, 195, 196, 199, 209
Gandhi, Rajiv, 154, 200, 201, 207
Ganga, 285
Garhwal Rifles, 97
General Officer Commanding, 203
General Services, 217
Germany, xii, 5
Golden Temple, 150, 196
Gracey, Douglas, 157
Greeks, 15
Gross Domestic Product, 216, 245
Gross National Product, 216
Gujarat, x
Gujjar, Siddoji, 77
Gulf War, 138
Gunther, John, x
Gupta, Bhupesh, viii
Gupta empire, 18
Gurdaspur, 262

Hall, Rear Admiral J. T. S., 114
Hariman, Averill, 36
Hattersley Mills, 101
Hemachandra, 14
Henderson-Brookes, ix
HMS Hercules, 121
Himalayas, ix, 3, 4, 5, 54, 151
Himalayan bastions, 145

Himalayan War, 239
Hindu, 5, 97
Hindu civilization, vi
Hindu king, iv
Hindu milieu, 13
Hindustan, 4
Hinduism, vi, 4
Hindustani dance, vi
Hitler, 44
HMSO, xix
Hodgson, Marshal, 11
Hong Kong, 91
Hoover Administration, xiv
Humayun, v
Hungary, xi, 33
Huntington, Professor Samuel,
    vi
Huntington thesis, vii
Hydaspes (Indus), 65
Hyderabad, 99, 101, 102
Hyderabad police action, 142

IAF, 130, 131, 133, 135, 138
IGMDP, 139
IMF, Managing Director of, 218
Imperial British, 146
Imperial Service Troops, 100
Incas, vi
Independent India's military
    operations, 142-212
India, iv, vi, vii, viii, xi, xiv,
    xv, 2, 3, 9, 14, 18, 20,
    26, 61, 85, 151, 194, 239,
    265, 266, 267, 286
India-China, 36, 241, 250
India-Pakistan, 244
Indians, iii, iv, 194, 195
Indian Army, ii, 20, 89, 93,
    135, 178
Indian Army Chief, 184
Indian Army Headquarters, x,
    252, 292
Indian Cabinet, 158
Indian Commissioned Officer
    (ICO), 93
Indian Citizenship Act, vi

Indian Defence Ministry, 184
Indian Government, 123, 214
Indian image, xiv
Indianization, 93
Indian Military Academy (IMA),
    95
Indian Muslim personnel, 98
Indian National Congress, 30
Indian Naval Staff, 119
Indian Navy, xix, 79, 113, 114,
    115, 116, 119
Indianness, 10
Indian Ocean, vii, 19
Indian Parliament, 165
Indian Peacekeeping Force,
    143, 195
Indian Peacekeeping Operations,
    155
Indian people, iv
Indian Prime Minister, 202
'Indian Sandhurst', 95
Indian tradition, iii
Indian Union Budget, 216
India's national security, iii
India's strategic culture, 1
Indo-China, 4
Indo-China Conference, 162
Indo-Gangetic plains, v, 14
Indo-Pak Agreement, 186
Indo-Pakistan War, 125
Indo-Soviet, ii
Indo-Sri Lanka Agreement, 202,
    207, 208, 209
Indo-Tibet, 149
Indonesian Archipelago, 4
Infantry Combat Vehicles, 253
Inside Asia, x
INSAS, 139
INS Gomti, 233
INS Mysore, 124
INS Vikrant, 121
Intelligence Bureau (IB), 288
Internal Military Operations,
    142
Inter-state wars, 142
International affairs, xvi

International Institute of
  Strategic Studies (IISS), 241
IPKF, 204, 205, 208, 210, 277
Iran, vii
Islam, vi
Islamic invasions, 3
Islamic rulers, v

Jahangir, 68
Jain scripturist, 13
Jainism, 4
Jambu-dveep-Bharat, 4
Jammu & Kashmir, xii, 31, 43,
  55, 104, 107, 150, 152,
  155, 156, 160, 172, 174,
  175, 176, 195, 213
Jammu-Rajauri-Poonch, 175
Jane's Information Group, 247
Japan, xii, 20
Japanese, the, 5, 6, 20, 45
Japanese invasion, 19
Jataka Kathas, 12
Jayewardene Government, 196,
  201
Jhelum, 154
Jinnah, M. A., 95
Jodhpur, 100
Johnston, Alastair Iain, 7
Joint Intelligence Committee,
  273, 288
Judaisam, vi, 5
Junagadh, 102
Junagarh deployment, 142
Junior Commissioned Officer
  (JCO), 93

Kabul, 14
Kakul, 98
Kamath, H. V., viii
Kameng Division, 162
Kanyakumari, 152
Karachi, 114, 128, 129, 157
Karnad, Bharat, xix
Kashmir, ii, x, xi, xiii, 17, 24,
  117, 150, 154
Kashmir Valley, 150, 153, 178

Katari, Vice Admiral R. D., 124
Kautilya, 12, 13
Kennan, George, 30
Kennedy, 169, 170
Khan, Afzal, 72
Khan, late Major General,
  Akbar, 158
Khan, Field Marshal Ayub, 174,
  175
Khan, General Yahya, 181
Khan, Liaquat Ali, 48
Khan, Sadiqu Lutfullah, 69
Khrushchev, 36, 169, 170
King Charles II, 82
King, Martin Luther, 44
Kohat, 128
Kohima, 19
Korean Armistice Agreement,
  143
Korean war, x, 123
Koregaum, 89
Kripalani, J. B., viii
Kshatriya, 62
Kumaon Regiment, 97
Kunzru, Pandit H. N., viii
Kushans, 150
Kutayuddah, 13

Labour Party, 28
Ladakh, 17, 162, 172
LaFontaine Committee, 137
Lahore, 128, 176, 177
Latin America, xiii
Leites, Nathan, 6
Liberation of Goa, 142
Liberation Tigers of Tamil Eelam
  (LTTE), 154, 196, 201,
  206, 207, 208, 210, 268,
  289
Light Combat Aircraft (LCA),
  139
Light Fleet Aircraft Carriers,
  114
Line of control, xiii
Lockhart, General Sir Robert,
  44

Lodi, Ibrahim, 67
Lohia, Ram Manohar, viii
London, 81, 85, 123, 241

MacArthur, General Douglas, x
MacFarqualer, R., xix, 169
Madras, 83
Madras Artillery, 90
Madras European Regiment, 82
Madras Fusiliers, 82
Mahabharata, The, 62
Maharashtra, 73
Major Military Operations (1947-97), 142
Major Peacekeeping Operations (1947-97), 143
Malacca, 193, 110
Malaya, 91
Maldives, the, 54, 147, 127
Malgaonkar, 76
Malraux, André, 24
Manekshaw, General, 184
Manipur, 286
Mao Dze Dung, x
Mao Zedong, 44
Maoris, vi
Maratha army, 87
Maratha guerrillas, 87, 88
Maratha Light Infantry, 97
Maratha Confederacy, 72
Maratha Navy, 266
Maratha spirit, 73
Marshal, General, 30
Marxist philosophy, 36
Masani, M. R., viii
Mason, Philip, 63
Mathura-Agra, 14
Matter of Honour, A, 63
Maurya, Chandragupta, 10, 11, 64, 65, 66
Mauryan, 18
Mayans, vi
McMahon Line, 160, 167
Meghalaya, 286
Mehta, Ashok, viii
Mehta, Jagat, xix, 22, 26

Menon, Krishna, 26, 27, 28, 35, 165, 166, 168
Messervy, Frank, 157
Mewar, 62
Mexican Indians, 3
Military Engineering Service, 53
Military Intelligence, ix, 288
Ministry of Defence (MoD), 103, 106, 114, 166, 222, 292
Ministry of External Affairs, 166, 201, 206
Mistri Airlines, 102
Mizoram, 151, 154, 286
Mornington, Lord, 88
Moscow, 188, 190
Mountbatten, Lady Edwina, 123
Mountbatten, Lord, 24, 30, 96, 113, 116, 118, 120, 121, 122, 123, 157
Mountbatten papers, xix
Mughal Army, 71
Mughal Empire, 11, 14, 81
Mughals, v, 10, 62, 64, 67, 70, 72, 78
Mughal-Rajput coalition, 68
Muzaffarabad, 155
Mukerji, H. N., viii
Mukti Bahini Control, 189
Muslims, iv, vii, 9, 74, 75, 97, 194
Muslim rule, iv
Myanmar, 24, 146, 151
Mysore, 100

Nagaland, 154, 155, 286
National Agenda, xvii, xviii
National Commission for Services, 294
Nationalism, v
National Security Council, (NSC), xv, xvi, xviii, 271, 272, 294
National Security Management, xvi
NATO, 31
Naval Headquarters, 121

Naval Staff, 124
Navy, 61, 134, 225, 226, 228, 234, 293
Nawanagar, 100 101
Nehru, B. K., viii, 23, 25, 27, 34
Nehru, Jawaharlal, i, ii, vii, viii, x, 22, 25, 26, 27, 28, 30, 34, 39, 40, 41, 42, 43, 44, 45, 49, 53, 56, 57, 58, 101, 111, 120, 123, 156, 167, 168, 172, 180, 267
Nehru, Pandit Motilal, 95
Nehru's Defence Policy, 22
Nehru's death, 35
Nehru's pronouncement, 56
Nepal, x, 50, 54, 143, 286
New Delhi, 187, 189, 190, 192 see also Delhi
New Zealand, 5
Nikator, Selukos, 65
Nizam, Osman Ali, 99
Nonalignment, ii, iii, viii
Non-Proliferation Treaty, 37
North African countries, 285
North-East, 17
North-Eastern Frontier Province, 160
North India, 3
Northern Army, 262
Northern Ireland, 121
NSC Secretariat, xvi
Nuclear Defence Policy, 273
Nyamkachu, 160

Observer Group in Lebanon, 143
Operation Bluestar, 142, 196
Operation Cactus in the Maldives, 143
Operation Gibraltar, xiii
Ottoman empire, 11

Padmavathi, xx
Pai, Nath, viii
Pakistan, iii, viii, x, xi, xii, xiv, 21, 26, 27, 49, 54, 104, 118, 125, 128, 153, 154, 174, 176, 177, 178, 186, 188, 239, 241, 244, 245, 257
Pakistan Army, 186
Pakistan Army Headquarters, 155
Pakistani Commander General, 184
Pakistani Navy, 114
Pakistani naval attack, 125
Pakistan naval ships, 125
Pakistani Prime Minister, 48
Panchsheel, 112
Panchatantra, 12
Panchendriya, 139
Pan-Indian, 18
Parliament, viii, xviii, 48
Parliamentary Secretary, 116
Parry, Vice Admiral, 115, 122
Partition, 20, 21, 24, 26, 27, 28, 29, 30, 31, 36, 39, 61, 92, 96-98, 99, 101, 102, 104, 105, 106, 113, 131, 150, 213
Partition Council, 113
Patel, Sardar Vallabhbhai, 43
Pathankot-Jammu-Srinagar road link, 178
Pearl Harbour, xiv
People's Liberation Army (PLA), 32
People's Republic of China, 17, 34, 39, 148, 152
Persian Gulf, 91
Peshawar, 128
Peshwa, 90
Pizey, Admiral Mark, 115, 123
Planning Commission, xv, xvi
Portugal, 99
Portuguese, the, 77, 78, 82
Post-Cold War, 276, 282
Prabhakaran, 208
Prime Minister's Office, 166
Prithvi, 139

PSAPDS, 139
Public Works Department, 53
Punjab, x, xii, 55, 154, 195, 262
Punjab Boundary Force, 142
Pye, Lucian, 6

Quasi-military forces, 88
Quetta, 98

Radhakrishnan, Dr Sarvepalli, 8, 34
Rajasthan, x
Rajput, 14, 62, 75
Rajput kingdom, 62
Ram, iv, 62
Ramayana, 62
Rand Corporation, iii
Ranga, N. G., viii
Rann of Kutch, viii
  operations, 143
Rau, Sir B. N., 26
Ravana, iv, 62
Rawalpindi, 157
Red Indians, 3
'Red Napoleons in Blue', x
Reorganized Army Mountain Infantry Division, 253
Reorganized Army Plains Infantry Division, 253
Research and Analysis Wing (RAW), 288
Rezung La, 162
Richard I, 63
Risalpur, 128
Roe, Sir Thomas, 68
Rose, Leo, 193
Rosen, Stephen Peter, 5, 7, 58, 84
Royal Air Force (RAF), 129, 130, 132
Royal Indian Air Force, 128
Royal Indian Army Service Corps School, 98
Royal Indian Navy, 113
Royal Institute, xvi

Royal Military College, 94
Royal Navy, 124
Russia, xi, xii, 5, 20, 39, 165, 127, 229, 282, 291

Safaid Iranian Muslim empires, 11
'Sanatana Dharma', 5
Sandys, Duncan, 36
Sanskrit, 4
Sanyasi, 88
Sarkar, Jadunath, 14
Sarva Bhauma (Emperor), vii
SEATO, 37
Second Chinese attack, 171
Second Indo-Pak War, 142, 155, 172, 180
Second President of India, 34
Second World War, ix, xv, 20, 31, 93, 96, 101, 110, 130, 131, 132, 159, 213, 248, 276
Sela-Bomdila, ix
Sherman Tanks, 248
Shimla Agreement, 186
Shiromani Akali Dal, 153
Shivaji, 72, 73, 74, 75, 76, 77, 79, 80
Shudra, 62
Siddies, 77
Sikhism, 4, 50, 143
Sikkim, 143
Sindhu (Indus), 3, 4
Sindis, 75
Singapore, 193
Singh, Air Commodore Jasjit, xix
Singh, Dr Manmohan, 218
Singh, Guru Gobind, 80, 14
Singh, Jaswant, i, iii, iv, viii, x, xi, xiii, xvi, xvii, xviii
Singh, Maharaja Hari, 156
Singh, Manmohan, 218
Singh, Ranjit, 72, 80, 81
Singh, Swaran, xix
Singh, Zorawar, 149

Sino-Indian border war, 142, 160
Sino-Indian dispute, 34
Sino-Indian relations, 43
Sino-Indian skirmishes, 143
Sino-Indian war, 133, 155, 267
Sino-Soviet dispute, ix
Sir Dorab Tata Trust, xix
Skeen, Sir Andrew, 95
Sleeman, 75
Slims, Field Marshal, xivth Army, 19
Somadeva, 13
Somalia, 277
South Asia, 146, 239
South Asia Command, 108
South Asia region, 29
South-East Asia, vii, 114
South-West Asia, 38
Soviet Union, ii, iii, 57, 116
Sri Lanka, x, 54, 126, 143, 147, 155, 194, 195, 196, 197, 198, 199, 200, 201, 202, 268, 286
Sri Lankan Agreement, 203
Sri Lankan Government, 207
Sri Lankan operation, 206
Sri Lankan policy, 209
Sri Lankan Tamils, 200, 208, 209
Srinagar, 156, 177
Srinagar Valley, 159, 262
Srinivasan, N., 280
Staff College, 98
Stalin, 44
Staunton, Captain, 89, 90
Stimson, Henry, xiv
Strategic culture, 1-60
Strategic Policy Group, 271
Stringer, Lawrence, 97
Subrahmanyam, K., xix, 22, 40, 50, 55
Sultan, Tipu, 87
Sumatra, 85
Sundarji, General K., 201
Sun Tzu, 12

Surat, 77
Surrey, 247

Taiwanese, the 169
Taj Mahal, vi
Tamil Nadu, x, 195, 198, 207, 209
Tanham, George, iii
Tashkent Declaration, 179
Tata Energy Research Institute (TERI), 285
Teen Murti, 101
Thagla Ridge, 160
Thailand, vii
Thapar, Romila, 16
Thapar, 166
Thimmaya, General, ix, 49, 96
Third Indo-Pak War, 142, 155
Third World, 25, 36
Third World unity, 29
Tibet, vii, 19, 50, 145, 148, 164
Travancore, 86, 99
Trishul, 140
Truce Agreement, 157
Truman Doctrine, 20
Twang, 160
Tyagi, Mahavir, 117

UK, xii, 36, 273
UN Angola Verification Mission, 143
UN Assistance Mission in Rwanda II, 143
UN Force in Egypt, 143
UN General Assembly, 188
UN Iraq-Iran Military Group, 143
UN military team for Mozambique, 143
UN Observers' Group, 143
UN Peace Enforcement Operations, 143
UN Peacekeeping in Angola, 143
UN Peacekeeping in Congo/

Zaire, 143
UN Peacekeeping in Somalia, 143
UN Peacekeeping Operations, 143
UN Security Council, 188
Unbalanced Force Development, 237
United Liberation Front of Assam (ULFA), 153, 195
US, ii, iii, vi, viii, xi, xii, xiv, xv, 5, 28, 36, 37, 42, 46, 116, 136, 169, 277, 285, 291, 294
USSR, 32, 37, 49, 134, 135, 136, 153, 169, 291
U. Thant, UN Secretary General, 176

Vaishnav Bhakti, 13
Vaishya, 62
Verba, Sidney, 6
Verma, Bharat, xix
Viceroy, 76
Viceroyalty of Lord Curzon, 181
Viceroy of India, 96
Viceroy's Commissioned Officer (VCO), 93
Victoria Cross, ix, 89
Victoria, Queen, iv

Vietnam, 24
'Vijay Divas' (Victory Day), 184
Vikramaditya's throne, xvii
Vindhyas, 3
Viproh Bahudha Vadanthi, vi
Vishakapatnam, 116, 126, 132

Wagah, 176
Warsaw Pact, 31
War Wastage Reserve (WWR), 222, 226, 228, 259
Washington Special Action Group (WSAG), 192
Weiner, Myron, 8
Wellesley, Arthur, 73, 87
Wellesley, Richard, 85
West Asian identity (of Pakistan), 28
West Bengal, 183, 286
Western Sector, 1965, 173
Whitehall, 20, 105
World Trade Organization, 269
World War II, 5

Xiao, Ambassador Liu, 169

Yalu, x

Zoroastrianism, vi, 4

Postscript

Clearly this is less an afterthought more an additionality, in which sense it is hardly a postscript, being in reality a continuation of an earlier, half articulated position. In the previous chapter is contained an outline of India's approach to the entire issue of 'nuclearisation', as one of the challenges of the future needing clarity and resolution, but it was really only as an outline. In that chapter were offered some broad integrals meriting attention: for instance, a reconciliation between India's security needs and valid international concerns about weapons of mass destruction; between a moralistic and the realistic approach to nuclear weapons; between a covert or an overt nuclear policy. 11th May, 1998 changed all that. A statement issued in New Delhi on that day announced that India had successfully carried out three underground nuclear tests at the Pokhran range. This was followed on 13th May by two more underground, sub-kiloton tests. The Government of India, thereafter, announced the completion of the series, and also a number of other steps. These five tests ranging from the sub-kiloton variety to fission to thermonuclear amply demonstrated India's scientific, technical and organizational abilities, until then only vaguely suspected. A fortnight later, on 28 and 30 May, with predictable inevitability, neighbouring Pakistan also carried out its tests in the bleak fastnesses of Chagai Hills in Baluchistan, bordering Afghanistan. With these developments of May 28, the strategic equipoise of the post cold war world got significantly unsettled; questions of fundamental importance to the entire non-proliferation regime, and the future of the disarmament debate got placed at the forefront of international agendas.

This postscript is, therefore, an attempt at assessing some of the strategic consequences of the May '98 developments in South Asia. What are the global implications of it; what lies at the heart of western concerns; what were the Indian national security reasons for these tests? What future then of the non-proliferation regime and of disarmament? Has South Asia become more unsafe or less so? Is the nuclear genie out of the bottle and are we back to the sterility of the cold war years? These are amongst some of the concerns that got voiced in the aftermath of the tests. These, therefore, are also the issues that we attempt to address. But for that we have to first trace the evolution of India's nuclear programme.

Development of India's nuclear energy programme

The roots of the Indian atomic energy programme go back to the early 40's; before even the country's independence from British colonial rule. The beginning was almost incidental. In 1944, Dr Homi Babha, premier nuclear physicist of his times wrote to the doyen of Indian industry, late JRD Tata, then Chairman of the Sir Dorabji Tata Trust, "suggesting the setting up of an institute devoted to basic scientific and technological research"[1]. In response was born the Tata Institute of Fundamental Research; and it this institute that gave Homi Bhabha the needed platform. "The experimental groups started by Bhabha deserve special mention because they became the forerunners of all indigenous technological activity in the country and heralded the beginnings of an extensive atomic energy programme in India",[2] says Raja Ramanna, who oversaw the first nuclear tests in 1974. The Tata Institute of Fundamental Research subsequently went on to even design and assemble India's first computer in 1957. The earliest of the laboratory scale nuclear experiments were also conducted during this period.

Soon after independence, in Aug '48, the Atomic Energy Commission of India (AEC) was constituted with Homi Bhabha as the first chairman. In these initial years it was the close intellectual bonding between Bhabha and the first Prime Minister, Jawaharlal Nehru, that laid the foundation of subsequent self-sufficiency in diverse scientific fields including nuclear energy. On 4 August 1956, Apsara, the 'swimming pool' reactor went critical. Outside of the Soviet Union this was the first to become so operational in Asia. Homi Bhabha's logic for the development of the Indian atomic energy programme was founded in the belief that as the country was not sufficiently endowed with resources of conventional fuel, development of nuclear energy sources for power production was vital. In course of time, the first nuclear power generating reactor came up at Tarapore in 1969. For this fuel was imported from the United States on the basis of a 1963 Treaty. But this contract also had other ramifications, as Raja Ramanna recounts, "As time went by, inspection clauses were constantly amended, unilaterally by the supplier countries, and included all kinds of engineering items... For instance, heavy water was considered on par with enriched uranium"[3]. In the meantime Canada assisted in the construction of the Candu-type reactors in Rajasthan, aware of India's established technical expertise in plutonium production. Similarly, whilst designing the Cirus reactor, Canada offered to help with the first fuel charge of natural uranium, as presumably "(India) would find the fuel technology too advanced to handle"[4]. Indian scientists, however, managed to demonstrate their ability again and developed the fuel for the reactor, and of a "better quality than had hitherto been offered'[5.]

On 23 January 1966, Dr Homi Bhabha died in an aircrash in the Swiss Alps. "A chapter in the history of Indian science and technology [came] to an abrupt end. Bhabha's valuable contributions to Indian science remain unquantifiable"[6].

In the early seventies Dr H N Sethna took over the reins of the AEC, with Dr Raja Ramanna becoming the Director of the recently renamed Bhabha Atomic Research Centre. This institute, established in 1957 as the Atomic Energy Establishment, and renamed only after Bhabha's death has, in subsequent years, proven itself as an example of inter-disciplinary scientific research in the country. The International Atomic Energy Agency had also come into being in 1958. India, became a founder member and has continued to play a very prominent role. This also resulted in a regime of inspections of nuclear installations in the country. Predictably, these became, or tended to be intrusive and sovereignty violative regimes. "In the proposals made to us, there was neither a note of persuasion, nor an attitude of give and take in the general interest of world non-proliferation. It was thrust upon us as though the superpowers were the chosen custodians to uphold the peace of the world... Although we were bitterly criticised by the West and were woefully short of time, experience and confidence involving high technology, self-reliance truly began at this point of time"[7].

Nuclear weapons and national security

In 1947, when India emerged as a free country to take its rightful place in the global community, nuclear age had already dawned. Indian leadership then opted for self-reliance, freedom of thought and of action. India rejected the cold war paradigm and instead of aligning with either bloc, chose the more difficult path of non-alignment. The foundation of this guiding principle of non-alignment lay in India's quest for retaining maximum autonomy of decision making in the realm of international affairs; to not get locked in any super-power rivalary, and to endeavour to attain an alternative global balance of power: a balance structured also around universal, non-discriminatory disarmament.

In any event, development of nuclear technology had already by then transformed the nature of global security. It has been reasoned that nuclear weapons are not actually weapons of war; that these weapons of mass destruction are in effect a military deterrent and a tool of possible diplomatic coercion. A nuclear-weapon-free-world would, therefore, enhance not only India's security but also the security of all nations. So it was asserted then and that basic doctrine remains as the foundational thought of Indian nuclear policy. In the absence of universal and non-discriminatory disarmament India could scarely accept a regime that created arbitrary divisions between nuclear haves and have-nots. Also, that it is the sovereign right of every nation to make a judgement regarding it's supreme national interests, in pursuance of which to then exercise sovereign choice. It is from this that the other tenet: of the principle of equal and legitimate security interests of all nations flows. This is what conflicts with the assertions of a self identified and a closed club, that of the P5 - the Permanent Five of the United Nations Security Council.

During the decade of the 50's, nuclear weapons testing routinely took place above ground. That characteristic mushroom cloud became the visible symbol of the age. India, even then took a lead in calling for an end to all nuclear weapon's testing, as that first essential step for ending a, by then, rampant nuclear arms race. On 2 April, 1954 shortly after a major hydrogen bomb test had been conducted, the then Prime Minister, Jawaharlal Nehru stated in the country's parliament that "nuclear, chemical and biological energy and power should not be used to forge weapons of mass destruction".[8] He called for negotiations for prohibition and elimination of all nuclear weapons and in the interim, a standstill agreement to halt all nuclear testing. The world had by then witnessed less than 65 tests. The call was, ofcourse, not heeded. In 1963, an agreement did finally emerge, the Partial Test Ban Treaty, but this became possible only because by then countries had sufficiently developed their technologies for conducting underground nuclear tests.

During the 60's, as we have seen in the earlier chapters, India's security concerns deepened. Then took place a major new development: the reality of the nuclear age arrived in India's neighborhood. As K Subrahmanyam in a recently published book reminiscences: "October 16, 1964 was one of the defining moments in the history of Indian nuclear policy. Upto that date India only thought of developing a capability which could be converted into a nuclear weapon option, if it became necessary. On that day when China became a nuclear weapon power it became imperative for Indian policy makers to give serious consideration [to] the country acquiring nuclear weapons. A few days later Dr. Bhabha talked of India being in a position to go nuclear in about eighteen months following a decision and that it would then cost only Rs. [1.8 million] per weapon.... As a Deputy Secretary in the Ministry of Defence I submitted a paper to the Defence Secretary urging that the Government set up a Committee under Dr. Bhabha to analyze the implications of the Chinese bomb to India's security and our response to it. Mr. K.R. Narayanan, at that time Director (China) in the Ministry of External Affairs (now the President of India) was also reported to have sent a note, making out a case for India exercising the nuclear option. As a result of [these] moves... a Secretaries' Committee was formed. [It is thus that] India's nuclear security concern goes back to 1964."[9]

Options for India were limited; to either address next door developments on its own; to persist with global disarmament and continue to remain 'non-nuclear;' or to seek international guarantees. "It is in this context that the then Prime Mininster Lal Bahadur Shastri was believed to have requested the British Prime Minister Harold Wilson for an extended deterrence by Britain, during his visit to that country during December 1964 but there was no favourable British response."[10]

Inevitably the nuclear debate within the country sharpened. It began to focus on the emerging nuclear reality. Voices began to be raised questioning both the validity and the continuing relevance of nuclear abstinence, and that too, by India alone. Besides, the sobering experience of 1962 continued to trouble the Indian political community. Prime Minister "Lal Bahadur Shastri withstood that pressure but made a slight modification on the earlier policy. He announced that India would not embark on the nuclear programme 'now', implying that the policy could change. At the same time he sanctioned the proposal put forward by Dr. Bhabha on investigating a 'Subterranean Nuclear Explosion Project' (SNEP)."[11] And thus was planted the seed for Pokharan I, of the peaceful nuclear explosion (PNE) of 1974. Efforts on the disarmament front, however, continued.

"In 1965 India along with other nations moved Resolution 2028 in the UN General Assembly, [aimed at halting] the spread of nuclear weapons. The Indian intention was to ensure that there was reciprocity of obligations between nuclear weapon powers who already possessed [these weapons] in 1965, and the small group of non-aligned countries."[12] India then put forward the idea of an international non-proliferation agreement under which the nuclear weapon states would agree to give up their arsenals provided other countries refrained from developing or acquiring such weapons. Alongwith were taken other initiatives. For instance soundings despite earlier failures, for security guarantees. These, predictably, yet again yielded no results. It needs to be recollected that in 1965 had occurred the Second Indo-Pak War, and that early in 1966, Prime Minister Shastri had died in Tashkent to be succeeded by Mrs Indira Gandhi.

The missions then commissioned by her and undertaken by Dr. Vikram Sarabhai, who had succeeded Dr. Bhabha as the Chairman of the Atomic Energy Commission, and L.K. Jha, who was then still secretary to the Prime Minister, during the winter 1966-67 were not successful. "They went to Moscow, Paris, London and Washington. They could not get the kind of joint assurance they wanted from the nuclear weapon powers across the Cold war divide.... this was also the time when France developed its own deterrent and proclaimed its lack of credibility in the US extended deterrence. The French very pertinently raised the query whether the US would risk New York or Washington to save Paris."[13]

In this backdrop the Non-Proliferation Treaty opened for negotiations. The country's parliament debated the issue on 5 April 1968. The then Prime Minister, Mrs. Indira Gandhi assured the House that "we shall be guided entirely by [enlightened self-interest] and... considerations of national security."[14] She highlighted the shortcomings of the NPT whilst reemphasising the country's commitment to nuclear disarmament. She warned the House and the country "that not signing the Treaty may bring the nation many difficulties. It may mean the stoppage of aid and stoppage of help. Since we are taking this decision together, we must all be together in facing its consequences."[15] This debate became, in effect, another turning point in India's nuclear journey, for national security in a proliferating nuclear environment.

During tortuous negotiations on the Treaty (NPT), "The US, Russia and UK twisted the proposal for a halt [to] the spread of nuclear weapons to suit their own agenda. [This] came in handy for the US to resist the demands of its NATO partners, especially Germany for a multilateral or an Atlantic nuclear force. Russia was also interested in preventing Germany and Japan [from] acquiring nuclear weapons. They converted the Non-proliferation Treaty into one licensing unlimited nuclear proliferation to the five nuclear weapon powers with a total ban on acquisition of nuclear weapons by all, by [any other] other nation. India fought against this hegemonic imposition of a discriminatory treaty dividing the world into five privileged ones and the rest. Others who initially found the treaty unacceptable finally succumbed to the pressure of the United States. This included Germany, Japan and Sweden."[16] It needs to be noted, also emphasised that "at that stage China did not join the NPT, and its delegation was excluded from participating in the UN. China was conducting atmospheric nuclear tests along with France defying the international norm which under the Partial Test Ban Treaty prohibited such tests."[17]

As K Subrahmanyam recollects again: "India had at that stage the Canada-India reactor and the Plutonium Reprocessing plant at Trombay in operation. A stockpile of weapon grade Plutonium was being built. Using this Plutonium, BARC had designed the Purnima reactor and operation of this reactor enabled the scientists to gather all data necessary to design a nuclear explosive device. The scientific establishment pressed for permission to conduct the subterranean nuclear explosion. At that stage both US and USSR were conducting a large number of experiments in peaceful nuclear explosions which were intended to be applied to civil engineering purposes, for benefaction of ores, releasing gas, liquefying shale etc. The Indian scientists had presented papers in international conferences on applications of peaceful explosions. It was accepted all over the world and Indian scientific establishment did not dispute it - that technology for peaceful explosions and weapons was the same. Since there was a commitment that the Canada - India reactor would not be used for purposes other than peaceful it appears to have been decided to go in for a peaceful explosion on the lines conducted by US and USSR. Peaceful nuclear explosions [do, afterall] find a place in the NPT. Finally Mrs. Gandhi gave the go ahead to the scientists some time in October 1972.... There are no papers to explain Mrs. Gandhi's decision."[18]

Hereafter, this Peaceful Nuclear Exposion of 1974, or Pokharan I as it has now come to be called is best described in the words of one of the principal participants: Dr Raja Ramanna. He describes the test with a sense of immediacy and vividity:

"After Vikram Sarabhai's death in 1971, India [had begun] to seriously consider conducting a PNE. Although we [India] had the design of the explosive device ready, the production of the plutonium alloy, the trigger device and the associated electronic devices was yet to commence.

Further, for the development of the implosion device we needed to liaise with the defence laboratories in the country as they were to fabricate the explosive lenses; thankfully, this became easy as Dr Nag Chaudhary, the head of the defence laboratories, was an old friend of mine. With his help the project was not difficult to streamline.

By 1973, when all material problems had been tackled, the most important aspect of the Pokhran experiment arose: the site to conduct the experiment. This was far from simple as one had to take both the political and the logistical angle into consideration. Finally, the army testing range in the Thar desert was chosen as the location as it was a closed area with a sparse human population; above all there was a very remote likelihood of water sources underground. The last condition was significant because it had been decided that the PNE would be an underground experiment.

It was found that there was hardly any detailed information available on the ground water sources of the Thar and that led us to try the "wild cat" method of prospecting in order to locate a place where there would be no water down to a hundred metres or more. A well was dug at a likely spot but water came gushing out at a comparatively shallow depth and the site had to be abandoned. Several days later it occurred to us that we could ask the villagers whether they knew of any abandoned, dry wells in the area. An old villager took us to one such place. Once again a few days were lost in assessing the spot but eventually the old man was proven right. We had found the location for the Pokhran experiment.

Work progressed well and the soon came for taking important decisions.... As the experiment demanded high-level secrecy, Mrs. Gandhi decided that only a few, select people be privy to it. Those who were present at the first round of meetings were: P.N. Haksar, the former Principal Secretary to the PM; P.N. Dhar, the incumbent Principal Secretary; Dr. Nag Chaudhary, Scientific Advisor to the Defence Minister; H.N. Sethna, the then Chairman of the Atomic Energy Commission and myself, [Dr Raja Ramanna]   In the initial meetings considerable discussion ensued on the economic repercussions and possible fallout of the experiment.

After discussing the various implications of the experiment a decision was taken to proceed. At these meetings it was also decided that, simultaneously with preparations to carry out the experiment, studies would also be conducted to determine the impact Pokhran would have on the Indian economy - in terms of the reactions of India's trading partners.

It was getting to be summer and there were strong north-easterly winds as the site was prepared for the Peaceful Nuclear Explosion. The winds were a good sign as it meant any fallout from the explosion would be prevented from drifting towards Pakistan. We had of course studied the geological strata in the region and the physicists responsible for safety measures ruled out any potential for large-scale damage. Mrs. Gandhi was then approached to convene a last meeting that would set the seal on the project. It was to be merely a formality as the preparations had advanced to such an extent that we could not have retraced our steps. For instance, with considerable difficulty, keeping all the safety and security measures in view, we had moved the plutonium alloy to the site giving the preparations, in effect, the final touch.

Like all important decision-making processes, the final meeting on Pokhran was one which involved heated discussions. P.N. Dhar was vehemently opposed to the explosion as he felt it would damage our economy; Haksar took the view that time was not ripe and gave his reasons; my own view was that it was now impossible to postpone the date given the expense, time and the critical stage the experiment had reached. Fortunately for my team. Mrs. Gandhi decreed that the experiment should be carried out on schedule for the simple reason that India required such a demonstration.

The day was fixed: 18 May 1974. A fortnight before D-day I visited Pokhran in order to supervise the final arrangements and found that the atmosphere was most relaxed. The morale of the scientists was excellent and they were confident of the operation's success. When I asked Dr. P.K. Iyengar (later Director, BARC) whether we had taken everything into consideration he remarked sharply in his usual style: 'This has to work or the laws of physics are wrong.' A group under Dr. Chidambaram [now Chairman, Department of Atomic Energy] had worked on the calculations in great detail and was certain about the experiment going off smoothly. The plutonium ball in its plastic cover looked beautiful (but no different from the dummy beside it) except that it was hot due to alpha activity.

Several scientists had worked themselves to the bone in order to bring the project to this stage; the chemistry of plutonium had been studied under Dr. Ramanaiah and the preparation of the alloy and its machining was taken up by the radio metallurgy division under P.R. Roy who was assembling the various parts alone in a makeshift radiochemical laboratory built at the site; the electronic system for the experiment was designed under the guidance of Dr. Dastidar; his assistant, the late Dr. Seshadri, was even now overexerting himself by carrying out all the operations manually (I had to tell him : 'Seshadri, we did not bring you here to pull cables, there are others who can do this. You are here to supervise that all the systems are indeed working.' But that was his characteristic style of working and it finally killed him a few years later); the neutron trigger had taken a long time to design - however, it was made ready on time by Dr. Roy and Dr. Murthy and was given a codename, 'Flower'. (The reason 'Flower' had taken so much time to fabricate was that it had to be an alpha-beryllium source of a certain shape and strength brought together at an appropriate time; the polonium for the alpha source had to be produced by irradiating bismuth in our reactors and this process proved to be somewhat tardy.)

For the Pokhran experiment we had had to collaborate with the Defence Research and Development Organization (DRDO). Prior to 1972, the Bhabha Atomic Research

Centre (BARC) and the DRDO had never worked together on any project involving high-level secrecy. This collaboration was thus surprising as the two were culturally opposed but thanks to Dr. Nag Chaudhary things went smoothly on the Pokhran project. The DRDO's contributions to the Pokhran experiment - the development of the lenses and the fabrication of the high explosives - were very significant.

On 18 May our team attended to the final details. We had to realign the lenses as they could not bear the weight over them and were giving way. We then faced some earthing problems between the generator and the power supply at the pit. Though these problems appeared small they were potentially dangerous - for instance the faulty earthing could have led to sparking which in turn could have activated the explosives. Displaying considerable courage Balakrishnan of the DRDO rectified these at the pit.

It was time now for the realization of our month of preparation. There was some argument about who would press the button to detonate the device but I put an end to it by suggesting that the person who had been responsible for fabricating the trigger should, in a manner of speaking, pull it. Dastidar was chosen to press the button after counting backwards from twenty. While he stood to one side of the observation scaffolding some four kilometres from the detonation spot, the other side was reserved for the photographing of the event. A wireless relay of the counting was made audible to the photographers so that they could prepare themselves when the count reached five. For some reason the photographers cut off the counting relay at six and after that we heard nothing. We thought the worst had happened and something had gone wrong but about five seconds later, right in front of us, the whole earth rose up as though Lord Hanuman had lifted it.

We knew that the experiment had succeeded and shook hands and started descending the scaffolding: in our excitement we'd forgotten all about the shock wave that follows a nuclear explosion - the vibrations of it hit us soon after and made us even happier. As far as we were concerned, it only confirmed the success of the operation. The seismic team under the direction of George Verghese placed the yield between twelve and fifteen kilotons.... The health physicist reported no radiation activity anywhere above ground level after the explosion.

Since 1974, several people have asked me about the strict silence we maintained on the Pokhran project and our ability to restrict its knowledge to a few persons. I suppose it was the magnitude of the operation and the enormity of its implications that led us all to honour the oath of secrecy so diligently. We also realized that had word got around about India's attempt to conduct a PNE, there would've been insurmountable pressures both from inside and outside the country to stall the experiment..... Pokhran came as a surprise to the world. They hadn't expected such an achievement from a developing nation."[19]

In this narrative of the decade of the 70's there is need to cite yet another development. In 1971 had occurred the Bangladesh Liberation War and the Third Indo-Pak conflict. It was on that occasion that the US had employed militarily (also nuclear?) coercive tactics against India. K Subhramanyam recollects how, "Dr. Kissinger [has] described in detail in his book, The White House Years [that] he pressed the Chinese to intervene against India and the Chinese refused to do so fearing [a] Soviet reaction. The US, then sent in its Task Force 74, headed by the nuclear aircraft carrier USS Enterprise, on board of which nuclear weapons were then standard equipment. Now we know that there were no specific operational directions to the Enterprise mission. But at that stage the Indian Government could not but assume the worst and treat it as an act of nuclear intimidation. We also know now what President Nixon disclosed subsequently, that he did contemplate the use of nuclear weapons at that stage. There are various accounts of the Soviet deterrent reaction to the Enterprise mission. A Soviet task force followed the Enterprise force. There are reports of the Soviet Naval headquarters having generated a lot of signals to their submarines with a view to enhancing the deterrent impact on the US... But this experience of nuclear intimidation must have influenced Mrs. Gandhi in giving the green signal to the Atomic Energy Department to go ahead with the nuclear test in 1972."[20]

It appears, however, that the decision about the PNE of 1974 could have been taken earlier. There being no records, as none have been made publicy yet, perforce we rely on memory. "Towards the end of August 1971 I had my last meeting with Dr. Sarabhai at a private dinner in Ashoka Hotel. The third person present was Sisir Gupta. During dinner Dr. Sarabhai told me that Mr. Krishan Kant [now Vice President of India] and I could relax and take it easy on our campaign on India exercising [the] nuclear option. He added that he was going to attend the next French nuclear tests at Mururoa. I asked him what conclusions I was to draw from that observation. He laughed and said that I could draw whatever conclusions I wanted. Dr. Sarabhai did not go to Mururoa. He died suddenly on 31 December, 1971."[21]

The Pokhran test, predictably, inspired a reaction in Pakistan, and Zulfiqar Ali Bhutto, the then Prime Minister initiated the weaponisation programme. Towards the end of this decade, [in] early "April 1979 Mr. Vajpayee [now Prime Minister, then] as Foreign Minister disclosed in Parliament that Pakistan's nuclear programme was not peaceful... A few days later, the US Government invoked the Symington amendment and imposed sanctions on Pakistan on the ground that there was evidence that Pakistan was engaged in Uranium enrichment for weapon purposes. In the seventies the world [had become] aware of [late] Prime Minister Bhutto's... efforts [at purchasing] a Plutonium reprocessing plant from France. A contract for [this] was signed and Dr. Kissinger warned Prime Minister Bhutto, in 1976, that if he persisted in pushing his efforts through on acquisition of nuclear weapons he would be 'made a horrible example of'. Bhutto, [later, gave voice to the sentiment] that his overthrow was partly ascribable to his drive for acquiring nuclear weapons."[22]

Earlier, in 1978, France had under US pressure canceled the contract with Pakistan for the reprocessing plant. "However, intelligence information was that 90 per cent of the drawings and bulk of the plant and equipment needed had already [by then] reached Pakistan. While all this was in public domain the Joint Intelligence Committee, (of which I was then the Chairman) assessed that Pakistan's preferred route was going to be Uranium enrichment and bulk of the equipment had already reached Pakistan. Simaltaneously, a book, Pakistan's Islamic Bomb appeared. This was the first book on Pakistan's effort. A few months later Mr. P.K.S. Namboodiri [the co-author] came up with a rare insight, that Bhutto's reference to the treaty he concluded after eleven years of negotiations, for which [he had asserted] he would be remembered with gratitude by future generations of Pakistanis', [was] to a treaty with China. A year later the British defence analyst, Edgar O'Ballance published an article confirming Mr. Namboodiri's hypothesis. He also disclosed that the Chinese collaboration with Pakistan slowed down following the execution of Bhutto but was resumed ....."[23]

In 1980, late "Mrs. Gandhi was returned to office. Presumably, by then she took the Pakistani threat more seriously than [had] Mr. Morarji Desai, the then Prime Minister. She sent back Dr. Ramanna from his post as the Scientific Adviser to the Defence Minister as Director of Bhabha Atomic Research Centre..... Dr. Arunachalam was selected to succeed him as the Scientific Adviser. At around the same time Dr. Ramanna persuaded A.P.J. Kalam to move over from the Department of Space to be the Director of the Defence Research and Development Laboratory, Hyderabad which was engaged in missile research. Presumably, at this stage Mrs. Gandhi authorized Dr. Ramanna to go ahead with preparations for yet another underground test. This finds confirmation in former President Venkataraman's disclosure 'how he went down the shaft at Pokhran in 1983 when he was the Defence Minister'. US Satellites, [however,] discovered

322 / DEFENDING INDIA

[these] preparations and Mrs. Gandhi came under US pressure not to conduct the test."[24]

Though it was perhaps not sufficiently well known at that time, information now available reveals that the intelligence community in the United States had reported to the administration, in 1983-84, the full extent of China - Pakistan nuclear cooperation. It is also now known from the disclosures of General Arif in his book Working with Zia that in 1981, the then US Secretary of State, "General Alexander Haig had assured Pakistan that US would not interfere with Pakistan's nuclear programme. The world media carried information about Dr. A.Q. Khan's conviction in the Netherlands,"[25] resulting from controversy on "documentation on the centrifuge technology and Pakistan's extensive purchases of equipment and materials in many countries of Europe. Two Israeli authors Steve Weissman and Herbert Krosney brought out their book on Pakistan's nuclear efforts and it made a world wide impact. However in India there [remained] certain ambivalence towards Pakistani nuclear efforts."[26]

It was in this period that India accelerated its missile development. In 1983 an integrated guided missile programme was formulated by the Defence Research and Development Organisation under the leadership of Dr. V.S. Arunachalam with A.P.J. Abdul Kalam as its mainstay. This programme included the entire spectrum of missiles, from an antitank, Nag, to two surface-to-air, Akash and Trishul, one medium range surface-to-surface, Prithvi, and an intermediate range missile, Agni. To well informed observers it was obvious that India was aiming at developing its nuclear option further. Agni missile would not make sense unless it had a nuclear warhead. Prithvi could be used in a dual role though it would be more cost effective with a nuclear warhead. This was the period when the debate on intermediate range missile was at its height in Europe. It is to be noted that this programme was sanctioned at about the same time [that] Mrs. Gandhi had asked for a nuclear test.

The decades of the 80's had meanwhile also, once

again, witnessed a gradual deterioration of India's security environment. In South Asia nuclear weapons increased and more sophisticated delivery systems were inducted. In the region there also then came into existence a pattern about clandestine acquisition of nuclear materials, missiles and related technologies. India, during this period, became the victim of externally aided and abetted terrorism, militancy and clandestine war through hired mercenaries.

In 1987, occurred a by now oft-cited instance of a false scare. This was during a routine military training exercise by India termed "Ex Brasstacks". In response, Pakistan deployed troops. "At [which] stage Mr. Mushahid Hussain, then Editor of Muslim arranged for Mr. Kuldip Nayar to meet Dr. A.Q. Khan. On 28th January, 1987 Dr. Khan told Mr. Nayar that Pakistan had nuclear weapon[s] and would use [them] to counter Indian aggression. [He] subsequently denied this interview. But both Mr. Kuldip Nayar and Mr. Mushahid Hussein stood by it. Unfortunately, for Pakistan the publication of the interview got delayed by more than a month by which time the Indo-Pakistan confrontation crisis had been defused."[27]

Almost simultaneously, increasing evidence surfaced of China-Pakistan nuclear technology cooperation. "There were reports in the US that China might have tested a nuclear device for Pakistan in Lop Nor. [Permissiveness about] of Pakistan's nuclear weapon acquisition was also becoming explicit. In 1985, US Senators John Glenn and Alan Cranston attempted to introduce [a] legislation to stop all aid to Pakistan because of its proven quest for nuclear weapons. [They were] out-manouvred with the Pressler amendment, which permitted continued military and civil aid to Pakistan subject to [an] annual certification that Pakistan had not reached nuclear explosive capability. This was a way of buying Pakistan more time to develop its nuclear weapon capability. [That is why this] Pressler amendment had [the] wholehearted endorsement of General Zia. Even after Pakistan assembled its nuclear weapon in early 1987, the US Administration, because of its need for Pakistani cooperation in assisting the Afghan Mujahideen to [persist with] their war against the Soviet forces in Afghanistan decided to [continue furnishing] certificates that Pakistan had not reached nuclear explosive capability. In 1989 the Soviets withdrew from Afghanistan and the US no longer needed Pakistani cooperation for Afghan operations"[28].

1988 was a decisive year in Prime Minister Rajiv Gandhi's life. He put forward his Rajiv Gandhi Plan for nuclear disarmament in the Third UN Special session on Disarmament. It was a comprehensive, phased programme of disarmament. "Apart from his active participation in the 'six nation five continents' initiative for a test ban treaty, he had also joined Michael Gorbachev in issuing the Delhi Declaration [of] November 1986 on progressing towards a non-nuclear and non-violent world. [This] plan was ignored by the five nuclear hegemonic powers...."[29]

Faced with these harsh realities Rajiv Gandhi appears to have given the go ahead to the DRDO, under Dr., Arunachalam and the BARC under P.K. Iyengar to proceed with the Indian nuclear weapons' programme. The Agni IRBM was successfully test fired in May 1989. "I happened to meet Rajiv Gandhi at the foreign affairs correspondents club at the Kerala House in May 1991, just a couple of weeks before his assassination. Manoj Joshi, the well known defence analyst raised the nuclear issue and asked Rajiv Gandhi what would be his policy if he returned to power which seemed very likely at that stage. Rajiv Gandhi replied that he was very perturbed by the implied nuclear threats held out during the Gulf crisis."[30] By that time the Pakistani nuclear capability was in the open with US President refusing to certify, in October 1990, that Pakistan had not reached nuclear explosive capability and through invoking the Pressler amendment against that country.

It can be assumed that the first Indian nuclear deterrent came into existence in early 1990, with Dr. Arunachalam heading the DRDO and Dr. P.K. Iyengar as, Chairman of the Atomic Energy Commission.

Dr. Chidambaram was Director, BARC. During the period 1987-1990, however, India was totally vulnerable to Pakistani nuclear threat. "It is possible the Pakistanis thought India already had nuclear deterrent capability. However we do not have all facts about this period to make a plausible assessment. Analysing all available facts of that period it would appear that Pakistanis attempted a nuclear blackmail in May 1990, when the Pakistan backed insurgency in Kashmir was at its peak. Discussions among the principal American participants in that crisis bring out that India had not [then] mobilised its ground forces for any action... Leading Indian officials of that time have gone on record that Robert Gates did not mention any possible nuclear confrontation with India during [his] visit to Delhi in May 1990. But there are indications that the nuclear issue could have been discussed in Pakistan by Gates with President Ghulam Ishaq Khan and General Aslam Beg. There are some pointers about the possibility of some implied nuclear threat from Pakistan at that time. There was a top secret analysis in India on the probability of Pakistani nuclear threat and it concluded it was not very significant..... Speaking in Rajya Sabha in May 1990 Dr. Ramanna, then as Minister of State for Defence, said while 'India would never use its nuclear capability against any neighbour, if any neighbour were to do so the country would rise to the occasion'. In these circumstances one is left to wonder [that] while the published US version of the 1990, alleged crisis may not stand upto scrutiny, there was something more to it than has been publicly disclosed so far."[31] Considering all factors it is reasonable to conclude that Narashmha Rao, when Prime Minister, had also ordered nuclear tests in 1995. Sattelite imagery, and some even suggest human intelligence from India, revealed the plans to the US government, which then was made public, and the premier backed-off. It is in this backdrop that the tests of May 11 and 13 were conducted.

The May tests and after

The end of the Cold War marks a watershed in the history of the 20th century. While it transformed the political landscape of Europe it did little to ameliorate India's security concerns. Early and mid eighties, and the period roughly upto 1995 was, infact, a greatly troubling period for India. The relative order and absence of conflict that arrived in the Americas and Europe was also not replicated in other parts of the globe. At the global level there is no evidence yet on the part of the nuclear weapon states about taking decisive and irreversible steps and moving towards a nuclear-weapon-free-world. Instead, the NPT, in 1995 was extended indefinitely and unconditionally, perpetuating the existence of nuclear weapons in the hands of five countries who are also engaged in programmes for modernisation of their nuclear arsenals. At this juncture, and after over 2000 tests had been conducted, a Comprehensive Test Ban Treaty was opened for signature in 1996, following two and a half years of negotiations in which India had participated actively. This treaty was neither comprehensive nor was it related to disarmament.

The range of options for India had, by then, narrowed critically. India had to take necessary steps to ensure that the country's nuclear option, developed and safeguarded over decades, was not permitted to erode by a self-imposed restraint. Indeed, such an erosion would have resulted in an irremediably adverse impact on national security. The Government of India, was thus faced with a difficult decision. The only touchstone that could determine its decision remained national security. The tests conducted on 11 and 13 May, had by then not only become inevitable they were, in actuality a continuation of the policies set into motion, from almost the earliest years of independence.

An examination of the first fifty years of Indian independence reveals that the country's moralistic nuclear policy and restraint did not really pay any measurable dividends. Consequently, this resulted in resentment within the country; a feeling grew that India was being discriminated against. In the political market place of India, nuclear weaponisation gained currency, and the plank of disarmament began to appear as both unproductive and unrealistic. It began to be argued that if the Permanent Five's possession of nuclear weapons is good, confers security to their respective countries, then how is the possession of nuclear weapons by India not good, or how does the equation reverse simply in this instance? There is also the factor of the currency of power. If the P-5 continue to employ this currency in the form of nuclear weapons, as an international communicator of force, then how is India, to voluntarily devalue its own state power, which it has to, afterall, employ for its own national security? It is this reasoning that lies behind the evolution of Indian nuclear thought in the past fifty years. India has also learnt from the experience of the West, their approach to, attitudes about and application of nuclear policy. Deterrence works in the West, or elsewhere, as it so obviously appears to, otherwise why should these nations continue to possess nuclear weapons at all. Then by what reasoning is it to be asserted that it will not work or cannot work in India? To admonitorily argue, thereafter, that India has to now 'fall in line' because there is now a new international agenda of discriminatory non-proliferation, pursued more on account of the demands of the political market place of some of these countries, as an extension also of their own internal agendas or political debates, is to assert the un-implementable. The rationale behind nuclear weapons powers continuing to have, and preaching to those that do not have, to have even less, leaves a gross imbalance between the rights of and obligations of nation states of the world community. Either, India counters by suggesting, global, non-discriminatory disarmament by all; or, equal and legitimate security for the entire world.

That alone is why, and it bears repetition, that India since independence, has been a consistent advocate of global nuclear disarmament, participating actively in all such efforts, convinced that a world without nuclear

328 / DEFENDING INDIA

weapons will enhance both national and global security. India was the first to call for a ban on nuclear testing in 1954, for a non-discriminatory treaty on non-proliferation in 1965, for a treaty on non-use of nuclear weapons in 1978, for a nuclear freeze in 1982, and for a phased programme for complete elimination in 1988. Unfortunately, most of these initiatives were not accepted by the nuclear weapon states who still consider these weapons essential for their own security. What emerged, inconsequence, has been a discriminatory and flawed non-proliferation regime which affects India's security adversely. For many years India conveyed its apprehensions to other countries but this did not lead to any improvement in its security environment. This disharmony and disjunction between global thought and the movement of India's thought is, unfortunately, the objective reality of the world. In the totality of state power, nuclear weapons as a currency of it is still operational. Since this currency is operational in large parts of the globe, therefore, India was left with no choice but to update and revalidate the capability that had been demonstrated 24 years ago in the PNE of 1974.

In undertaking these tests, India has not violated any international treaty obligations. The Comprehensive Test Ban Treaty, to which India does not subscribe, also contains provisions permitting states parties to withdraw if they consider their supreme national interests being jeopardised. In any event, in the evolution of the present South Asian situation 1995 was a watershed year. By forcing an unconditional and indefinite extension of the Non-proliferation Treaty on the international community, India was left with no option but to go in for overt nuclear weaponisation. The Sino-Pakistan nuclear weapon collaboration, continued with in violation of the NPT, made it obvious that the NPT regime had collapsed, and critically in India's neighbourhood. "Since it is now argued that NPT is unamendable it is obvious that the legitimization of nuclear weapons, implicit in the unconditional and indefinite extension of the NPT, is also irreversible. While India could have lived with a nuclear option but without overt weaponization in a world where nuclear weapons had not been formally legitimised, that course was no longer viable in a world of legitimised nuclear weapons. Unfortunately, the full implications of the legitimisation of nuclear weapons were not debated either in India or abroad. This fatal set-back to nuclear disarmament and progress towards delegitimisation of nuclear weapons was hailed by most of the peace movements abroad as a great victory."[32]

In negotiations on the CTBT, for the first time the Indian Ambassador's statement of June 20, 1996 in the Conference of Disarmament stated "that the nuclear issue is a national security concern for India and advanced [that] as one of the reasons why India was unable to accede to the Comprehensive Test ban Treaty".[33] Presumably this persuaded the nuclear hegemons to introduce a clause at the last minute, "that India along with 43 other nations should sign the treaty to bring it into force. This clause was coercive and a violation of the Vienna Convention on Treaties which stipulates that a nation not willing to be a party to a treaty cannot be imposed obligations arising out of the treaty. It should be remembered that this clause was [introduced] at the insistence of China - the nuclear proliferator to Pakistan. The international community approved that coercive CTBT."[34] That was a major deterioration in India's security environment.

As the decade of the nineties advanced the situation for India became more pressing. In 1997 more evidence surfaced on China-Pakistan proliferation linkage and about US permissiveness. The very fact that the US administration insisted on a separate agreement with China, during President Jiang Zemin's visit to Washington, on its proliferation to Iran and Pakistan, and that the Chinese signed such an agreement, instead of protesting their innocence establishes that Chinese proliferation was a reality affecting India's security. After all these assurances, according to a testimony given by the US Deputy Assistant Secretary of State for Non-proliferation to the House of Representatives on 4th February 1998, it had to be asserted that though China did not proliferate MTCR class missiles it was continuing to proliferate missile technology and components to Pakistan. Despite this, US Administration continued to express willingness to certify that China was not proliferating, or, for India, worse that the US was either unable or unwilling to restrain China. As the range of options for India narrowed so, too, did the difficulties of taking corrective action.

Today, India is a nuclear weapon state. This adds to its sense of responsibility as a nation that is committed to the principles of the UN Charter and to promoting regional peace and stability. Efforts for closer engagement will, ofcourse, have to be intensified covering the entire range of issues which require collective consideration. During the past 50 years there have been a number of decisive moments. 1968 was one such moment in India's nuclear chapter; as was 1974, and now 1998. At each of these moments, India took the decision guided only by national interest, and supported by a national consensus. The May tests of 1998 were born in the crucible of earlier decisions and made possible only because those decisions had been taken correctly, and in time.

Let it be repeated that India's nuclear policy remains firmly committed to a basic tenet: that the country's national security, in a world of nuclear proliferation lies either in global disarmament or in exercise of the principle of equal and legitimate security for all. The earliest Indian articulations on the question of nuclear disarmament were admittedly more moralistic than realistic. The current disharmony, therefore, between India's position and the position that the rest of the globe has seemingly adopted is that whereas India has moved from the totally moralistic to a little more realistic, the rest of the nuclear world has arrived at all of its nuclear conclusions entirely realistically. They now have a surplus of nuclear weapons, also the technology for fourth generation weapons, and are now thus beginning to move towards a moralistic position. It is of this that is born lack of understanding about the Indian stand. The first, and perhaps, the principal obstacle in understanding

India's position lies in an absence of due and proper recognition of the country's security needs; also in this nuclearised world for a balance between the rights and obligations of all nations; of restraint in acquisition of nuclear weaponry; of ending this unequal division between nuclear haves and have-nots. No other country in the world has demonstrated the kind of restraint that India has for near about a quarter of a century after the first Pokhran test of 1974. In the years preceding that PNE and in subsequent decades, consistently, India continued to advocate the basic tenet of its nuclear strategy.

Now, in the nineties, and as the century turns, the country was faced by critical choices. India had been witness to decades of international unconcern and incomprehension even as the overall security environment of the country, both globally and in Asia deteriorated. The end of the cold war resulted in the collapse of the then existing bipolarity, it created the appearance of unipolarity but it also led to the rise of additional power centres. The fulcrum of international balance balance of power shifted from Europe to Asia; Asian nations began their process of economic resurgence. Asia-Pacific as a trade and security rim became a geo-political reality. In 1995, the Nuclear Non-proliferation Treaty, essentially a cold war arms control treaty, with a fixed duration of 25 years, was extended indefinitely and unconditionally. This legitimised, in perpetuity, the existing nuclear arsenals; in effect an unequal nuclear regime. Even as nations of the world acceded to the treaty, the five nuclear weapons powers stood apart and three undeclared nuclear weapon states were also unable to subscribe. Meanwhile, in the intervening decades had persisted reports of the transfer of nuclear weapon powers technology from declared nuclear weapon powers to preferred states. Neither the world nor the nuclear weapons powers succeeded in halting this process. NPT notwithstanding, proliferation in the region spread.

Since nuclear weapon powers that assist proliferation, or even condone it are not subject to any penalty, the entire non-proliferation regime became flawed. Nuclear technologies became, at their worst, commodities of international commerce, at best lubricants of diplomatic fidelity. Such proliferation in India's neighbourhood has been enumerated in strategic literature and cited in numerous Congressional testimonies. India noted with concern that not only did the CIA refer to them, indeed, from the early nineties onward the required presidential certification in this regard could not be provided. India is the only country in the world to be situated between two nuclear weapon powers.

Today most nations of the world are also the beneficiaries of a nuclear security paradigm, From Vacouver to Vladivostock stretches a club: that of a security framework with four nuclear weapon powers as partners in peace providing extended deterrent protection. The Americas progress under the US nuclear deterrent protection, as members of Organisation of American States. South Korea, Japan and Australasia also have the benefit of US extended deterrence. By itself, China is a major nuclear weapon power. Only Africa and southern Asia remain outside the exclusivity of this new international nuclear paradigm, where nuclear weapons and their currency in international conduct is, paradoxically, legitimised. How to accept these differentiated standards of national security or a regime of international nuclear apartheid is a challenge not simply to India but to the inequality of the entire non-proliferation regime.

In the aftermath of the coldwar a new Asian balance of power is emerging. Developments in this region create new alignments, new vacuums. India, in exercise of its supreme national interests, has acted, and timely, to correct this imbalance, to fill a potential vacuum. It's endeavour is to contribute to a stable balance of power in Asia, which it holds will contribute meaningfully to a furtherance of the democratic process.

On India's western flank lies the Gulf region, one of the most critical sources of the world's energy requirements; to its north the Commonwealth of Independent States, a yet to be fully developed reservoir. With both these regions India has ancient linkages. It also has extensive energy import requirements. The Gulf provides employment to Indian labour and talent. However, this region too, and its adjoining countries have been targets of missile and nuclear proliferation. Long range missiles of 2500 km range were proliferated to this area in the mid 80's. Unfortunately, from 1987 onwards nuclear proliferation, with extra regional assistance, has continued unchecked.

Faced as India was, with a legitimisation of nuclear weapons by the haves, by a global nuclear security paradigm from which it was excluded, trends towards disequilibrium in the balance of power in Asia, and a neighbourhood of two nuclear weapon countries acting in concert, India had to protect its future by exercising its nuclear option. By doing this India has brought into the open the nuclear reality which had remained clandestine for atleast the last eleven years. India could not accept a flawed non-proliferation regime, as the international norm, when all objective realities asserted conclusively to the contrary.

India's policies towards its neighbours and other countries have not changed. The country remains fully committed to the promotion of peace, stability, and resolution of all outstanding issues through bilateral dialogue and negotiations. The tests of May 11 and 13, 1998 were not directed against any country; these were intended to reassure the people of India about their own security. Confidence building is a continuous process; with India remaining committed to it.

India is now a nuclear weapon state; as is Pakistan. That is a reality that can neither be denied, nor wished away. This category of a Nuclear Weapon State is not, in actuality, a conferment; nor is it a status for others to grant, it is an objective reality. This strengthened capability adds to India's sense of responsibility; the responsibility and obligation of power. India, mindful of its international obligations, is committed to not using these weapons to commit aggression or to mount threats against any country; these are weapons of self-defence, to ensure that India, too, is not subjected to nuclear threats or coercion.

India has reiterated its undertaking of a 'no-first-use' agreement with any country, bilaterally, or in a collective forum. India shall not engage in an arms race; ofcourse, it shall also neither subscribe to nor reinvent the sterile doctrines of the Cold War. India remains committed to the basic tenet of its foreign policy - a conviction that global elimination of nuclear weapons will enhance its security as well as that of the rest of the world. It will continue to urge countries, particularly other nuclear weapon states to adopt measures that would contribute meaningfully to such an objective. This is the defining difference; it is also the cornerstone of India's nuclear doctrine.

That is why India will continue to support such initiatives, taken individually or collectively, by the Non-Aligned Movement which has continued to attach the highest priority to nuclear disarmament. This was reaffirmed most recently at the NAM Ministerial meeting held at Cartagena soon after India had conducted its present series of underground tests. The NAM ministers "reiterated their call on the Conference on Disarmament to establish, as the highest priority, an ad hoc committee to start in 1998 negotiations on a phased programme for the complete elimination of nuclear weapons with a specified framework of time, including a Nuclear Weapons Convention". This collective voice of 113 NAM countries reflects an approach to global nuclear disarmament to which India has remained committed. One of the NAM member initiatives, to which great importance is attached, was the reference to the International Court of Justice resulting in the unanimous declaration as part of the Advisory Opinion handed down on 8 July, 1996, that "there exists an obligation to pursue in good faith and bring to a conclusion negotiations leading to nuclear disarmament in all its aspects under strict and effective international control". India was one of the countries that appealed to the ICJ on this issue. No other nuclear weapon state has supported this judgement; in fact, they have sought to decry its value. India has been and will continue to be in the forefront of the calls for opening negotiations for a Nuclear Weapons Convention, so that this challenge can be dealt with in the manner that has dealt with the scourge of other weapons of mass destruction - the Biological Weapons Convention and the Chemical Weapons Convention. In keeping with its commitment to comprehensive, universal and non-discriminatory approaches to disarmament India is an original State Party to both these conventions. In recent years, in keeping with these new challenges, India has actively promoted regional cooperation - in SAARC, in the Indian Ocean Rim-Association for Regional cooperation and as a member of the ASEAN Regional Forum. This engagement will also continue. The policies of economic liberalisation introduced in recent years have increased India's regional and global linkages and India shall deepen and strengthen these ties.

India's nuclear policy has been marked by restraint and openness. It has not violated any international agreements either in 1974 or now, in 1998. This restraint exercised for 24 years, after having demonstrated a capability in 1974, is in itself an unique example. Restraint, however, has to arise from strength. It cannot be based upon indecision or doubt. Restraint is valid only when doubts are removed. The series of tests undertaken by India have led to the removal of doubts. The action involved was balanced, in that it was the minimum necessary to maintain what is an irreducible component of the country's national security calculus.

Subsequent to the tests the Govenment of India has already stated that it will now observe a voluntary moratorium and refrain from conducting underground nuclear test explosions. It has also indicated willingness to move towards a de-jure formalisation of this declaration. The basic obligation of the CTBT are thus met: to refrain from undertaking nuclear tests.

India has also expressed readiness to participate in negotiations in the Conference on Disarmament, in Geneva, on a Fissile Material Cut-off Treaty. The basic objective of this treaty is to prohibit future production of fissile materials for use in nuclear weapons or nuclear explosive devices. India's approach in these negotiations will be to ensure that this treaty emerges as a universal and non-discriminatory treaty, backed by an effective verification mechanism.

India has maintained effective export controls on nuclear materials as well as related technologies even though it is neither a party to the NPT nor a member of the Nuclear Suppliers Group. Nonetheless, India is committed to non-proliferation and to the maintaining of stringent export controls to ensure that there is no leakage of its indigenously developed know-how and technologies. In fact, India's conduct in this regard has been better than some countries party to the NPT.

India has in the past conveyed its concerns on the inadequacies of the international nuclear non-proliferation regime. It has explained that the country was not in a position to join because the regime did not address the country's security concerns. These could have been addressed by moving towards global nuclear disarmament, India's preferred approach. As this did not take place, India was obliged to stand aside from the emerging regime so that its freedom of action was not constrained. This is precisely the path that it has continued to be follow, unwaveringly, for the last three decades. That same constructive approach will underlie India's dialogue with countries that need to be persuaded of India's serious intent and willingness to engage so that mutual concerns are satisfactorily addressed. The challenge to Indian statecraft remains that of reconciling India's security imperatives with valid international concerns in regard to nuclear weapons.

What collapsed prior to the Pressler Amendement cannot now be reinvented. Let the world move towards finding more realistic solutions: to evolving a universal common security paradigm for the entire globe. Since nuclear weapons are not really useable, paradoxically the dilemma lies in their continuing deterrent value; and this paradox further deepens the concern of public men having the responsibility of governance: how to employ state power in service of national security and simultaneously address to international concerns. How, thereafter, to evolve to an order that ensures a peaceful present and an orderly future. How then to reconcile with an objective global reality that as these weapons do have a deterrent value, some are the owners of this value, others not; yet a lasting balance has to be founded even then. For, though humanity is, indivisible, national security interests, as sovereign expressions, have not the same attribute. That is why the assertion that it is not possible to have two standards for national security-one based on nuclear deterrence and the other outside of it.

NOTES

1. Raja Ramanna, *Years of Pilgrimage* [New Delhi:Viking, 1991) p. 55.
2. Ibid., p. 56.
3. Ibid., p. 70.
4. Ibid., p. 71.
5. Ibid., p. 71.
6. Ibid., p. 75.
7. Ibid., p. 94.
8. Lok Sabha Debates April 1954.
9. Jasjit Singh, *Nuclear India* [New Delhi: Knowledge World, 1998] p. 16-35.
10. Ibid., p. 16-35.
11. Ibid., p. 16-35.
12. Ibid., p. 16-35.
13. Ibid., p. 16-35.
14. Lok Sabha Debates April 1965.
15. Ibid.
16. Jasjit Singh, op. cit., p. 16-35.
17. Ibid., p. 16-35.
18. Ibid., p. 16-35.
19. Raja Ramanna, op. cit., p. 92.
20. Jasjit Singh, op. cit., p. 16-35.
21. Ibid., p. 16-35.
22. Ibid., p. 16-35.
23. Ibid., p. 16-35.
24. Ibid., p. 16-35.
25. Ibid., p. 16-35.
26. Ibid., p. 16-35.

27.   Ibid., p. 16-35.
28.   Ibid., p. 16-35.
29.   Ibid., p. 16-35.
30.   Ibid., p. 16-35.
31.   Ibid., p. 16-35.
32.   Ibid., p. 16-35.
33.   Ibid., p. 16-35.
34.   Ibid., p. 16-35.